Acclaim for

Brain Health From Birth

"A well researched book that offers evidence-based advice for parents and doctors alike to navigate the complexities of optimizing infant brain health, with guidance on everything from reducing the risk of preterm birth to choosing the best formula and probiotics for newborns. The concise end of chapter summaries make it easy to implement meaningful changes."

—ADRIENNE L. SIMONE, MD, BOARD CERTIFIED OB-GYN AND AUTHOR OF THE NEW RULES OF PREGNANCY: WHAT TO EAT, DO, THINK ABOUT, AND LET GO OF WHILE YOUR BODY IS MAKING A BABY.

"An engaging explanation of the latest research on infant neurodevelopment, covering important topics such as delayed cord clamping and the need to detect and treat anemia during pregnancy."

—JUDITH S MERCER, PHD, FELLOW OF THE AMERICAN COLLEGE OF NURSE-MIDWIVES, PROFESSOR EMERITA, UNIVERSITY OF RHODE ISLAND, ADJUNCT PROFESSOR OF PEDIATRICS, BROWN UNIVERSITY

"Brain Health From Birth walks us through the latest research on infant brain development, translating the science into practical steps for parents to nurture their baby's brain when it matters most. With her latest book, Rebecca empowers parents with the knowledge to make the best decisions to help their babies thrive - body, mind & spirit!"

—ELISA SONG, MD, INTEGRATIVE PEDIATRICIAN, FOUNDER OF HEALTHYKIDSHAPPYKIDS.COM AND THE EVERYDAY HOLISTIC PEDIATRICS COURSE.

"An easy-to-read guide to how environmental chemicals can impact the developing brain and how parents can make safer choices when buying products for their new baby."

—BETH GREER, BEST-SELLING AUTHOR OF SUPER NATURAL HOME AND ENVIRONMENTAL TOXINS EXPERT.

BRAIN

HEALTH

FROM BIRTH

Nurturing Brain Development During
Pregnancy and the First Year

REBECCA FETT

FRANKLIN
FOX

For Emily

Brain Health from Birth
Copyright © 2019, Rebecca Fett
First Edition.

www.brainhealthfrombirth.com

Published in the United States by Franklin Fox Publishing LLC, New York.
Cover design: Shuma Malik
Cover images: Karolina Yen, Kay Photography
Editors: Jenna Rose Robbins and Meredith Tennant

This book is intended to provide helpful and informative material. It is not intended to provide medical advice and cannot replace the advice of a medical professional. The reader should consult his or her doctor before adopting any of the suggestions in this book. The author and publisher specifically disclaim all responsibility for any liability, loss, or risk, personal or otherwise, which is incurred as a consequence of the use and application of any of the contents of this book.

ISBN-13 (print): 978-0-9996761-3-4
ISBN-10 (ebook): 978-0-9996761-5-8

Contents

PART 1

Brain Health & Why It Matters

Introduction

During pregnancy and the first few months of life, a baby produces new brain cells at an astonishing rate. On average, the brain grows by more than 250,000 nerve cells *per minute* during pregnancy, to form a total of more than 100 billion neurons by the time a baby is born. Even then, the building process continues—during the first three months, a baby's brain is still increasing in size by 1 percent per day.

Over the next six months of babyhood, the focus shifts from producing new brain cells to connecting them together. This process builds the extraordinarily complex network of pathways that will carry thoughts, memories, and emotions for life.

As you might expect, building a brain from scratch is a delicate process that can be easily disrupted. For instance, some babies that are born extremely premature will have critical areas of the brain that are much smaller than normal, a difference that remains even as these children grow older.[1] That makes preterm birth, unsurprisingly, one of the major risk factors for autism, intellectual disability, and other developmental disorders.

But premature birth is also something we can help prevent. As you will learn in this book, cutting-edge science shows that with sufficient vitamin D during pregnancy, the risk of very early preterm birth plummets.[2] It follows that supplementing with vitamin D is one way to give your baby the best opportunity to develop a healthy brain. Yet there are also many other ways to minimize the chances of premature birth and protect the delicate brain-building process.

If you are currently trying to conceive, are pregnant, or have a new baby, you have a golden opportunity to provide a safe and nurturing environment for this extraordinary process to take place, uninterrupted. By providing enough of the key nutrients needed for brain building, reducing the odds of preterm birth, and avoiding certain toxins, you can go a long way toward removing many of the major risk factors for autism and ADHD, two conditions that are becoming more common with each passing year.

Doing so will have many other benefits too. That is because the same factors that influence the risk of autism and ADHD can also cause more subtle neurological changes in all children. By protecting your baby's brain when it is most vulnerable, you will not only reduce the risk of significant developmental disorders but may also help nurture a healthy brain that will one day be capable of extraordinary things.

My Story

My fascination with exactly how the brain works runs deep. Long before studying cellular neuroscience as part of my degree in biochemistry and molecular biology at the University of Sydney, I vividly remember peppering my father with questions about neurons and nerve signaling on family walks when I was five years old.

To give some context to this rather unusual behavior, I grew up knowing that my grandfather, Dr. Paul Fatt, had contributed to key discoveries about how brain cells communicate with each other (discoveries for which several of his research partners were awarded the Nobel Prize). My grandfather's obituary in the journal *Nature*

Neuroscience describes him as "one of the founders of modern cellular neuroscience" and "among the most distinguished neuroscientists and biophysicists of the twentieth century."[3]

Growing up with an awareness of neurons and neurotransmitters has profoundly shaped my worldview. Yes, the human brain is more than the sum of its parts, but first and foremost it is a biological structure. How we think, feel, communicate, and experience the world is really the product of cells, chemicals, physics, and biology. This book explores the forces that influence your baby's brain from that perspective.

Although I have always been fascinated with the biology of the brain, I became particularly interested in autism and ADHD once I found out my husband and I were expecting a baby boy and learned of the troubling statistics. In the United States, boys born today face at least a 3 to 4 percent chance of developing autism.[4] My son probably had much worse odds, looking at the laundry list of factors that seem to be associated with autism risk. In particular, my family history of several autoimmune diseases and my husband's age were working against us.

During the time our surrogate was pregnant with my first son, I was also deep into researching and writing my first book, *It Starts with the Egg*. The book describes how common toxins such as BPA and phthalates negatively influence fertility and may contribute to miscarriages. In the course of conducting research for that book, I came across troubling data that linked the same toxins to compromised brain development in children.

Fortunately, it is relatively easy to avoid many of these toxins once you know how. Our surrogate was on board with replacing plastic kitchenware with stainless steel or glass and switching to fragrance-free cleaning and skin-care products. She was also happy to adopt other measures suggested by the research, such as adding a daily omega-3 supplement.

Yet after my son was born, the autism concern remained. It

quickly became clear that my tiny baby had a propensity toward gastrointestinal problems and inflammation. By three months old, he had severe eczema and could not hold down any formula we tried. He cried in pain for six to eight hours per day from what we could only guess was severe reflux, although the medication we gave him seemed to make no difference. For reasons that are not fully understood, inflammation, gastrointestinal problems, and autism seem to go hand in hand. Everything about my son indicated he was beginning down a worrying path.

With that backdrop, I did everything I could to further reduce the burden of chemicals on his system, support his immune system, and reduce inflammation. Given the benefit of hindsight (and the new research discussed in this book), it is clear there is even more I could have done, but in the end, the basic steps I took were enough to turn his health around.

I am incredibly grateful that my son is now a bright, thriving, and healthy little boy. I know that many of the strategies I adopted to lower his overall level of inflammation probably helped nurture his developing brain too, such as giving him specific infant probiotics and avoiding chemicals in our home. I followed the same approach when my second child was born and thankfully now have two healthy boys who show all the characteristic signs of having had an optimal environment during pregnancy and early childhood. These signs include a long attention span, the ability to remain calm and focused, and early language development.

I attribute these positive characteristics to the steps we took to avoid certain toxins and ensure adequate nutrients during pregnancy. This is not just wild conjecture. The latest research clearly shows the effects of toxins such as BPA and phthalates on infant brain development, along with the many other measures discussed in this book. I feel compelled to share this science with as many parents and future parents as possible, so our children can all reach their full potential.

I feel a particular responsibility to ease the path for those who are becoming parents after reading *It Starts with the Egg*. I know that for many people, reading the book created a sense that there was finally something positive to do in the world of infertility, where everything normally feels helpless and beyond our control. But for others, the new information on BPA, phthalates, and other toxins became a source of worry.

It is not my goal to scare you about toxic chemicals lurking around every corner. If you read *It Starts with the Egg*, you are probably already concerned enough. Instead, this book offers practical advice on how to carry a nontoxic lifestyle through pregnancy and parenting, based on the latest scientific research linking common chemicals to impacts on childhood development. I would like this book to be your guide to what matters most during this extraordinary time, explaining what to focus on and what you can let slide without guilt.

I also want to ease any anxiety you may have about the new epidemic of autism and ADHD. The odds are truly cause for concern, but if we pay attention to the science, it is clear that there is so much we can do to protect our children's developing minds. That is particularly true if we take action during the time they are most vulnerable.

Doing so will not only reduce the risk of autism and other significant developmental problems but will also help protect cognitive function. In practical terms, this means preserving all the abilities needed for a child to form strong social bonds and live a happy and productive life.

Protecting Cognitive Function

In our modern world, where far too many children are affected by significant developmental disorders such as autism or ADHD, any discussion of brain health will naturally focus on what is causing these disorders and what we can do to prevent them. But the concept of brain health is actually much broader. The ultimate goal is not just to prevent the most serious problems but to give your child the best start in life.

By taking steps to nurture your baby's brain health during pregnancy and early infancy, you will help safeguard all the abilities that fall under the broad umbrella of "cognitive development." This term refers to factors such as

- IQ
- attention span
- memory
- creativity
- language development
- nonverbal communication skills
- impulse control
- emotional regulation

When considering all of these facets, it is clear that the outcomes from nurturing brain health go far beyond boosting a child's future academic success. The implications for a child's life are much greater.

Studies consistently show that one of the most important factors that determine long-term happiness is having positive relationships with friends and family.[5] Studies also show that the ability to form these important bonds depends largely on cognitive function.[6] More specifically, it hinges on the capacity to express our thoughts, interpret nonverbal cues, empathize, and regulate our emotional state. These skills are all considered to be reflections of "executive function" within the overall umbrella of cognitive function.

Communication skills and other executive functions are no doubt heavily influenced by what children experience after they are born. How we interact with our children clearly shapes the development of their brain. This is particularly true when it comes to how much time parents spend talking to their child, teaching them to recognize and regulate their own emotional state, and encouraging imaginative play and social interaction with other children. (For more on this topic, see the excellent books *Brain Rules for Baby* by John Medina and *The Whole Brain Child* by Daniel Siegel.)

Clearly, the learning experiences we provide to babies and toddlers are important, but they can only go so far. Based on the biology of their brains, children will innately have differing potential to develop cognitive skills.

Autism is one example of this phenomenon, where there is a biological influence at play that affects key aspects of cognitive function. Yet it is important to recognize that all children will fall somewhere within a broad range when it comes to their natural capacity to learn new words, interpret nonverbal cues, and express themselves. The same is true for many other aspects of cognitive function, including IQ and the ability to regulate emotions and maintain focused attention.

Your child's potential to develop these abilities is partly genetic, but biological and chemical influences during pregnancy and early infancy have a powerful impact too. These influences include pre-term birth, toxin exposures, nutritional deficiencies, and hormone disruptions. As you will learn throughout this book, these factors can leave lasting effects on children's IQ scores, behavior, attention span, and learning ability.

Closing the Gap Between Scientific Research and Real Life

The sheer volume of research on early brain development is staggering, but that allows us to cast a skeptical eye on scientific findings. There is now a vast amount of data on factors during pregnancy and infancy that can compromise brain health and raise the risk of autism, ADHD, or developmental delays. On the flip side, there is also a vast amount of data showing the ways we can positively influence our baby's brain development, including providing key hormones and nutrients that are often overlooked.

As a result, we are no longer left clutching at straws or extrapolating from isolated animal studies. The advice in this book is based on research findings that have been replicated again and again, in a variety of different contexts (with citations provided so you can read the actual studies for yourself). You will learn about clear patterns seen in large observational studies and then confirmed in randomized controlled trials, where researchers divide pregnant women into two groups, change some factor in one group, and then follow the development of their children for many years.

In autism research in particular, the urgent need for answers causes many people to rush to judgment on the basis of isolated research findings. We have all seen the dramatic headlines claiming that something causes autism, only to read another headline six months later suggesting the exact opposite. This book will cut through the noise, weighing all the evidence and allowing you to make your own informed decisions on the major controversies such as vaccines, ultrasounds, Tylenol, and folic acid supplements.

You will also hear from several pioneering obstetricians and pediatricians who have changed the way they practice in light of the new evidence on baby brain health. One of these pioneers is Dr. Elisa Song, a Stanford-, NYU-, and UCSF-trained pediatrician with one of the most highly regarded holistic pediatrics practices in the country. I am honored to give you the benefit of her many years of experience.

In an ideal world, we would all have a knowledgeable doctor guiding us through the important decisions we encounter as new parents. Perhaps you do, and you can use this book as a tool to provide background information for your conversations with your obstetrician and pediatrician. But most doctors do not have the time to stay up to date on all of the latest research or delve deeply into issues as soon as a red flag is raised by new studies.

The unfortunate reality is that we simply cannot rely on standard medical advice to keep our baby's brains safe. As just one example, new studies are beginning to suggest a possible link between autism and the use of acetaminophen (also known as Tylenol) during pregnancy or infancy. Even though we do not yet have a clear answer on the issue, the research that has been done so far is enough to raise a red flag. Any pediatrician who claims there is no risk in giving babies acetaminophen is simply not paying attention to this research. As noted by Dr. William Parker of Duke University School of Medicine, "Even the best-trained pediatricians are generally unaware that the long-term effects of acetaminophen were never tested in children in controlled trials."[7]

I also firmly believe that it is important to approach scientific studies with the right dose of skepticism, but that we should still be willing to take action as soon as the evidence becomes sufficiently persuasive. In conventional medical practice, it is typical to wait for decades of incontrovertible proof before the standard advice changes. When it comes to addressing the epidemic of developmental disabilities affecting children today, any delay is a profound disservice to the babies that will be born this year and next. We simply have to act on the best available evidence before it is too late.

The goal of this book is to allow you to do just that, by bringing together all of the latest findings in the scientific literature and translating complex science into plain English, to provide evidence-based guidance on supporting your baby's brain development when it matters most.

To some extent, the biological and chemical influences on your child's cognitive abilities will continue their whole childhood. Factors such as nutrition, physical activity, and even continued exposure to toxins will always have some degree of impact. But at no time will the external world influence your baby's brain as much as during pregnancy and the first few months of life.

We know, for example, that very low blood sugar in the first few days of life is still evident in cognitive abilities seven years later (as chapter 13 explains). Blood sugar disruptions in older babies, however, have little to no long-term impact on brain function. External factors during early life have an outsized impact on brain function because the brain is growing and changing so rapidly during this time.

The stage from conception through the first year is undoubtedly the most critical window to ensure lifelong brain health. During this time, our goal is not just to avoid the extreme disruptions to infant brain development that are reflected in autism and ADHD, but to nurture the ability to focus, remember, communicate, and regulate emotions. All of these mental processes are crucial to your child's ability to form strong social bonds and live a happy and productive life.

Overview of Chapters

Before exploring the practical steps to support your baby's growing brain, it is helpful to see the broader picture and understand the problem we are facing as modern parents. To that end, chapter 1 provides an overview of the epidemic of developmental disorders we are currently facing and explains the common thread linking various risk factors.

Chapters 2 to 9 then guide you through the steps to take during pregnancy to nurture and protect your baby's developing brain, including

- how to ensure you are providing the nutrients that are key to infant brain development, such as choline, vitamin D, and omega-3 fatty acids.
- the importance of testing for thyroid function and anemia during pregnancy.
- the latest science on the potential risks posed by prolonged use of acetaminophen.

- why you should feel comfortable with prenatal vaccines
and ultrasounds.

If your baby has already arrived, you may choose to skip over chapters 2 through 9 and pick up with chapter 10, which provides guidance on how to create a nontoxic home by minimizing chemicals with the potential to compromise brain development.

The next step is setting up the baby's nursery. Chapters 11 and 12 help you choose the safest crib mattress, furniture, diapers, bottles, skin-care, and other gear, before discussing whether it is really worth spending more for organic bedding and clothing.

Chapters 13 and 14 guide you through the current science on formula feeding, explaining why aggressive efforts in hospitals to promote breastfeeding can sometimes backfire, along with detailed advice on how to choose the best formula.

Chapters 15 through 16 address the other crucial matters you will face in the first few months with your baby, such as infant vaccines, antibiotics, and pain medication. Chapter 17 then explores the links between the beneficial gut microbes, the immune system, and brain health, explaining simple ways to support your newborn's microbiome.

By the end of the book, you will have learned about many small changes that can have a big impact on the health of your child's brain. You will be armed with all the knowledge you need to make truly informed decisions, to give your child the best possible start in life.

Chapter 1

Threats to Brain Health

The modern world is somehow compromising our children's brains on an unprecedented scale. One reflection of this is the rapid rise in autism, a developmental disability that used to be incredibly rare.

If you are in your thirties or forties and living in a developed country, there is a very good chance that one of your friends, neighbors, or work colleagues has a child with autism. In our parents' generation, this would have been unheard of.

The rise in autism is not simply a matter of improved diagnosis. Research shows there has been a true increase in cases—and at an extraordinary rate. In the United States, the number of children diagnosed with autism used to be 1 in 10,000.[8] Now it is 1 in 40.[9] The odds are even worse for boys, with the latest numbers released from the Centers for Disease Control (CDC) showing that autism will affect 1 in 27 boys born today.[10]

In parallel, there has also been a troubling rise in attention-deficit/hyperactivity disorder (ADHD), which now affects more than 7 percent of children in the United States.[11] In 2016, there were more than 5.4 million American children with ADHD, of whom two-thirds were taking medication.[12] And it doesn't end there. The CDC has reported that the total number of children in the United States with any form of developmental disability, including speech and language impairments, intellectual disabilities, cerebral palsy, and autism, is 1 in 6.[13]

This is a dire situation that cannot be ignored. There is an urgent need to figure out what is happening—what has changed in recent decades that is compromising the developing minds of so many children? That is a question many researchers have been grappling with and the answer, it seems, is a multifaceted one. There is not one single cause, but a variety of external risk factors that can cause autism, ADHD, and other developmental problems, especially in children who are genetically vulnerable.

The good news is that we have the power to change many of these risk factors. New science is emerging every day that reveals ways to dramatically reduce the risk of developmental disabilities by ensuring adequate nutrients during pregnancy, reducing the risk of preterm birth, and minimizing exposure to toxins. The research is also revealing many common threads that tie together seemingly unrelated threats to infant brain health, as this chapter explains.

Before exploring those common threads, I want to briefly address the argument that autism is not actually caused by factors unique to the modern world, such as toxin exposure, but is instead something that existed throughout human history but simply went unrecognized.

Is There Really an Autism Epidemic?

In his book, *Neurotribes: The Legacy of Autism and the Future of Neurodiversity*, reporter Steve Silberman argues that autism merely reflects natural variations in the human brain function. "Whatever autism is, it is not a unique product of modern civilization. It is a strange gift from our deep past passed down through millions of years of evolution."[14]

Silberman advocates for a view of autism as a type of "neurodi-versity" rather than an impairment, noting that "Autistic people, for instance, have prodigious memories for facts, are often highly intelligent in ways that don't register on verbal IQ tests, and are capable of focusing for long periods on tasks that take advantage of their natural gift for detecting flaws in visual patterns. By autistic standards, the 'normal' human brain is easily distractible, is obsessively social, and suffers from a deficit of attention to detail."

There may be some truth to Silberman's view, at least for many individuals on the autism spectrum, but to parents of children with more severe forms of autism, this concept of "neurodiversity" is far from reality. As one such parent, J.B. Handley, comments in his book *How to End the Autism Epidemic*, "I resent the way Mr. Silberman…and many neurodiversity advocates are romanticizing a devastating disability."[15]

To be diagnosed with autism, a child must show "persistent deficits in social communication and social interaction."[16] The severity of language and social impairment can vary widely, with some autistic children being able to communicate well and others not able to speak at all. Other common characteristics include repetitive body movements (such as flapping, rocking, and spinning), unusual interest in specific objects, difficulties with changes in routine, and extreme sensitivity to sensory inputs such as light, sound, taste, and touch. Approximately one-third of children with autism also have significant intellectual disability.

It is perhaps unsurprising then that autism can have far-reaching impacts on a child's life. In their 2017 book, journalist Dan Olmsted and autism parent Mark Blaxill note that "most with an autism diagnosis will never be employed, pay taxes, fall in love, get married, have children, or be responsible for their health and welfare."[17] This view is supported by the data.

Research shows that the average cost of supporting an individual with autism over the course of their lifetime is $1.4 million.[18] Around one-third of children with the disorder are unable to speak, and more than half are prone to physical aggression, with many also hurting themselves.[19]

In reality, the term "autism" encompasses a wide variety of abilities and challenges. We can acknowledge the extraordinary gifts of many individuals with autism while at the same time recognizing that it is often a serious and lifelong disability that is worth preventing.

The vast weight of scientific evidence suggests that autism is not a natural state of affairs but the result of harm to a developing brain. As you will learn throughout this book, there are many steps we can take to protect a child's brain health and reduce the odds of developing autism. Silberman's argument that autism merely reflects natural diversity in human cognitive function "passed down through millions of years of evolution" just does not fit with the facts.

The one grain of truth to this contention is that there is a genetic component to autism. Having a sibling with the disorder is probably the single biggest risk factor.[20] But genes alone do not cause autism. Some external triggering factor or combination of factors is required. Simply put, genetics cannot explain why almost 3 percent of boys in the United States today will have autism, whereas before the 1970s, the number was 1 in 10,000. In many countries, the prevalence of autism has increased exponentially in recent years, even though the human gene pool remains much the same.[21]

As Handley notes, "Ask any teacher, doctor, nurse, or coach who has been working for three decades or more and you'll always hear the same thing: something new and very different is happening with children today."[22] Even now, the percentage of children with autism continues to rise each year. Specifically, the prevalence of Autism Spectrum Disorder in US children aged three to 17 years was 2.24 percent in 2014, 2.41 percent in 2015, and 2.76 percent in 2016.[23]

The rise in autism is particularly troubling when we go further back and graph the number of autism cases by year of birth, as shown in Figure 1.

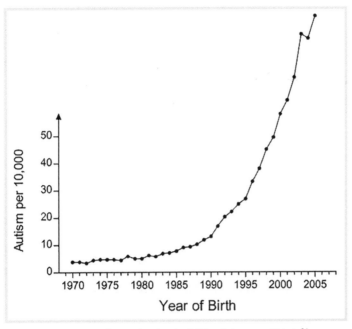

Figure 1: Prevalence of autism in California by year of birth.[24]

This graph shows that autism, which used to be quite rare, has become disturbingly common. We can also see that the inflection point was somewhere around the 1980s, with an exponential rise throughout the subsequent decades.

Some have questioned whether this exponential rise is a true increase in cases, or whether we have simply started categorizing more children as autistic. It is true that the diagnostic criteria have expanded, with the creation of the broader umbrella term "autism spectrum disorder" to capture milder cases and children with Asperger's Syndrome, for example. In addition, there is likely a greater awareness of the problem amongst parents and doctors, so fewer children go undiagnosed.

These factors may have accounted for a small rise in the prevalence of autism, but nowhere close to the exponential rise that has occurred in the past 30 years. Rigorous studies clearly show that what we now regard as autism was exceedingly rare before the 1980s.[25]

According to Dr. Cynthia Nevison, an environmental researcher at the University of Colorado, approximately 75 to 80 percent of the increase since 1988 is due to an actual increase in the disorder rather than changes in how autism is diagnosed.[26]

Perhaps the most concerning feature of the autism prevalence data is that it appears we have not yet reached "peak autism." At the time of writing, the percentage of children diagnosed with autism continues to climb. Simultaneously, we are also witnessing a rise in other neurological and behavioral disorders that reflect problems with early brain development, particularly attention-deficit/hyperactivity disorder (ADHD).

The prevalence of ADHD has not been rising as quickly as autism, but it affects far more children. It is the most common developmental disorder, now impacting at least 7 percent of children in the United States.

Children with ADHD will typically have difficulty staying focused and paying attention. They may also have greater difficulty regulating their own behavior or emotional state. In practice, this may lead to hyperactive, impulsive, and aggressive behavior. By some estimates, more than half of children with ADHD will display significant aggressive behavior.[27] As we might expect, this has been found to severely limit a child's ability to build friendships and succeed in school.[28]

Common Threads Underlying Autism and ADHD

The explosion in the number of children facing developmental disorders has fortunately sparked a flurry of scientific research to try to find the possible causes. Much of the funding has been devoted to research studying possible genetic causes, which in some ways makes sense, given that autism often runs in families. Yet understanding the genetic contributors will take us only so far. Our genes have not changed dramatically in the past 30 years, yet the number of children with autism has.

Clearly the exponential rise is not the result of genetics but some external factor in the world around us or, more likely, a combination of factors. Some of the genes involved in autism could just make some children more vulnerable to those external factors.

To start unraveling the mystery of what is causing the rise in autism, the most logical starting point is to consider potential risk factors that have changed the most since the early 1980s, when autism rates began to rise exponentially. This suggests several possibilities, including

- a rise in autoimmune and inflammatory conditions amongst pregnant women.
- an increase in the number of people having children later in life.
- an expansion of the newborn vaccine schedule, resulting in very young babies receiving a much higher dose of aluminum.
- replacing aspirin with acetaminophen (also known as Tylenol/Panadol) as the pain and fever medicine of choice in babies.
- an increase in the use of pesticides on food crops.
- an increase in exposure to flame-retardant chemicals.

For some of these possibilities, the link with autism is no more than speculation, as in the case of aluminum in vaccines. But research published in just the past couple of years has now provided direct evidence that some of the other factors listed above could indeed increase the risk of autism.

For example, we know that autoimmune disease in mothers is a major risk factor. Specifically, a mother's history of autoimmune thyroid disease, diabetes, psoriasis, or rheumatoid arthritis is associated with a 50 percent higher risk of autism.[29] The same conditions also appear to increase the risk of ADHD.[30]

The rates of all of these autoimmune diseases have skyrocketed since the 1980s, which may account for some of the increase in developmental disorders. (In my second book, *The Keystone Approach*, I explain some of the causes for autoimmunity, such as vitamin D deficiency and a decline in the number of beneficial gut microbes.)

The connection between a mother's autoimmunity and autism also hints at a bigger force at play: inflammation. The term "inflammation" refers to a system of defense mechanisms normally triggered by infections, damaged cells, or chemical irritants. The immune system switches to damage-control mode to remove the problem and initiate healing. Yet collateral damage can sometimes occur, particularly if inflammation continues unchecked for too long. For an infant, this collateral damage could include harm to their developing brain.

Autoimmunity is, however, only one possible cause of inflammation. Another cause is infection. There is now clear evidence that serious infections during critical developmental stages can increase the risk of autism, ADHD, and other mental disorders.[31]

This link between infections and autism supports the overall paradigm that inflammation harms the developing brain, but it cannot explain the rise in the number of cases. That is because infectious diseases have existed throughout human history and their prevalence has been falling as autism has been rising.

Likewise, the recent rise in autoimmune disease only accounts for a small fraction of the autism and ADHD cases seen today. There is something much more pervasive at play, with a more widespread reach. Many experts now believe that the culprit may be exposure to environmental toxins.

Cynthia Nevison is one researcher who has been analyzing the rise in autism cases in the United States and comparing that to our level of exposure to environmental toxins over the same time period.

Dr. Nevison notes that most of the suspected environmental toxins she looked at have actually decreased over the time period of interest, including lead, certain pesticides, and air pollution from vehicles. In many ways, our world is actually getting cleaner and less toxic.

But Dr. Nevison also reports there are some toxins that have increased in parallel with the rise in autism, notably: flame retardants, aluminum in vaccines, and the pesticide glyphosate, which is now heavily sprayed on wheat, corn, soy, and oats.[32] Acetaminophen also became the pain and fever reliever of choice during the 1980s–1990s, when autism began to skyrocket.

The fact that young children have been exposed to greater levels of these chemicals over the same time frame that autism has increased is obviously not sufficient to establish that any one of these toxins causes autism. However, for several toxins, such as pesticides, we actually do have direct evidence that exposure to high levels during pregnancy is a risk factor for autism, as will be discussed in the chapters that follow.

For other chemicals, where the evidence is more ambiguous, it may be the case that exposure only contributes to autism in particularly vulnerable children. This vulnerability may be because of genetics or because the children already have higher levels of inflammation due to nutrient deficiencies, the mother's autoimmunity, infections, or exposure to other chemicals.

When we zoom out and look at the bigger picture, it appears that it is probably the *combination* of many different factors that contributes to autism risk. Any one factor alone may not be sufficient to cause autism, but when combined with other assaults that also trigger inflammation, it may be too much for a vulnerable brain to handle.

That is why we can have such a powerful influence with relatively simple steps. By minimizing exposure to certain toxins, we can reduce the risk posed by other factors that also cause inflammation. By ensuring adequate nutrient intake, we reduce the potential harms of toxins even further. In short, by changing the risk factors that are relatively easy to address, our children will be less vulnerable to other factors that are out of our hands.

That leads to one overarching philosophy to keep in mind as you learn about all the various ways to protect your baby's brain development: you can pick and choose what to focus on. You do not have to do everything discussed in this book to make a big impact. Even a few small changes will go a long way toward providing a safe and protective environment for your baby's brain to grow. These changes can be as simple as taking the right supplements during pregnancy, as the next chapters explain. (For a broad overview of supplement recommendations, a summary list is provided at the end of chapter 6.)

PART 2

Brain-Making Nutrients & Hormones During Pregnancy

Chapter 2

Folate & Choline for Brain Development

Folate for Detoxification

In 2016, Johns Hopkins University caused quite a stir with a dramatic press release linking folic acid supplements and autism.[33] The headline read, "Too Much Folate in Pregnant Women Increases Autism Risk, Study Suggests." The press release went on to state that "Researchers found that if a new mother has a very high level of folate right after giving birth—more than four times what is considered adequate—the risk that her child will develop a condition on the autism spectrum doubles." Since prenatal folic acid supplements became popular around the same time autism rates began to increase, the press release obviously set off alarm bells.

Yet the study does not actually show that prenatal supplements contribute to autism risk. Looking at the broader picture, we know from several other much larger studies that mothers who take a folic acid supplement before conceiving and during early pregnancy are in fact *less* likely to have a child with autism. Three separate studies have found that taking folic acid during this critical time can actually halve the risk of autism.[34]

This is likely because folate, also known as vitamin B9, plays a key role in detoxification. Specifically, folate helps the body process byproducts of normal metabolism. One of those byproducts is homocysteine, an amino acid that is generated from chemical reactions that occur in every cell in the body. High levels of homocysteine can be harmful, so our cells use folate and vitamin B12 to convert it into more useful amino acids, namely cysteine or methionine. Without enough folate during early pregnancy, this detoxification process can be compromised and homocysteine can accumulate at high levels. This can lead to birth defects, inflammation, and, in all likelihood, a greater risk of autism.

Even the most conservative members of the medical establishment now recognize the "detoxification" theory of how folate protects against autism. The National Institutes of Health (NIH) notes that "Periconceptional use of folic acid might mitigate the potentially increased risk of [autism spectrum disorder] in children exposed to certain drugs and neurotoxins,"[35] including pesticides and air pollution.

As just one example of how folate can reduce the risk posed by toxins, a 2017 study reported that exposure to household pesticides during pregnancy more than doubled the risk of autism, but this risk factor was reduced in mothers with a higher folic acid intake.[36]

How, then, do we explain the Johns Hopkins study, which potentially links very high folate levels at birth with a higher rate of autism? One important point to note is that the 10 percent of mothers in the high-risk group had blood folate levels far above the normal range; we would not expect to see such high levels just from taking a prenatal supplement. Perhaps these women had a genetic variation in folate metabolism or had consumed a lot of processed food fortified with additional folic acid. They may have even had a folate deficiency, which can sometimes cause a falsely elevated folate level on blood tests.

Importantly, and not mentioned in the press release, the study actually found that both high *and* low folate levels in the mother shortly after birth were associated with a heightened risk of autism.[37] Taking a moderate dose of folic acid was actually protective, especially when taken during the first trimester.

Even the researchers involved in the study did not want to undermine the value of prenatal vitamins. "We are not suggesting anyone stop supplementation," said Daniele Fallin, one of the Johns Hopkins researchers.

There are simply too many unanswered questions with this study. Even so, we do not want to completely ignore a potential red flag. It is worth considering the question: If folate during early pregnancy is so important to autism prevention, how could high levels at birth possibly contribute to higher autism risk?

Researchers at the University of Northern Iowa suggest that if there is a problem, it may lie with excessive intake of *synthetic* folic acid during later stages of pregnancy.[38] In other words, it comes down to a matter of timing and the specific type of folate in supplements.

To understand this theory, it is important to recognize that the term "folate" actually encompasses a group of closely related compounds. Folic acid, the type of folate found in most supplements, is a man-made compound that is simply not the same as the natural folates found in foods such as vegetables. The two types are absorbed and processed differently.

Before the body can use synthetic folic acid for detoxification and other reactions, it must be converted into an active form by a series of enzymes. The activity of these enzymes can vary significantly between individuals. In people who are less efficient at performing the conversion, or if too much is taken, synthetic folic acid can build up in the bloodstream. Some studies indicate this can then interfere with the activity of natural-food folate (although this is a controversial issue).

According to the NIH, the safe upper limit of synthetic folic acid is 1,000 micrograms per day. The NIH notes that consuming more than this amount of synthetic folic acid can "increase the risk of adverse health effects."[39]

During pregnancy, these adverse effects may include compromising infant brain development, as new research reveals. Even setting autism risk aside, there could be more subtle effects on children's cognitive abilities. A recent study in Spain reported that when women took more than 1,000 micrograms per day of synthetic folic acid during pregnancy, their children showed reduced cognitive development at ages four to five.[40] The difference in cognitive abilities was relatively minor, but the authors concluded that the use of more than 1,000 micrograms per day of synthetic folic acid during pregnancy "should be monitored and prevented as much as possible."

Since most prenatal supplements contain 400 or 800 micrograms of folic acid, one might think it would be relatively easy to keep folic acid intake below this threshold. The problem is that synthetic folic acid is also added to many foods by law in more than eighty countries, including the United States. The net result is that anytime you are eating highly processed grains such as bread, crackers, or cereal, you are probably consuming a significant amount of synthetic folic acid.

To make matters worse, some manufacturers have voluntarily decided to add much more folic acid than the regulations require. For example, many brands of cereal contain 100 percent of the recommended daily intake (400 micrograms) in a one-cup serving. With a prenatal supplement containing 800 micrograms, a generous bowl of fortified cereal, and one or two other servings of fortified grains during the day, it becomes easy to consume vastly more folic acid than the recommended upper limit.

One helpful way to limit synthetic folic acid is to choose a prenatal that contains methylfolate or natural folate instead. If your prenatal has one of these natural forms, you are much less likely to go over the safe upper limit of synthetic folic acid, regardless of your diet. The preferred amount of methylfolate to look for is 800–1,000 micrograms, although even 400 micrograms may be sufficient in combination with a healthy diet. (For recommended brands, see brainhealthfrombirth. com/supplements)

Alternatively, you may decide to continue with a standard prenatal but limit your intake of processed grains, particularly those that are heavily fortified with folic acid. To see how much has been added to any particular food, check the percentage of the recommended daily intake of folic acid on the nutrition data panel.

The Harvard School of Public Health recommends avoiding foods fortified with more than 100–200 micrograms of folic acid, which would be shown as 25 percent to 50 percent of the daily value on the nutrition data panel.[41] Avoiding heavily fortified foods could mean replacing your usual breakfast cereal with old-fashioned oatmeal or granola, which do not usually have folic acid added. As a general rule, the less processed and refined a grain is, the less likely it is to contain a large amount of added folic acid.

Keeping synthetic folic acid within the safe limit of 1,000 micrograms per day is probably most relevant later in pregnancy. The most plausible theory explaining the apparent contradiction in studies on folic acid and autism is that it is only exposure to high levels during the second and third trimester that is problematic.

Before conception and in the earliest stages of pregnancy, having sufficient folate is so critical to development that even synthetic folic acid is clearly beneficial, as it reduces the risk of autism and serious birth defects. (This is true even in mothers with genetic variations in folate metabolism.)[42] The balance may shift later in pregnancy, when high doses of synthetic folic acid could possibly compromise development.

There does not seem to be the same concern with natural folate, which is found in leafy greens, broccoli, asparagus, avocado, chickpeas, and lentils. Although the NIH has advised that folic acid in supplements and fortified foods should not be consumed in amounts above the upper limit, it has not set an upper limit on natural food folate "because high intakes of folate from food sources have not been reported to cause adverse effects."[43]

This distinction is supported by the Spanish study mentioned earlier, which investigated the link between prenatal folate intake and cognitive function in four- to five-year-olds. Although more than 1,000 micrograms of synthetic folic acid appeared to compromise cognitive development, the reverse was true for natural folate. A higher intake of natural food folate was associated with significantly better scores in verbal memory and several other key measures of cognitive function.[44]

It also helps to choose a prenatal multivitamin that contains methylfolate or natural food folate instead of synthetic folic acid. In addition to protecting your baby's brain development, this type of prenatal may have other advantages. For example, researchers have shown that supplementing with methylfolate plus additional vitamin B12 is much more effective at preventing anemia during pregnancy than supplementing with a standard prenatal vitamin. In one study, less than half of the women taking methylfolate and B12 became anemic by the second trimester, compared to three-quarters of women taking a standard prenatal.[45] Preventing anemia is important for nurturing brain development, as further discussed in chapter 6.

Choline for Brain Building

Choline is another B vitamin that is absolutely critical for infant brain development. In the context of prenatal care, the importance of choline is often neglected, overshadowed by its more well-known cousin folate. Although it does not get nearly the same press, choline actually functions very similarly to folate in detoxification reactions and is therefore just as critical to preventing birth defects. Choline and folate are in fact so closely related that a deficiency of one will compromise our supply of the other.

But choline's importance during pregnancy goes much further. It is actually one of the major building blocks a baby needs to produce new brain cells and neurotransmitters. That is because it forms the backbone of the molecule phosphatidylcholine, which is the main raw material needed to produce nerve cells. Choline is also the basis for the important neurotransmitter acetylcholine, a signaling molecule that regulates the function of brain cells. A growing fetus, therefore, needs a constant supply of choline.

During pregnancy, the baby actually becomes a choline vacuum, sucking up a huge proportion of its mother's supply.[46] A healthy baby will be born with six to seven times the level of choline in the bloodstream as her mother.[47]

When a growing baby cannot obtain enough of this critical nutrient, the consequences can be very serious. One of the reasons why alcohol use during pregnancy is so harmful for infant brain development is that it depletes the supply of choline. A severe deficiency can also have many of the same effects as a folate deficiency, likely because they both perform the same detoxification reactions.

We know, for example, that a lack of choline in very early pregnancy increases the risk of neural tube defects.[48] (These are birth defects involving the brain or spine, such as spina bifida.) In a March of Dimes study, mothers with the lowest intake of choline had a fourfold higher risk of having a baby with a neural tube defect.

Most pregnant women will get enough choline to prevent these and other serious problems with neural development, but mild deficiencies that compromise brain building in more subtle ways are shockingly common. According to the NIH, the bare minimum amount of choline needed during pregnancy is 450 milligrams per day. By current estimates, more than 90 percent of pregnant women do not get enough.[49]

One of the researchers who has helped to reveal the extent of choline deficiencies in pregnant women is Dr. Taylor Wallace, Affiliate Professor in the Department of Nutrition and Food Studies at George Mason University. "Our research shows that only heavy egg consumers (i.e., those who consume two or more whole per day) even come close to meeting choline requirements," he says. "This is an enormous public health risk given the vital role choline plays in cognitive development of the infant."[50]

One would expect this is just the type of problem we should be able to solve with a good prenatal supplement. Unfortunately, the companies that manufacture prenatals are still largely ignoring the fact that choline is one of the nutrients pregnant women need most and are most likely to lack from their diets. At the time of writing, most prenatals contain only 10 to 55 milligrams of choline, if they contain any at all. This is far short of the 450 milligrams pregnant women need every day.

The American Medical Association (AMA) is so concerned about this gulf that in 2017, they passed a unanimous resolution advocating for greater amounts of choline in prenatals. This is an important step, and one that may have far-reaching benefits for future children. According to Dr. Carl Bell, a psychiatrist and professor of public health who has spent many years focusing on the prevention of fetal alcohol syndrome, "Should this AMA recommendation gain the traction it deserves, the American people might see a substantial decrease in the prevalence of premature and low-birth-weight infants, intellectual disability, ADHD, speech and language difficulties [...] – all of which seem to be tied to choline deficiency."[51]

Ensuring sufficient choline during pregnancy is also likely to have the bonus effect of supporting cognitive development in healthy children. We know from research in mice that in the second half of pregnancy, choline facilitates development of the hippocampus, the memory center of the brain.[52] Rats born to mothers who were supplemented with choline during pregnancy had better visual and spatial memory throughout their lifetimes.[53]

We have not yet seen the same dramatic results in humans, although there have been some promising studies. In 2012, researchers found a significant link between the mother's level of choline during the second trimester and cognitive scores at 18 months.[54] There is also some evidence of beneficial effects later in childhood. A group of researchers at the Harvard School of Public Health reported that higher choline intake during the first and second trimester was associated with better visual memory in 7-year-olds.[55]

Ensuring you get enough choline throughout pregnancy is one of the best ways to support your baby's developing brain. If you eat eggs on a daily basis, you are probably getting enough, but otherwise you are likely to need a supplement.

When it comes to supplementing, one strategy is to find a pre-natal that already contains a good amount of choline, although this can be difficult. As noted by Lily Nichols, a registered dietician and the author of *Real Food for Pregnancy*, nutrients such as choline "are bulky and, therefore, manufacturers leave them out or put in minimal amounts to keep the total number of pills down."[56]

A solution is to take a stand-alone choline supplement. Good-quality brands of choline supplements include Nested, Nature's Way, and Solgar. The dose found in separate choline supplements is typically between 350 and 500 milligrams. Taking a 350 milligrams supplement, combined with a diet that includes minor sources of choline such as meat, should be sufficient to reach the minimum daily requirement. Vegetarians and vegans may need a higher supplement dose, such as 500 milligrams.

If you breastfeed your baby, it is very important to ensure adequate choline throughout the time you are nursing. Choline is a key ingredient in breast milk, but the amount present varies widely depending on the mother's choline supply. The minimum recommended intake of choline for breastfeeding mothers is 550 milligrams per day.

Points to Remember

- Getting enough folate in early pregnancy significantly lowers the risk of autism.

- Choose a prenatal that contains methylfolate or natural food folate, rather than synthetic folic acid.

- The preferred amount of methylfolate in a prenatal is 800–1000 micrograms.

- Consuming more than 1,000 micrograms of synthetic folic acid per day late in pregnancy could possibly compromise brain development, although the evidence for this is relatively weak.

- To err on the safe side, if you are taking a prenatal with synthetic folic acid, reduce consumption of heavily processed grains fortified with large amounts of folic acid.

- On the other hand, consuming more foods that are naturally rich in folate likely boosts cognitive development. These foods include dark leafy greens, broccoli, asparagus, avocado, chickpeas, and lentils.

- As a critical nutrient for brain building, choline can help prevent birth defects in much the same way as folate.

- The recommended minimum intake of choline during pregnancy is 450 milligrams per day. It is typically difficult to reach this level without supplements, unless you eat eggs on a daily basis.

- Most prenatals contain very little choline. Look for a brand that contains at least 300 milligrams, add a stand-alone choline supplement, or eat eggs more often.

- Recommended brands of choline supplements include Nested, Nature's Way, and Solgar.

Chapter 3

The Surprising New Science on Vitamin D & Preterm Birth

In the United States, one in ten babies will be born premature. With many extraordinary advances in medical care in recent decades, premature babies have a better chance than ever of going on to lead healthy lives, without any adverse health consequences.

Yet even with the best available treatment, babies who are born extremely early often have compromised brain development. Those born before 32 weeks, for example, are seven times more likely to have severe intellectual disability.[57]

Autism is also particularly common in children born preterm, possibly because a premature baby's brain simply does not have enough time to form critical areas of neurons.[58] Researchers have observed such a pattern in brain MRI images of autistic children who were born premature. The images showed that key areas of the brain were much smaller than normal, including areas involved in social interactions and behavior.[59]

Although premature babies will be at a higher risk of significant intellectual disability and autism, these are still relatively rare outcomes. A much more common scenario is that children who are born premature develop typically but then show reduced cognitive abilities once they reach school age. Researchers have observed that preschoolers who were born at 30 to 34 weeks commonly have lower scores on intelligence tests, visual perception, attention span, memory, and vocabulary.[60]

By the time they reach 7 years old, up to a third of children born between 32 and 35 weeks will also have noticeable difficulty with hyperactivity, fine motor skills, mathematics, speaking, reading, and writing.[61]

It is clear that the best place for an infant's brain to develop is in the womb. The longer they remain there, the more opportunity a baby will have to build a healthy brain that can focus, remember, solve problems, and learn new skills. Preventing preterm birth is clearly a laudable goal, but is it really something we can influence?

Some of the major risk factors for preterm birth are largely beyond our control, such as infections and twin pregnancies. But groundbreaking new research has revealed one likely contributor that is easy to address: vitamin D deficiency.

Researchers were originally suspicious that vitamin D deficiency could play a role in preterm birth because of the racial disparity in preterm birth statistics: black infants are 60 percent more likely to be born preterm than white infants. We also know that individuals with darker skin tones need significantly more UV exposure to produce the same amount of vitamin D, so they are much more likely to become deficient. One study of pregnant women in Pittsburgh found that black women were six times more likely to have a severe vitamin D deficiency than white women were.[62]

Troubled by this pattern, doctors and researchers at a hospital in South Carolina conducted a bold experiment. In September 2015, the hospital initiated a new standard of care for pregnant women that included routine vitamin D testing and providing free supplements. Doctors gave patients personalized dosing recommendations based on their current vitamin D levels, with the ambitious goal of raising vitamin D levels to more than 40 nanograms per mililiter (ng/mL).[63]

This is significantly above the level traditionally considered to be sufficient, which is 20 ng/mL. Many experts now believe that the conventional target, which is based on the amount of vitamin D needed for bone health, is far too low, as will be discussed later in this chapter.

The results of the South Carolina experiment were staggering. When the researchers looked at the data from more than 1,000 pregnancies after introducing the program, they found that the women who were able to get their vitamin D level above 40 ng/mL had a 60 percent lower risk of preterm birth.[64] On average, the higher the vitamin D level, the longer the women made it through pregnancy.

A similar trend has also been witnessed by several other groups of researchers in population-based studies.[65] The South Carolina researchers also went back and looked at the data from two earlier trials of vitamin D supplements in pregnant women and found the same phenomenon: women with vitamin D levels above 40 ng/mL had a 57 percent lower risk of preterm birth than those with a vitamin D deficiency.

This evidence also fits together with studies finding that supplementing with vitamin D can help prevent other related complications during pregnancy, including low birth weight and preeclampsia, a condition involving high blood pressure during pregnancy, typically due to immune and hormonal disruptions. Until recently, little was known about how to prevent this potentially life-threatening condition.

Taking a bird's-eye view of the evidence in this area, a recent review of randomized controlled trials of vitamin D in pregnancy found that, compared to those taking a placebo, women taking a vitamin D supplement during pregnancy had[66]

- nearly half the risk of developing preeclampsia.
- half the risk of preterm birth.
- a significantly lower risk of low-birth weight infants.

No one is quite sure why vitamin D is so useful for preventing pre-term birth and these other complications, but one likely explanation is that it helps rebalance the immune system. Specifically, vitamin D calms excessive inflammation while also reducing the chance of infections, both of which have long been known to contribute to preterm birth.[67]

New research also suggests a similar relationship between vitamin D and recurrent miscarriage: a deficiency is more common in women who experience multiple pregnancy losses.[68] It is also apparent that a lack of vitamin D increases the risk of specific immune problems that can cause miscarriage, such as antiphospholipid antibody syndrome.[69]

Vitamin D and Autism

Preventing preterm birth, preeclampsia, and miscarriage is reason enough to ensure sufficient vitamin D during pregnancy, but doing so may also help prevent autism. So far, the research connecting vitamin D and autism has been limited to observing patterns in populations, rather than in controlled trials, but the findings are intriguing nonetheless.

In one of these observational studies, published in 2017, researchers in the Netherlands measured the vitamin D levels of more than 4,000 mothers during the second trimester of pregnancy.[70] When the children were 6 years old, they were screened for traits typically associated with autism, such as impaired social communication, repetitive behaviors, and difficulty with changes in routine. Those children with behavioral scores that raised concerns were referred for diagnosis by medical specialists.

When the children were 9 years old, the researchers then returned and combed through the medical records to find out how many were ultimately diagnosed with autism spectrum disorder and to determine if there was a correlation with the mother's vitamin D level. What they found was fascinating: when mothers were vitamin-D deficient during pregnancy, their children were more than twice as likely to be autistic.

A similar pattern linking vitamin D deficiency in pregnancy with a higher rate of autism has also been reported by other researchers in China and Sweden.[71] This consistent trend led the Dutch researchers to speculate that prenatal vitamin D supplementation may one day help reduce the rate of autism, just as folate supplementation has reduced the rate of many serious birth defects.[72]

Although there are not yet any randomized controlled trials confirming that suspicion, it is highly plausible, given that we know vitamin D reduces inflammation and preterm birth, both of which are significant risk factors for autism.

Even without incontrovertible proof that vitamin D can indeed help prevent autism, we already have good reason to supplement with this vitamin: to prevent pregnancy complications such as preterm birth and preeclampsia. Unfortunately, the studies linking vitamin D deficiency in pregnancy to autism, preterm birth, and preeclampsia have not gained the traction they deserve.

Even if preventing preterm birth is the only reason to supplement with vitamin D, this is an incredibly compelling reason, since preterm birth has so many potential downstream consequences, including risk of infections, hearing loss, serious intellectual disability, autism, ADHD, and even milder cognitive impairments.

As registered dietitian Lily Nichols notes in her book, *Real Food for Pregnancy*:

> *In some areas of the world, vitamin D deficiency affects up to 98 percent of pregnant women. At the same time, supplementing with this nutrient is effective at reversing deficiency and is incredibly inexpensive. It's perplexing to me that identifying and correcting vitamin D deficiency is not the norm, especially given that it puts you at higher risk for preeclampsia, having a low-birth weight infant, and gestational diabetes.[73]*

Given what is at stake and the ease of testing for and treating vitamin D deficiency, this is an issue all pregnant women should be made aware of. Hopefully medical practice will soon catch up and we will see not only universal screening of vitamin D levels in pregnancy, but also official guidance on the supplement dosage that is needed to raise levels high enough to prevent preterm birth.

This could be challenging because there is still a great deal of controversy over how high we should be aiming for with vitamin D levels. The Endocrine Society suggests that a level of 30 ng/mL should be the target for pregnant women.[74] Using that guideline, two-thirds of pregnant women in the United Kingdom would be characterized as deficient in vitamin D.[75]

Yet the studies on vitamin D and preterm birth show that 30 ng/mL is still too low. To reduce the odds of delivering early, vitamin D should be at least 40 ng/mL—and an even higher range may be better. Many integrative and holistic doctors recommend keeping vitamin D levels between 60 and 80 ng/mL, in order to better regulate the immune system. This strategy is supported by a large body of research finding that higher vitamin D levels can reduce inflammation, improve immunity against infections, and offer a range of other health benefits.[76]

If you suffer from an inflammatory or autoimmune condition, such as asthma, thyroid disease, or type 1 diabetes, it makes sense to aim for this higher range of at least 60 ng/mL. Doing so could potentially help reduce the severity of your condition while also protecting your growing baby from the harmful effects of inflammation during pregnancy. This is, however, somewhat speculative.

What we know for sure is that the bare minimum we should be aiming for is 40 ng/mL. Higher is probably better, but everyone should at least reach that baseline target for reducing the risk of preterm birth.

The only way to know if you are on the right track is to get your vitamin D level tested. Elisa Song, a Stanford- and NYU-trained pediatrician who founded one of the first and most highly regarded integrative pediatrics practices in the United States, gives the following advice to pregnant women:

> *Please ask your OBs to check your vitamin D levels. And don't just take "it's normal" at face value. Ask for the level because if it's a 25, that might be considered normal, but that's certainly not optimal for your baby's brain health, or for yourself—for mood support, immunity, and hormone balance.*

In an ideal world, your doctor will both test your vitamin D level and advise on the optimal supplement dose. However, many doctors are unfortunately still not familiar with the new studies in this area and so may not be able to provide specific guidance. If you are on your own, what is the best dose to start with?

The studies suggest that most women will require at least 5,000 IU per day to reach optimal levels during pregnancy. A randomized controlled trial that was published in the *Journal of the American Medical Association* in 2016 gave pregnant women 4,000 IU per day. At this dose, the average vitamin D level was close to 40 ng/mL, but a quarter of the women were still deficient, with levels below 30 ng/mL. Since we would like everyone to be over 40 ng/mL, the minimum level to prevent preterm birth, this study indicates that 4,000 IU per day will often be too low.

Beginning with 5,000 IU per day is a conservative next step. At that dose, most women will eventually reach the minimum threshold level. If you have a significant deficiency, however, your doctor may recommend an even higher dose in the short term to address the problem more quickly. For those with significant deficiencies, the Endocrine Society guidelines specifically recommends treatment with 6,000 IU of vitamin D per day for two weeks, followed by a lower ongoing maintenance dose.[77] The guidelines also advise that up to 10,000 IU per day is generally safe.

This is in line with the recommendation of Dr. Cedric Garland, one of the world's leading authorities on vitamin D. He suggests that those with a significant vitamin D deficiency usually need to take 5,000–10,000 IU per day, which is equivalent to what we would naturally produce from ten to twenty minutes of midday sun exposure in summer.[78]

You can also try to raise your vitamin D levels by spending this time in the sun each day, but only if you live in the right part of the world. As Dr. Garland notes, "In Boston, you cannot make any vitamin D from November through March, even if you were standing naked in the middle of the city."

A dose of 5,000 IU per day has also been used in one successful trial where vitamin D was given to pregnant women who previously had a child with autism.[79] In families where one child has autism, there is a 20 percent chance that younger siblings will be affected too. In this small trial, the mothers were given 5,000 IU per day throughout pregnancy and the younger siblings 1,000 IU per day from birth to age three. At the end of the study, only 5 percent of the children developed autism, a rate far lower than we would expect. This trial was not placebo-controlled and is too small to draw any firm conclusions, but it lends further support to the idea of supplementing with a dose of 5,000 IU per day while pregnant.

Because vitamin D facilitates calcium absorption, the main concern with using too high a dose of vitamin D long-term is raising blood calcium levels, but this is very unlikely to occur at just 5,000 IU per day (or even at 10,000 IU per day), especially since pregnancy increases the demand for calcium.

When choosing a supplement, note that the preferred form is vitamin D3, which is more effective than vitamin D2 in raising blood concentrations.[80] For even better absorption, it is best to choose an oil-based gel capsule or liquid drops. Good-quality brands include Jarrow, Doctor's Best, Pure Encapsulations, and Thorne Research.

Note that once your baby is born, she will likely also need her own vitamin D supplement, as this vitamin plays many critical roles during infancy and early childhood, including building strong bones and calibrating the immune system. Babies should typically be given 400 IU per day of vitamin D (typically one drop of a supplement designed for infants), starting in the first days of life. This is discussed in further detail in chapter 17.

Points to Remember

- Ensuring adequate vitamin D levels during pregnancy can significantly reduce the risk of preterm birth, one of the major risk factors for autism and developmental delays.

- The optimal level for preventing preterm birth is likely at least 40 ng/ml.

- An even higher range—60 to 80 ng/ml—may be beneficial, particularly for mothers with autoimmune or inflammatory conditions.

- Most women will require a vitamin D supplement during pregnancy. Ideally, the dose should be based on your current levels, but 5,000 IU per day represents a good starting point.

- Recommended brands include Jarrow, Doctor's Best, Pure Encapsulations, and Thorne Research.

- Babies should typically be given 400 IU per day of vitamin D, starting in the first days of life.

Chapter 4

Baby Brain Food: Fish & Omega-3 Fats

The Faroe Islands, a series of remote and rocky islands in the North Atlantic, with a population of just 50,000 people, might sound like an unlikely place for scientific breakthroughs. Yet it has two unique characteristics. The women there eat a lot of fish. They also have one of the lowest rates of preterm birth in the world. Dr. Sjurdur Olsen, then a researcher at a university on the islands, was the first to suggest that there may be a link between the two, publishing a paper in 1986 hypothesizing that high intakes of omega-3 fats from fish could lower the risk of preterm birth.[81]

It has taken decades to prove that he was right, but we now have a convincing body of evidence that omega-3 fats do indeed help prevent preterm birth. Numerous randomized controlled studies have demonstrated that increasing omega-3 fats during pregnancy lowers the risk of delivering before 34 weeks by more than 40 percent.[82]

Consuming more omega-3 fats is likely to be even more beneficial for women who would otherwise be very deficient. We know this from the latest research of Dr. Olsen, still focused on the question of omega-3 fats and preterm birth, thirty years after his initial discovery in the Faroe Islands. Now an adjunct professor at The Harvard School of Public Health, Dr. Olsen and his colleagues directly measured the levels of omega-3 fats in women's blood during the first and second trimesters of pregnancy. In a study published in 2018, he reported that the women with very low omega-3 fats were 10 times more likely to deliver prematurely.[83]

This research has far-reaching implications for brain health because premature babies are at higher risk of a range of long-term conditions including visual impairment, developmental delays, autism, and learning difficulties. Preventing preterm birth is one of the best ways to avoid these problems.

According to Philippa Middleton, Associate Professor of Pediatrics and Reproductive Health, "There are not many options for preventing premature birth, so these new findings are very important for pregnant women, babies, and the health professionals who care for them."[84]

Although it has taken far too long for the link between omega-3 fats and preterm birth to come to light, and the information is still not being shared widely enough, many pregnant women are already taking a step in the right direction by supplementing with DHA (docosahexaenoic acid).

DHA, one of the main omega-3 fats found in fish, is commonly recommended during pregnancy in order to support brain growth. This is because DHA is one of the building blocks used to produce new brain cells. A growing baby needs a steady supply of DHA throughout pregnancy but especially during the third trimester, when the brain accumulates DHA at an astonishing pace: a baby accumulates more DHA over these three months than in the 18 months after they are born.[85]

Supplementing with DHA during pregnancy is thought to support the important brain-building process, with the hope that this translates into higher IQ scores. The evidence on that point is somewhat mixed, but overall the studies do indicate that supplementing with

DHA during pregnancy improves cognitive development.[86] As one example, in a study where mothers were supplemented with fish oil containing approximately 1200 milligrams of DHA during pregnancy, their 4-year-olds scored significantly higher on intelligence tests.[87]

Thanks to Dr. Olsen's discovery in the Faroe Islands and the decades of research it sparked, it appears that supplementing with omega-3 fats is likely to have the added benefit of reducing the chance of preterm birth and all of its potential downstream consequences. (It may also have other benefits, including reductions in asthma and eczema.)

Given the desire to support brain growth, DHA is now added to many brands of prenatal multivitamins. Yet if our goal is also preventing preterm birth, there are two problems with relying on a standard prenatal to provide DHA.

The first problem is that many supplements intended for pregnant women contain only DHA, not the other important omega-3 fat, EPA (eicosapentaenoic acid). It is likely that both are helpful for preventing preterm birth because they each reduce inflammatory mediators known as prostaglandins, which stimulate labor. Both EPA and DHA can help regulate the production of prostaglandins, in slightly different ways. By taking only DHA, we are not getting the full benefit of the fats naturally found in fish.

The other problem is a question of dose. A prenatal multivitamin that proudly claims to provide DHA in order to support brain development typically contains only 50–200 milligrams. This falls far short of the amount needed to reduce your odds of delivering very early.[88] As noted by Dr. Middleton, who analyzed all the studies on omega-3 fats and preterm birth in 2018, "Our review found the optimum dose was a daily supplement containing between 500 and 1000 milligrams of long-chain omega-3 fats (containing at least 500 milligrams of DHA)."[89]

One way to ensure you are getting enough of these important fats is by taking a good quality fish oil supplement. There are three key questions to ask when choosing a fish oil supplement:

1. Does the manufacturer ensure the oil is not contaminated with mercury and other pollutants?

2. Does the manufacturer take steps to protect the fragile oils from becoming oxidized (i.e., rancid) and test to confirm low oxidation levels in the finished product?

3. Is the supplement concentrated enough to provide approximately 500 milligrams of DHA in one or two capsules and at least 200 milligrams of EPA?

One brand that excels on all of these fronts is Nordic Naturals Prenatal DHA, which is recommended by The American Pregnancy Association. Other good choices include Garden of Life Minami Prenatal Omega-3 Fish Oil, NOW DHA-500, and Best Nest Wellness One Fish Two Fish. These supplements contain approximately twice as much DHA as EPA, but the specific ratio is likely not that important. What matters more is getting enough DHA along with at least some EPA. (For the most up-to-date brand recommendations and information about where to buy these products, see brainhealthfrombirth.com/supplements).

If you are vegetarian or vegan, look for an omega-3 supplement made from algae oil, such as Nordic Naturals Algae Omega. The human body can produce a very small amount of DHA from other plant-based omega-3 fats, including flaxseed oil, but not nearly enough to meet a growing baby's needs. Studies have confirmed that supplementing with flaxseed oil does not significantly increase DHA levels in pregnant women,[90] so opt for an omega-3 supplement made from algae oil instead.

As with any supplement, especially when you are pregnant, check with your doctor before adding omega-3 to your regime. One common concern is that fish oil may increase bleeding risk in those taking blood-thinning medication such as Lovenox. However, this appears to be a matter of conjecture: there is actually very little evidence to support this concern.[91] As a result, many obstetricians do allow their patients to combine blood-thinning medications with 500–1,000 milligrams of fish oil.

If you have previously delivered early and the cause was not known or was attributed to immune problems, your doctor may recommend an even higher dose of fish oil. In a study of high-risk women who had previously delivered early, supplementing with 2.7 grams (2,700 milligrams) of combined EPA and DHA per day reduced the chance of another preterm birth by a third.[92]

Getting Omega-3s Directly from Fish

It is possible to get all the omega-3 fats that you and your baby need just by eating cold-water fish such as salmon and sardines. The question is how much fish you need to eat for supplements to become unnecessary.

If your goal is obtaining at least 500 milligrams of DHA per day, you would need to eat at least 9 ounces of high omega-3 fish per week, equivalent to two or three servings. Fish with high omega-3 levels include

- Salmon
- Sardines
- Atlantic mackerel
- Herring

Most other types of fish and seafood are much lower in omega-3 fats and would make it quite difficult to reach the equivalent of 500 milligrams of DHA per day. If you eat only tuna, shrimp, or flaky white fish such as cod, you would need to eat at least 30 ounces per week, or one serving every day, to get enough DHA. In the case of tuna, this would put you over the safe level of mercury.

It is well known that excessive mercury during pregnancy can compromise the developing brain.[93] But this should not discourage you from eating fish during pregnancy. It just means that it is important to choose varieties that are lower in mercury. Salmon is one of the best choices, since it is very low in mercury but high in beneficial omega-3 fats. A comparison of the mercury and omega-3 content of other common fish is shown in the tables below, categorized according to how often they can be eaten during pregnancy and listed in order of highest omega-3 and lowest mercury.

Very Low Mercury (3 or more servings per week)

Fish	DHA + EPA per 100 g (3.5 oz.)	Mercury (ppm)
Atlantic salmon, farmed	2.1	0.02
Atlantic salmon, wild	1.8	0.05
Herring	1.7	0.06
Sardines	1.5	0.08
Atlantic mackerel	1.2	0.05
Sockeye salmon, wild	1.2	0.04
Farmed trout	1.2	0.03
Coho salmon, wild	1.1	0.04
Atlantic cod	0.12	0.03

Moderate Mercury (1 serving per week)

Fish	DHA + EPA per 100 g (3.5 oz.)	Mercury (ppm)
Mackerel, chub	1.8	0.1
Sablefish (black cod)	1.8	0.2
Halibut, from Greenland	1.2	0.2
Sole	0.5	0.09
Flounder	0.5	0.1

Hake	0.5	0.2
Skipjack tuna	0.3	0.2
Tuna, light, canned	0.3	0.1
Tuna, yellowfin, canned	0.3	0.1
Perch	0.3	0.1
Snapper	0.3	0.2
Haddock	0.2	0.2

High Mercury (1–2 servings per month)

Fish	Mercury (ppm)
Halibut, Pacific	0.3
Tuna, albacore, canned	0.3
Grouper	0.4
Bass, Chilean	0.4
Mackerel, Spanish	0.4
Orange roughy	0.5

Very High Mercury (avoid entirely)

Fish	Mercury (ppm)
Tuna, bluefin	0.8
Swordfish	0.9
Mackerel, king	1.1
Marlin	1.5

For decades, governments have been warning pregnant women that mercury in fish can harm their baby's brain, but it now appears that these warnings may have caused more harm than good. That is because many women simply stopped eating fish when pregnant, depriving their infants of all-important DHA. Studies have now revealed that a lack of omega-3 fats is actually a much bigger threat to brain development than the low amounts of mercury found in most fish.

One of the largest studies demonstrating this effect was published in the prestigious medical journal *The Lancet* in 2007.[94] Researchers tracked seafood consumption in almost 12,000 pregnant women and then assessed developmental, behavioral, and cognitive outcomes in their children from age 6 months to 8 years. The results showed that when mothers consumed little to no seafood, the children had lower IQ scores and worse performance on a variety of measures of development, including communication and social behavior.

In light of this important finding, governments were lobbied to modify their recommendations on seafood consumption during pregnancy. It would take another seven years for the FDA to update its advice, but now the official recommendation is that all pregnant women should be eating fish regularly. "The latest science strongly indicates that eating 8 to 12 ounces per week of a variety of fish lower in mercury during pregnancy benefits fetal growth and development," said the FDA's Acting Chief Scientist, Stephen Ostroff, M.D.[95]

Is It Safe to Eat Sushi and Smoked Salmon During Pregnancy?

Pregnant women have long been told to avoid eating raw and smoked fish, out of concern that these foods may harbor parasites or bacteria that could cause food poisoning. While it is true that food poisoning is more likely when pregnant, and can in some cases harm an unborn baby, current recommendations are somewhat illogical.

In the United States, the FDA advises that raw fish and shellfish are not safe to eat while pregnant because they can contain parasites, salmonella, or other types of bacteria. While this is a legitimate concern in the case of shellfish, consuming sushi-grade raw fish is actually very low risk, particularly if the fish was previously frozen. The British National Health Service has in fact updated their guidance on this point, and now advises that "It's usually safe to eat sushi and other dishes made with raw fish when you're pregnant."

Smoked salmon is another matter, however, because it can contain *Listeria*. This is a type of bacteria that is not typically found on raw salmon, but it can contaminate processing equipment and thrives at refrigeration temperatures. *Listeria* is the reason why pregnant women are typically told to avoid deli meats and soft cheeses made from unpasteurized milk. The chance of any of these foods actually containing *Listeria* is remote but still a factor to consider, since *Listeria* infection while pregnant can cause miscarriage, stillbirth, or preterm delivery.

In recent years, the popular advice in this area has shifted slightly, based on claims that deli meats are no longer a concern when it comes to *Listeria*, but 2018 and 2019 saw several *Listeria* outbreaks traced back to deli meats, causing multiple hospitalizations and one death.[96] The unfortunate fact is that this bacteria is so dangerous and the stakes are so high that it is still safest to avoid deli meats altogether during pregnancy.

Points to Remember

- DHA, one of the main omega-3 fats found in fish, serves as an important building block for the developing brain.

- When babies get an abundant supply of this omega-3 fat during pregnancy, the risk of preterm birth decreases and the children have higher scores on intelligence tests many years later.

- Ensuring adequate omega-3 levels can also help reduce the risk of early premature birth by about 40 percent.

- To reap the full benefits of omega-3 fats, choose a good-quality fish oil supplement providing at least 500 milligrams DHA, along with at least some EPA.

- Nordic Naturals Prenatal DHA is a brand recommended by The American Pregnancy Association. Other good choices include Garden of Life Minami Prenatal Omega-3 Fish Oil, NOW DHA-500, and Best Nest Wellness One Fish Two Fish. If you are vegetarian or vegan, look for an omega-3 supplement made from algae oil, such as Nordic Naturals Algae Omega.

- Alternatively, you can get enough omega-3 fats by eating lower-mercury cold-water fish, such as salmon, at least two or three times per week.

- Fish with moderate and high mercury levels should be avoided during pregnancy.

- Good quality sushi made from low-mercury fish is fairly safe, but smoked salmon and deli meats should still be avoided due to concerns over *Listeria*.

Chapter 5

Iodine, Thyroid Hormones, & Your Baby

There is currently a heated debate among physicians as to whether all women should have their thyroid hormones checked as soon as they find out they are pregnant—or even as soon as they start trying to conceive.

Many obstetricians only offer thyroid testing for women they consider "high risk," namely those with obvious symptoms such as fatigue, dry skin, constipation, and cold sensitivity. But research has found that this approach misses a huge proportion of women who have hypothyroidism (low thyroid function) and need treatment.

In the United States, 2 to 3 percent of pregnant women are hypothyroid, which amounts to at least 80,000 cases per year, but many go undiagnosed because they are never tested. This is a significant problem because during early pregnancy, a baby is entirely dependent on its mother's supply of thyroid hormones: a baby does not begin making its own thyroid hormones until the second trimester.

In addition to regulating metabolism in the human body, thyroid hormones also play many important roles during pregnancy, including ensuring proper development of the placenta. If thyroid function is suppressed in early pregnancy when the placenta is forming, this appears to increase the risk of miscarriage and preterm birth.[97]

Thyroid hormones also support the baby's prenatal brain development. A mother's low thyroid function during pregnancy has been linked to lower IQ scores in young children, as well as a higher risk of autism, ADHD, and other developmental problems.[98]

As explained by Dr. Elizabeth Pearce, an expert on thyroid hormones in pregnancy and board president of the American Thyroid Association:

> Severe hypothyroidism can be associated with higher rates of pregnancy loss [miscarriage and stillbirth]. And we also know that thyroid hormone is critical for fetal neurodevelopment or brain development, so that children born to very profoundly hypothyroid mothers may have developmental delays. So the concern about brain development is really paramount when we're thinking about hypothyroidism in pregnant women. We want to make sure the fetus is getting adequate thyroid hormone throughout pregnancy.

When doctors can detect the problem and start treatment with supplemental thyroid hormone, the risks are dramatically reduced. We know, for example, that when women previously diagnosed with hypothyroidism go into pregnancy with their thyroid hormones well managed through medication, their children have no greater risk of autism.[99] Two recent studies also found that when pregnant women with low thyroid function are treated with thyroid medication starting in early pregnancy, the rate of miscarriage and preterm birth dropped to normal levels.[100]

The Controversy over Thyroid Testing

Universal screening is the only reliable way to ensure that all pregnant women at risk of complications from hypothyroidism are detected and treated, to support brain development and reduce the odds of preterm birth. Dr. Peter Taylor, a researcher at Cardiff University who has spent many years investigating the impact of thyroid disease during pregnancy, notes that "Fortunately, thyroid dysfunction is readily diagnosed with reliable blood tests and easily corrected with safe, inexpensive and available treatments."

Given that, why aren't doctors testing all pregnant women for low thyroid function? In some countries, they already are, but in the United States, wider testing is not recommended because of concerns over triggering unnecessary treatment in women with borderline test results. When TSH (thyroid stimulating hormone) is only slightly elevated, it is difficult to know whether treating with supplemental thyroid hormone has any benefit for the mother and baby.

The level of TSH, which is produced by the pituitary gland in your brain, increases as the thyroid gets more sluggish. If thyroid hormone levels are low, the brain produces more TSH to try to jump-start the thyroid, and this will be reflected in higher TSH levels on a lab test. During the first trimester, a TSH over 4 indicates low thyroid function, a level between 2.5 and 4 is borderline, while TSH below 2.5 means the thyroid is probably functioning well.

Doctors who argue against widespread screening believe that detecting mild and borderline cases (so called "subclinical hypothyroidism") may cause needless anxiety and lead to unnecessary prescriptions for thyroid medication, in much the same way that government guidelines on mercury in fish caused a detrimental overreaction, with the result of pregnant women unnecessarily avoiding fish.

The American Thyroid Association, a group of leading physicians that develops treatment guidelines, has been grappling with this question for many years. In 2017, it issued guidelines stating that currently there is not sufficient evidence for or against universal screening.[101] The guidelines instead recommend testing thyroid function in pregnant women who meet any one of a range of extremely broad criteria, including

- A history of infertility, miscarriage, or preterm birth
- A history of an autoimmune condition
- Family history of hypothyroidism
- More than two previous pregnancies
- Aged over 30
- Any symptoms suggestive of low thyroid function (fatigue, constipation, dry skin, cold intolerance, frequent muscle aches, or thinning hair)

In reality, the vast majority of pregnant women will meet one or more of these criteria, so it seems that the current recommendation comes very close to advocating universal screening. If you meet any of the criteria, you should feel comfortable asking your doctor for a TSH test even if they do not suggest it. As long as you recognize that mildly suppressed thyroid hormones are not reason for worry, there seems to be little downside in gathering as much information as possible about the health of your pregnancy.

Having your thyroid hormone level tested does of course often raise the question of what to do when the results are ambiguous, which is another area of controversy that the American Thyroid Association has been trying to address. What level of hypothyroidism justifies treatment with medication? "We are still trying to figure out whether or not it's necessary to treat women with milder hypothyroidism, but right now the data is really not conclusive," says Dr. Pearce.

There may be more value in treating these borderline cases if further testing shows that thyroid antibodies are present. In developing countries, the major cause of low thyroid function is iodine deficiency. Iodine is a trace mineral naturally found in fish, seaweed, and certain other foods. It also happens to form an essential component of thyroid hormones. By some estimates, more than 1.9 billion people are iodine deficient, including more than 40 percent of people in Africa and Eastern Europe.[102] If iodine deficiency is the cause of low thyroid function, the simplest solution is correcting the deficiency, rather than giving medication.

Yet in countries such as the United States, where table salt is iodized and women take prenatals containing iodine, the most common cause of low thyroid function is autoimmunity. This occurs when the immune system generates antibodies against the thyroid and those antibodies interfere with thyroid function. (In some cases, these antibodies can instead cause the thyroid to be overactive, but this is relatively rare and the impacts on pregnancy are not as clear.)

When women have only slightly abnormal thyroid hormone levels but also have thyroid antibodies, doctors are more likely to recommend medication. As Dr. Pearce notes, "That's a group that we think may have a higher risk for miscarriage and possibly for premature delivery, for reasons that are really not very well understood." As a result, the guidelines advise that giving thyroid medication to women with a history of miscarriage plus thyroid antibodies but normal hormone levels "may be considered given its potential benefits in comparison with its minimal risk."

The current evidence also suggests that treatment should be considered even when there is no history of miscarriage, based solely on the goal of reducing the risk of preterm birth. In one recent study, giving thyroid medication to women with thyroid antibodies but only slightly abnormal TSH reduced the risk of preterm birth by 70 percent.[103]

In explaining the findings, the study authors noted: "It seems that women who are positive for thyroid antibodies before pregnancy may have subtle preexisting thyroid dysfunction that could possibly worsen during pregnancy." Even though they may have normal hormone levels initially, the higher risk of complications may arise because these women may not be able to adequately respond to the higher demand for thyroid hormones during pregnancy, and they can very easily slip into hypothyroidism.

This raises an important point for women who were diagnosed with hypothyroidism even before becoming pregnant and are already taking medication: you will likely need to increase the dose of your medication by 25 to 30 percent during early pregnancy.

"A woman who is hypothyroid before she becomes pregnant, even if she's got perfectly controlled thyroid blood tests before she conceives, is likely going to need an increase in her thyroid hormone dose as soon as she knows she is pregnant," says Dr. Pearce. "That's important because she needs that thyroid hormone for her baby's brain development." The increased need for thyroid hormone starts at around seven weeks, so "we typically recommend a woman starts a higher dose as soon as she knows she's pregnant and continues that with frequent monitoring until she delivers."

Iodine for Thyroid Function

Although most thyroid disorders in developed countries are caused by autoimmunity, iodine deficiency can still be a problem for some women. Pregnancy places significant demands on the thyroid to produce more hormones than usual, which increases the need for iodine.

Without enough iodine to keep up with this demand, a baby's cognitive development can suffer.[104] In a long-term study of pregnant women in Bristol, England, researchers found that children of iodine-deficient mothers were significantly more likely to have low scores of verbal IQ, reading accuracy, and reading comprehension.[105] The lower the mother's concentration of iodine, the lower the average scores for IQ and reading ability in the children.

According to Professor Margaret Rayman, who led the research: "Our results clearly show the importance of adequate iodine status during early pregnancy, and emphasize the risk that iodine deficiency can pose to the developing infant." This is particularly troubling given how widespread iodine deficiency was in the study. When iodine levels were measured against World Health Organization standards, they found that two-thirds of pregnant women were deficient. This study was conducted in Bristol in the 1990s, and the situation has improved in recent years, but iodine deficiency is still relatively widespread in the United Kingdom.

Iodine deficiency is less common in the United States, because iodine is added to table salt. Even so, approximately one-third of pregnant women in the United States are marginally iodine deficient.[106] For this reason, the recommendation of organizations such as the American Academy of Pediatrics, the Endocrine Society, and the American Thyroid Association is for all pregnant women to take a prenatal supplement that contains 150 micrograms of iodine. Together with dietary sources, this is thought to be sufficient for most women to get the total amount they need each day, which is around 250 micrograms.

According to a 2017 study, only 60 percent of the top-selling prenatals contained iodine, and many do not contain the full amount.[107] If your prenatal does not contain a significant amount of iodine, you can probably obtain enough by using iodized salt and eating fish or dairy a few times per week.

Seaweed is also a rich source of iodine, but the amount can be unpredictable and certain varieties, such as kelp, kombu, and wakame, may actually contain too much. An extreme excess of iodine can be counterproductive when it comes to supporting thyroid health, because it can cause oxidative damage to thyroid cells .[108] As a result, government bodies have advised pregnant women to eat seaweed no more than once per week.[109]

Avoiding large doses of iodine may be especially important if you have an autoimmune thyroid condition, because excessive iodine can occasionally exacerbate the problem. In cases where thyroid autoimmunity causes an overactive thyroid, as with Graves disease, some doctors even recommend avoiding small doses of supplemental iodine, which would mean looking for an iodine-free prenatal (such as Mama Bird Iron & Iodine Free). In the case of Hashimotos, however, which typically suppresses thyroid function, it is likely beneficial to continue taking a prenatal that includes iodine. Seek your endocrinologist's advice on this point, but the research so far suggests that supplementing with low doses of iodine (up to 200 micrograms) can actually reduce thyroid antibodies in those with Hashimotos.[110]

Points to Remember

- Ask your doctor to check your TSH level as soon as possible during pregnancy.

- If your TSH is over 2.5, ask your doctor to test for thyroid antibodies and discuss whether you should take thyroid medication.

- If your TSH is only slightly elevated but you have thyroid antibodies, it is possible that thyroid medication may lower the risk of miscarriage and preterm birth.

- Check that your prenatal multivitamin contains 150 micrograms of iodine. If it does not, use iodized salt and eat fish or dairy regularly to meet your daily iodine needs.

Chapter 6

Iron, Anemia & When to Cut the Cord

Iron is another nutrient that is particularly important for your baby's brain development. Pregnancy dramatically increases the need for iron, especially during the second and third trimester when the mother needs to make a vast number of new red blood cells to carry oxygen to the placenta. In an average pregnancy, a mother's blood volume increases by 50 percent during this time.[111]

Producing all of these new red blood cells requires a steady supply of iron. That is because iron is a key component of hemoglobin, the molecule in red blood cells that carries oxygen. If a pregnant woman is lacking iron, she will not produce enough hemoglobin to make new red blood cells. The result is iron-deficiency anemia, a condition that impacts about one in five pregnancies.

Anemia during pregnancy is problematic for both mother and baby. For the mother, it causes fatigue and reduces immunity to infections.[112] For the baby, it is linked to lower birth weight and increased risk of preterm birth. It can also compromise brain development, resulting in lower cognitive scores.[113]

Iron deficiency seems to have the most impact on infant brain development when it occurs during the third trimester of pregnancy. This is not only an important time for brain growth but also a time in which the baby is supposed to be building up its own iron stores to carry it through the first months of life. A baby born to an iron-deficient mother is more likely to be anemic during the six months after he is born, which has further repercussions for brain development.[114]

Anemia in newborn babies is unfortunately quite common. It is also a problem that is much easier to prevent than to solve after a baby is born. Breast milk and formula contain small amounts of iron, but only enough to keep pace with minimum needs, not enough to address a major deficiency. Once a baby becomes deficient, pediatricians usually recommend liquid iron supplements. The problem is that most babies will reject these foul-tasting liquids. Even if your baby willingly takes an iron supplement, it may then cause painful constipation. The best solution is prevention—to give babies the opportunity to build up sufficient iron stores during pregnancy to carry them through their first months.

Prenatal Iron Supplements

Unless you are vegetarian or have a medical condition that can impair iron absorption (such as celiac disease or inflammatory bowel disease), chances are your iron intake will be sufficient and you will not need an additional iron supplement beyond the small amount typically found in prenatals.

Even so, it is safest to have your doctor test your iron levels at some point in the second half of pregnancy (usually by measuring your level of ferritin, which is a protein that reflects iron stores). You can also ask for a blood test at any time during pregnancy if you notice several symptoms of anemia, such as fatigue, weakness, paleness, rapid heartbeat, dizziness, or an unusual craving to chew ice. If a blood test shows that you are anemic or iron deficient, your doctor will likely recommend an additional iron supplement.

What often happens next is that the iron supplement causes digestive side effects such as constipation or nausea, and understandably, many women are reluctant to continue taking it. But addressing anemia in pregnancy is important for your energy levels, your immune system, and your baby's brain growth. The key is choosing an iron supplement in the optimal form.

The cheapest and most common forms of iron found in supplements, such as ferrous sulfate, are poorly absorbed and can often cause constipation or nausea. A much better option is iron in a form called amino acid chelate, such as iron bisglycinate. This is just as effective as standard iron, even at a much lower dose. It is also very well tolerated and rarely produces side effects.[115] In one randomized trial, a dose of 25 milligrams per day of iron bisglycinate was as effective as 50 milligrams of standard iron supplements, without the negative side effects.[116]

If your doctor recommends supplementing with iron, suggested brands include

- Thorne Iron Bisglycinate
- Solgar Gentle Iron
- Country Life Easy Iron

Another form of iron supplement that appears to be significantly more effective than ferrous sulfate, with fewer side effects, is iron bound to lactoferrin.[117] A protein naturally produced in humans and many other animals to transport iron, lactoferrin is found in particularly high levels in breast milk. It is nearly identical in humans and cows, so it can be isolated from cow's milk and taken in supplement form to treat anemia. Although typically more expensive than iron bisglycinate, lactoferrin can be a suitable backup option should you experience any problems taking iron bisglycinate. One recommended brand for this type of iron supplement is Jarrow Formulas Ironsorb + Lactoferrin.

When to Cut the Cord?

Addressing anemia during pregnancy is one way to help ensure that babies are born with enough iron, but there is one more factor that can have a profound impact on a baby's iron stores. It turns out that the standard medical practice of clamping the umbilical cord soon after birth may be robbing babies of all-important iron.

For decades, the conventional approach has been to clamp and cut the umbilical cord within the first minute after birth to prevent excessive maternal blood loss and reduce the risk of hemorrhage. There is, however, very little evidence supporting this practice. Whether the cord is clamped within one minute or after three minutes actually makes no real difference to the risk of hemorrhage for the mother.[118]

The timing of cord clamping does, however, make a difference for the baby. Specifically, a delay of a couple of minutes allows more of the baby's blood that is retained in the placenta to return to the baby, increasing iron stores. This can continue to benefit the baby for much longer than you might expect. In babies who are delivered with delayed cord clamping, higher iron stores are still evident after 12 months.[119]

A greater store of iron not only significantly reduces the risk that a baby will become anemic in the first year but also supports infant brain development.[120] The benefits for brain health are clearest in regions where iron deficiency is common. For example, a 2018 randomized controlled study in Nepal reported that delaying cord clamping by three minutes improved children's overall neurodevelopment at 12 months.[121]

Experts believe a similar benefit will also be seen even in developed countries where iron deficiency is less common. Danish researchers have noted that "delayed cord clamping seems to benefit full-term infants even in regions with a relatively low prevalence of iron deficiency anaemia."[122]

The first clear evidence supporting this theory came in December 2018, with a study led by Judith Mercer, Clinical Professor of Nursing at the University of Rhode Island. The study showed for the first time that delayed cord clamping helps brain development even in healthy full-term infants with no risk factors for anemia.[123] Delayed cord clamping not only increased iron stores at four months but also increased the brain's levels of myelin, a fatty substance that insulates nerves and helps them communicate efficiently. Abnormally low levels of myelin are associated with a range of childhood developmental disorders, including dyslexia and autism. It turns out that the cells that produce myelin in the brain need a sufficient supply of iron to function properly.

The Rhode Island researchers were able to see the effect of iron on myelin production by first randomly assigning infants to either standard or delayed cord clamping (with a five-minute delay.) This clearly boosted iron stores, as would be expected. "When we wait five minutes to clamp the cords of healthy babies, there is a return of the infant's own blood from the placenta, and one of the results is a return of up to 50 percent of the baby's iron-rich blood cells," said Professor of Nursing and nurse-midwife Debra A. Erickson-Owens, who conducted the research.

But the more surprising finding came when the babies were four months of age and the researchers took MRI images of their brains. The infants in the delayed cord-clamping group had significantly more myelin in early developing areas of the brain associated with motor, visual, and sensory processing function. There was also a clear link between an infant's level of iron stores and the myelin content in these areas of the brain. As explained by Erickson-Owens, "Our study shows that waiting five minutes or more before clamping the umbilical cord, while infants are held skin-to-skin with the mother, leads to more myelin development."

Since myelin acts as critical insulation around brain cells, scientists believe that the better the myelination, the more efficiently the brain can function. Given that, the new study helps explain how delayed cord clamping may benefit cognitive function.

The strong evidence that delayed cord clamping benefits infant brain health is unfortunately not yet widely known amongst obstetricians. As Erickson-Owens noted in 2019, "I presented six times (at major conferences) on this topic last spring, and I am still concerned with the number of clinicians who do not put this evidence-based research into their day-to-day practice."

The fact that delayed cord clamping is not yet the norm is even more surprising given that this method has been officially blessed by The American College of Obstetricians and Gynecologists (ACOG), which issued an opinion stating that:[124]

> *Delayed umbilical cord clamping appears to be beneficial for term and preterm infants. In term infants, delayed umbilical cord clamping increases hemoglobin levels at birth and improves iron stores in the first several months of life, which may have a favorable effect on developmental outcomes.*

The ACOG went on to explain that the benefits are even more significant for preterm infants, because delayed cord clamping reduces the risk of a variety of serious health problems. The main downside is that it may slightly increase the risk of a baby becoming jaundiced, which needs to be monitored and sometimes treated. The main treatment is light therapy, where babes are placed under UV lamps for several hours to help break down bilirubin, the blood by-product that causes jaundice.

Delayed cord clamping may also reduce the amount of cord blood available for storage, although one of the main providers of this service in the United States, CBR, reports that "In our experience, healthcare providers have been able to collect a sufficient volume of cord blood for storage even when practicing delayed cord clamping, giving your baby the best of both opportunities."[125]

Ultimately, when weighing the pros and cons, delayed cord clamping wins out. The American College of Obstetricians and Gynecologists unequivocally states that they "now recommend a delay in umbilical cord clamping in vigorous term and preterm infants for at least 30-60 seconds after birth."[126]

This may not be quite enough time to reap the full benefits, however. The World Health Organization currently recommends clamping the umbilical cord between one and three minutes after birth.[127] That should provide enough time to top up your baby's iron stores and set them up for healthy brain development over the next year.

Points to Remember

- Ask your doctor to test your iron levels at least once during the second half of pregnancy, or if you are unusually tired, pale, dizzy, or experience other symptoms of anemia.

- If testing shows that you are iron deficient and your doctor recommends taking additional iron, look for a supplement in the form of bisglycinate to reduce side effects.

- Recommended brands of iron supplements include Thorne Iron Bisglycinate, Solgar Gentle Iron, and Country Life Easy Iron.

- Although typically more expensive than iron bisglycinate, iron bound to lactoferrin can be a good backup option should you experience any problems taking iron bisglycinate.

- Ensure your obstetrician or midwife is aware of the advantages of delayed cord clamping, and discuss your wishes in advance of the birth.

Prenatal Supplement Summary

1. Prenatal Multivitamin

- Choose a prenatal containing 800 to 1,000 micrograms of methylfolate, rather than synthetic folic acid.

- Check that your prenatal contains at least 150 micrograms of iodine. If it does not, use iodized salt and eat fish or dairy regularly.

2. Choline

- Unless you eat eggs on a daily basis, supplement with 300–500 milligrams per day, whether as part of your prenatal or as a stand-alone supplement.

3. Vitamin D

- The optimal vitamin D level for preventing preterm birth is likely at least 40 ng/ml.

- Many women will need to supplement with 5,000 IU per day to reach that level.

- Look for a soft gel or liquid version containing vitamin D3.

4. Fish Oil/Omega-3 Fatty Acids

- Choose a good-quality fish oil supplement providing at least 500 milligrams DHA, along with at least some EPA.

- Alternatively, eat lower-mercury cold-water fish, such as salmon, at least two or three times per week.

5. Iron

- Most women will get enough iron from their diet and prenatal multivitamin, so there is no need to take a separate iron supplement unless blood tests suggest a deficiency.

- If you are anemic and your doctor recommends taking additional iron, look for iron bisglycinate, a form with fewer digestive side effects.

6. Probiotics

- As will be discussed in Chapter 17, adding a probiotic is optional but may help reduce the odds of testing positive for Group B streptococcus and therefore requiring antibiotics at delivery.

- For that purpose, take a probiotic containing a combination of *Lactobacillus rhamnosus GR-1* and *Lactobacillus reuteri RC-14* during the third trimester.

For up-to-date brand recommendations, see brainhealthfrombirth.com/supplements

PART 3

Protecting Baby's Brain During Pregnancy

Chapter 7

Acetaminophen & Antidepressants During Pregnancy

One of the most difficult decisions to make during pregnancy is whether it is safe to continue taking medication. The FDA recommends that women seek their doctor's advice on weighing the benefit of each medication against the potential risks, but the reality is that doctors often have very little solid data to guide their advice.

The risk/benefit analysis is particularly challenging, and perhaps even more important, for medicines that work by targeting the brain, such as those used to treat pain or mental illness. These medications are more suspect because the very reason they work is by acting in the mother's brain, so they may have an impact on the baby's brain too. This chapter discusses the current state of the evidence on the two most common types of medication in this category, namely acetaminophen and antidepressants. For recommendations on the safety of various other types of medications during pregnancy, see mothertobaby.org, a website operated by a group of world-renowned researchers and pediatricians.

The Acetaminophen/ Autism Connection

Acetaminophen is currently the most widely used medication during pregnancy. This pain and fever reliever, sold under the brand name Tylenol or Panadol and called paracetamol outside the United States, is currently used in half of all pregnancies.

Although there is still a surprising amount of uncertainty over exactly how acetaminophen works to reduce pain, it is clear that it involves the brain.[128] Rather than reducing inflammation, as other common painkillers do, it appears to reduce the activity of brain areas involved in the perception of pain.

Acetaminophen has long been considered the safest option for treating headaches and other types of pain in pregnancy, but a series of recent studies have raised concerns that this may be problematic. Specifically, the alarm has been raised that it may increase the risk of autism and ADHD. In 2015, the FDA issued the following caution:

> FDA understands the concerns arising from recent reports questioning the safety of prescription and over-the-counter (OTC) pain medicines when used during pregnancy...we evaluated research studies published in the medical literature and determined they are too limited to make any recommendations based on these studies at this time. Because of this uncertainty, the use of pain medicines during pregnancy should be carefully considered.[129]

Now, several years later, this issue has been investigated in at least seven groups of mothers and children, spanning 130,000 pregnancies in the United States and Europe.[130] This growing body of evidence indicates that prolonged use of acetaminophen during pregnancy can in fact impair brain development in infants, evident in slightly higher risks of ADHD and autism.[131]

This is no doubt cause for concern, but there are two important points to bear in mind:

1. The overall increase in risk of autism and ADHD is still relatively small.

2. It is only prolonged use that is problematic, not occasional or short-term use.

Starting with the first point, epidemiologists have now analyzed all of the combined data from the prior studies in what is known as a meta-analysis and concluded that the overall risk from prolonged use of acetaminophen in pregnancy is modest.[132] Specifically, prolonged exposure to acetaminophen during pregnancy was associated with a 30 percent increase in "relative risk" for ADHD and a 20 percent increase in "relative risk" for autism spectrum disorders (ASD).

This concept of "relative risk" refers to a percentage on a percentage, so the numbers are not actually as bad as they sound. As explained by Dr. Ilan Matok, the epidemiologist who led the meta-analysis, "In absolute terms, the risk for ASD is about 1 percent, and the risk from prolonged gestational acetaminophen use rises to about 1.2 percent."

It is also important to note that the risk comes from *prolonged* use of acetaminophen during pregnancy. "Use of a few days to relieve pain or fever is fine," Matok says. That view is supported by several studies, including one led by Dr. Eivind Ystrom, Professor of Genetics, Environment, and Mental Health at the Norwegian Institute for Public Health.[133]

Dr. Ystrom's study, published in the journal *Pediatrics*, found that using acetaminophen for less than eight days did not increase the risk of ADHD, whereas there was an increased risk from long-term use. The odds of children being diagnosed with ADHD increased with the length of time the medication was used.

For mothers taking acetaminophen for longer than eight days, the risk of children being diagnosed with ADHD increased with the number of days exposed; those who had 29 or more days of prenatal acetaminophen exposure were more than twice as likely to be diagnosed with ADHD. The impact of the number of doses is likely to be similar in the context of autism.

What about other effects on the developing brain? We know by now that any factor that raises the risk of autism and ADHD is also likely to compromise brain development in other ways. Small initial studies suggest this may also be true for acetaminophen. Specifically, taking this medication during pregnancy may slightly lower children's IQ and increase the risk of language delay.[134] It also appears to increase the risk of children having hyperactivity and behavioral and emotional problems.[135]

But again, the effect likely depends on the duration of use. In one study, three-year-old children whose mothers used acetaminophen for more than 28 days during pregnancy were found to have poorer communication skills, behavior, and gross motor development.[136] In contrast, children exposed to fewer than 28 days showed only a minor reduction in gross motor development.

Timing may also matter. The research so far indicates that an infant's developing brain may be most sensitive to acetaminophen in the third trimester, when the most brain growth occurs.[137]

With all of this new research raising concerns about the implications of taking acetaminophen during pregnancy, official guidelines are in a state of flux. Most guidelines state that occasional and short-term use is likely safe, but advise pregnant women to consult their doctor for advice if longer-term use is needed.

In the United Kingdom, the National Health Service states that paracetamol/ acetaminophen remains the preferred choice to treat mild or moderate pain and high fever, "but as with any medicine taken during pregnancy, use paracetamol at the lowest effective dose for the shortest possible time."

In the United States, the Society for Maternal Fetal Medicine issued the following guidance in 2017:

> *Based on our evaluation of these studies, we believe that the weight of evidence is inconclusive regarding a possible causal relationship between acetaminophen use and neurobehavioral disorders in the offspring. As with all medication use during pregnancy, communication regarding the risks versus the benefits of prescription and over-the-counter medications use should occur between patient and provider.* [138]

Unfortunately, doctors have very little information to go on when advising patients on this subject, unless they have time to analyze all of the latest scientific studies. They also have few good alternatives to offer patients with chronic pain.

The other common pain relievers, such as opioids and nonsteroidal anti-inflammatories (NSAIDs), are likely no safer during pregnancy—and may in fact be worse. In a 2017 study led by the Centers for Disease Control, researchers found that compared to acetaminophen, the use of opioids or NSAIDs during pregnancy increased the risk of several birth defects.[139] (This concern does not apply to low-dose aspirin, which is commonly recommended in pregnancy.)

In the future, it is possible that research may uncover ways of minimizing the potential risks to the brain associated with long-term use of acetaminophen. In animal models, research suggests that acetaminophen is more harmful when there is a deficiency of certain nutrients, including sulfate, cysteine, S-adenosyl methionine, and glutathione, which all play key roles in detoxification by the liver. Although we are still a long way from being able to apply these findings, it is possible that by supporting the liver with good nutrition or even supplements, we may be able to minimize the impact of acetaminophen on the developing brain.

At the moment though, the best option is probably to focus on addressing the source of the pain, to reduce the need for medication as much as possible. For headaches and muscle aches, magnesium supplements and massage may be helpful. Migraine sufferers can often find significant relief by eliminating trigger foods such as artificial sweeteners and foods high in histamine or tyramine (including chocolate, aged meats, and cheese).

Back pain is probably the most common source of chronic pain during pregnancy. Hundreds of studies have found that physical therapy is usually the best way to reduce this pain, particularly when treatment combines manual therapy (such as massage) with exercises to strengthen the muscles that stabilize the pelvis and spine.[140]

The question mark hanging over the safety of Tylenol is unfortunately not limited to pregnancy. After a baby is born, there is the separate issue of the risks posed by giving this medication directly to newborns, such as to treat pain from circumcision. Some experts believe that doing so may in fact contribute more to autism risk than exposure during pregnancy. The nature of this risk and alternatives for treating pain and fever in infants will be covered in chapter 15.

The Great Antidepressant Debate

Many women also find themselves having to weigh the potential benefits of medication against uncertain risks to brain development when it comes to antidepressants, a broad group of medications used to treat depression and anxiety. (If this is not an issue you face, you may wish to skip ahead to the next chapter.)

Assessing the risks and benefits of taking antidepressants during pregnancy poses unique challenges, because some doctors feel that these medications are not essential to the health of the mother, so the benefit cannot justify any risk at all. This common perspective of doctors is at odds with the experience of patients, who feel that psychiatric medications are just as essential as medicines that treat physical health problems.

In an article for *Slate*, journalist Laura Turner described her experience needing anxiety medication during pregnancy: "From my perch as a patient, I often felt that doctors practiced maternal fetal medicine in name only—the overriding concern is for the fetus, often at the expense of the mother, who is reduced to a mere vessel for a baby."[141]

Turner went on to explain that "some doctors refuse to prescribe even SSRIs [a common class of anti-depressants] to their pregnant patients. Others urge caution or refer patients to psychiatrists who specialize in treating pregnant people. This lack of consistency in the medical establishment means that women in need might receive entirely different care for no standard reason. This is confusing to patients in need, who, like any other confused patient, often end up on the internet looking for answers."

One of the questions these patients want answered is whether taking antidepressants while pregnant can increase their child's risk of autism. The concern over this issue rose to prominence in 2016, when a study by four Montreal researchers concluded that "the use of antidepressants, specifically selective serotonin reuptake inhibitors [SSRIs], during the second and/or third trimester increases the risk of [autism spectrum disorder] in children."[142]

In an interview following the study's publication, study senior author Anick Bérard of the Université de Montréal firmly advocated avoiding antidepressant use during pregnancy: "Depression needs to be treated during pregnancy but with something other than antidepressants in the majority of cases. The risk/benefit ratio is clearly leaning towards no use."

The study has been widely criticized, however. As journalist Emily Underwood wrote in *Science*, "the critical flaw in the [Montreal study] is that it doesn't fully account for the fact that women suffering from psychiatric illnesses already have a greater risk of having children with autism spectrum disorder."[143]

According to Dr. Roy Perlis, a professor of psychiatry at Harvard University, the study authors did not control for the severity of the mother's depression. The children of mothers taking SSRIs may have been at greater risk of autism simply because their mothers had more severe depression.

Several studies, including from Dr. Perlis's group, have found no increased risk of autism from SSRI use during pregnancy, when controlling for the severity of maternal depression. As Dr. Perlis told *Science*, "The risk travels with the disease, not the treatment."[144] More recent research lends further support to the view that antidepressants do not increase autism risk.[145]

Despite all the reassuring data, there is still a chance that antidepressant use during pregnancy has some negative impact on brain development, separate from autism risk. (For example, a 2019 study in mice found that treatment with Prozac during pregnancy produced behavioral changes.[146]) There is also a clear link between depression itself and a slightly increased risk of autism, so letting depression go untreated may not be the best answer.

One possible explanation for this link is inflammation. It could be excessive immune activity that drives both conditions. As discussed in earlier chapters, there is clear evidence that a high level of inflammation during pregnancy can increase the chance of a child developing autism or another developmental disorder. Many experts now believe that inflammation can be the underlying cause of depression too.

This view is supported by decades of research finding higher levels of inflammatory markers in people with depression.[147] In 2018, this higher level of inflammation was specifically observed in the context of pregnant women with depression.[148] In addition, there is a body of research showing that when people are injected with proteins that spur inflammation, such as interferon, many go on to develop depression.[149]

Connecting the dots between these phenomena, inflammation may be the underlying culprit, causing both depression in mothers and autism in their children.

If that is the case, what is the practical advice for expecting mothers affected by depression? One approach is to adopt dietary and lifestyle changes aimed at addressing the root causes of inflammation, as advocated by Dr. Kelly Brogan, a board-certified psychiatrist and author of the *New York Times* bestseller *A Mind of Your Own: The Truth About Depression and How Women Can Heal Their Bodies to Reclaim Their Lives.*

Dr. Brogan's approach is to help women slowly wean themselves off antidepressant medications and heal the gut through a series of dietary and lifestyle changes, as she discusses further below.

Addressing the Root Causes of Depression
by Dr. Kelly Brogan

We all recognize that anxiety or nervousness can impact our guts—most of us have had butterflies before a date or even diarrhea with extreme performance anxiety. We are just learning that this relationship is bidirectional: the gut can also communicate its state of calm or alarm to the nervous system.

If you suffer from depression, it is highly likely that your depression is a nonspecific symptom of chronic illness and inflammation, driven by poor gut health. The gut is in fact the gatekeeper of the inflammatory response. It houses at least 70 percent of our immune system, along with the vast community of beneficial microbes. These microbes, collectively known as the microbiome, perform countless functions for our body, not least of which is helping to regulate the immune system.

There are many factors that impact the health of your gut and the makeup of your microbiome, for better or worse, including antibiotics, toxins, and diet. We can address depression and other symptoms by addressing these factors.

As a starting point, I advise my patients to begin with three steps to start healing the gut and addressing the root causes of depression:

1. Eliminate processed foods, particularly refined grains and sugars.

2. Add more whole foods, such as fresh fruits and vegetables, root vegetables, pastured meats, wild fish, eggs, nuts, seeds, and traditional fats such as olive oil.

3. Add fermented foods or probiotics.

I also encourage my patients to practice daily meditation. The effects of relaxation, even through listening to a 20-minute guided meditation, can be far-reaching. Several studies have also demonstrated that meditation boosts expression of anti-inflammatory genes and suppresses inflammation.

In my practice, through these and other interventions, antidepressants have become obsolete.

For further details on building a healthy gut microbiome during pregnancy, see chapter 17.

Points to Remember

- The use of acetaminophen/paracetamol during pregnancy may increase the odds of autism and ADHD, but the magnitude of the increased risk is likely small, and it is only prolonged use that is problematic.

- Acetaminophen is likely still the safest choice to treat pain and fever during pregnancy, but it should be used at the lowest effective dose and for the shortest possible time.

- The use of antidepressants during pregnancy does not appear to increase the risk of autism or ADHD, but there are still unanswered questions and it may be worth considering alternative treatments.

- Severe depression in mothers during pregnancy is a risk factor for autism, likely because inflammation drives both conditions.

- Natural approaches to tackling inflammation can significantly improve depression.

Chapter 8

Vaccine Decisions During Pregnancy

Current guidelines advise women to receive two vaccines during pregnancy: the flu vaccine and the tetanus, diphtheria, and pertussis (Tdap) vaccine. Only about 50 percent of women receive either, in part because they are never told just how important these vaccines are for protecting newborns from potentially life-threatening infections. Some expectant mothers may also forego the vaccines due to concerns over autism, but the evidence on this point is generally reassuring, as this chapter explains.

The Risks and Benefits of the Influenza Vaccine

In 2017, a high-profile study investigating the link between prenatal flu vaccines and autism was published in the journal *JAMA Pediatrics*.[150] It concluded that "There was no association between maternal influenza vaccination anytime during pregnancy and increased ASD risk." But others have questioned whether the data really supports that conclusion, because the study could be interpreted as showing a slightly increased risk of autism when the vaccine is given in the first trimester.[151] On this point, the study states that "In trimester-specific analyses, first-trimester influenza vaccination was the only period associated with increased [autism] risk. However, this association could be due to chance."

If the flu vaccine actually does increase autism risk when given during the first trimester (which still seems unlikely based on the weight of the evidence), it could be because the vaccine provokes a mild inflammatory response. We know that a higher level of inflammation in pregnancy increases the risk of autism. But the inflammatory response following a flu vaccine has been described as "mild and transient" and no different among pregnant or nonpregnant women.[152] Inflammatory markers return to the baseline level within three days after vaccination. These same inflammatory markers would be raised for significantly longer during an actual flu infection.

For those reasons, proponents of the vaccine argue that it may actually help prevent autism because infections during pregnancy are a known risk factor. The link between infections and autism has actually been studied quite extensively. In one analysis of pooled data from many prior studies, researchers concluded that "maternal infection during pregnancy was associated with an increased risk of ASD in offspring…particularly among those requiring hospitalization." Looking more specifically at the types of infections, those from influenza were associated with a marginal increase in autism risk.[153] By preventing some of these infections, the flu vaccine would theoretically lower the autism risk.

Nevertheless, some pregnant women remain nervous about the flu vaccine, with concerns that it could also possibly increase the risk of miscarriage. The majority of studies have found no link between the two. However, there is one outlier to briefly mention: a small study published in 2017 found a higher rate of miscarriage in women who received a specific H1N1 flu vaccine early in pregnancy during the 2011 flu season.[154]

That result could have simply occurred by chance, due to the size of the study, or there could be something unique about that year's vaccine that did actually contribute to miscarriages. A broader link between vaccines and miscarriage seems unlikely, since many other studies have specifically looked at this issue and found no increased risk.[155] It is also clear that flu infection itself does increase the risk of losing a pregnancy,[156] so getting vaccinated is probably the safer course if you are pregnant during a severe flu season.

As Dr. John Merrill-Steskal, vaccine fellow of the American Academy of Family Physicians, summarizes, "the preponderance of medical research tells us that receiving influenza vaccine during early pregnancy is safe and is more likely to save both the mother's, as well as developing infant's, life."[157]

This of course depends on the flu vaccine actually being effective, which can vary somewhat from year to year. One study of pregnant women in California was unable to find any reduction in hospital visits for flu-like illness or pneumonia in women who were vaccinated.[158] But a much larger international study, published in 2018, collected data on flu hospitalizations among pregnant women in Australia, Canada, Israel, and the United States, from 2010 through 2016. This study found that the flu vaccine was about 40 percent effective in preventing flu-related hospitalization during pregnancy.[159]

On balance, the evidence suggests that it is worth getting the flu vaccine while pregnant. There is, however, one additional factor to consider that tips the balance even further in favor of the vaccine, namely the ability to protect your baby from flu after she is born. If you are vaccinated against flu during the second half of pregnancy, the antibodies you produce will be transferred across the placenta and will help protect your baby in her first few months of life, when influenza can be quite serious.

As the CDC notes, "Pregnant women are at increased risk for flu complications and a flu shot will protect them from illness, but it also has been shown to protect their newborn from flu for the first several months after they are born."[160]

Influenza can potentially lead to life-threatening complications in newborns, but babies cannot receive the vaccine themselves until they are six months old. If a woman receives a flu vaccine during the second or third trimester, the antibodies she develops will be transferred to the baby, providing ongoing protection for many months after birth.[161]

This lasting protection was demonstrated in a 2016 study published in the journal *Pediatrics*. Looking at records from 250,000 pregnancies, the study found that when mothers received a flu shot while they were pregnant, their baby was 80 percent less likely to be hospitalized for influenza in its first six months.[162]

Researchers have found that for the purpose of providing antibodies to the baby, the ideal time to get the flu vaccine is when you are anywhere from five to eight months pregnant.[163] Within this broad timeframe, the precise timing will vary depending on when flu season occurs and the availability of the vaccine (which is typically released at the end of summer). Getting vaccinated earlier in the second trimester also offers good protection to the baby, although the antibody levels appear to be slightly lower.[164]

It is not yet known how much protection babies get from vaccinations during the first trimester. Even so, if your early pregnancy overlaps with the peak of flu season it may still make sense to be vaccinated earlier, to protect yourself from infection during that time. This is a matter of weighing the pros and cons and discussing the preferred timing with your doctor.

When you do have your flu shot, it is best to request the vaccine in the form of a single-dose vial, rather than a multi-dose vial. Governments typically advise that the only form of flu vaccine not recommended for pregnant women is the live nasal mist; all brands of flu shot are considered safe. Yet some pharmacies draw up each individual dose of the vaccine from a multi-dose vial, which contains a small amount of mercury-based preservative. The harm posed by this preservative is not clear, but it is easy to avoid simply by asking for a single-dose form of the flu shot, from either your doctor or pharmacy.

The Tdap Vaccine During Pregnancy

The other vaccine that is commonly recommended for pregnant women is Tdap, which protects against tetanus, diphtheria, and pertussis. The main reason it is given to pregnant women is to protect newborn babies from the pertussis bacteria, which causes whooping cough. This is a highly contagious respiratory disease that can result in serious illness or death in infants.

Katie VanTourhout, a mother who lost her daughter Callie to whooping cough at just a month old, urges all pregnant women to get the vaccine. It was never offered to her during her own pregnancy, so she has spoken out to raise awareness of this important issue. "We want to help somebody else, before someone else's baby goes through this and parents suffer the loss of their miracle baby," VanTornhout said. "We believe that every new mom should be required to get this new vaccination. I'm going to do it in Callie's name."[165]

The reason why vaccination during pregnancy is so critical is that babies cannot receive the Tdap shot themselves until they are two months old. As result, they are unprotected during those first months, the precise time when whooping cough can be most dangerous. When mothers are vaccinated toward the end of pregnancy (ideally between 27 and 36 weeks), the antibodies are passed along to the newborn. This is more than 90 percent effective in providing some immunity to infants until they are two months old.[166]

As with the flu vaccine, the concern about autism has led to some suspicion over the Tdap vaccine for pregnant women, but that concern appears to be unfounded. In 2018, a large retrospective study that looked at 80,000 mother-child pairs who had delivered in

Southern California between 2011 and 2014 found no significant difference in the autism rate where the mother received the Tdap vaccine during pregnancy.[167] In fact, there was a slightly lower rate of autism in the vaccinated group.

Unlike some of the vaccine decisions to be made once your baby arrives (discussed in detail in chapter 16), the decision whether to get the Tdap vaccine during pregnancy is a relatively easy one. There is clear evidence that the vaccine helps prevent life-threatening infections by a very common and highly contagious illness, and the evidence points to no increased risk of autism when mothers receive the vaccine.

Points to Remember

- There is little evidence that getting a flu vaccine during pregnancy increases the risk of autism. It may even reduce the odds of autism by preventing serious infections, a known risk factor.

- Getting vaccinated against flu in the second or third trimester may also help protect your baby during their first six months, when flu can be particularly dangerous.

- It is best to request the flu vaccine in the form of a single-dose vial, rather than a multi-dose vial, due to a mercury-based preservative in the latter.

- The Tdap vaccine during pregnancy does not appear to increase autism risk and provides important protection to your baby against whooping cough.

- The ideal time to receive the Tdap vaccine is between 27 and 36 weeks.

Chapter 9

The Risks & Benefits of Ultrasounds

Ultrasounds have long been suspected of playing a role in autism, partly because their use has expanded dramatically over the same time period in which autism rates have spiked. Animal studies have also raised concerns, with researchers finding that ultrasounds can slightly raise the temperature of fetal tissues and interfere with brain development in mice. But it is far from clear that the same thing occurs in humans in real-world scenarios, or whether such effects could contribute to autism.

On the contrary, the human studies so far indicate that routine ultrasounds do not raise the risk of autism. In a 2018 study published in the prestigious journal *JAMA Pediatrics*, researchers found that, on average, children with autism had actually been exposed to *fewer* ultrasounds and ultrasounds of shorter duration.[168]

Dr. Sara Webb, an Associate Professor of Psychiatry at the University of Washington, who was not involved with the study, commented that "at this time, there is no evidence that ultrasound is a primary contributor to poor developmental outcomes when delivered within medical guidelines." Several prior studies also failed to find a connection between ultrasound and increased risk of autism.[169]

Yet Dr. Webb has commented that this body of research only means that ultrasounds are not a sufficient cause of autism on their own—it is still possible that ultrasounds have a negative effect in children who have a unique vulnerability.[170] This question over how ultrasounds may interact with genetics is an issue flagged by Webb's own research.

In 2017, Webb found that children with a specific genetic predisposition to autism who received ultrasounds during early pregnancy had more severe autistic symptoms than the children not exposed to ultrasound.[171] This link seemed to be limited to scans performed in the first trimester; there was no association between severity of autism and the number of scans in the second or third trimester.

Webb notes that her findings support the FDA's recommendation that ultrasounds should only be performed when medically necessary. "It's worthwhile to consider why a first-trimester ultrasound is being done. The pictures do provide some bonding [between the parents and their child], but if it is not medically necessary, you should wait until later in the pregnancy," she says.

The American College of Obstetricians and Gynecologists (ACOG) also advises that ultrasounds should only be performed for valid medical reasons. Their recent committee opinion states that ultrasounds "should be used prudently and only when use is expected to answer a relevant clinical question or otherwise provide medical benefit to the patient."[172]

When exactly an ultrasound will provide medical benefit remains a murky issue. Large-scale reviews have failed to demonstrate much benefit to any routine ultrasound screenings.[173] For example, a recent review analyzed a dozen prior studies involving almost 35,000 women who were randomly selected to ultrasound screening or a control group. The review concluded that:

> *Existing evidence shows that routine ultrasound, after 24 weeks' gestation, in low-risk or unselected women does not provide any benefit for the mother or her baby...Babies' birth weight, condition at birth, interventions such as resuscitation, and admission to special care were similar between groups. Infant survival, with or without congenital abnormalities, was no different with and without routine ultrasound screening in late pregnancy.*[174]

A review on ultrasounds earlier in pregnancy reached similar conclusions.[175] It is hard to reconcile this bird's-eye view with the fact that ultrasounds can sometimes provide useful information in individual cases. An ultrasound may, for example, find a rare anatomic problem that can be corrected with surgery, either in utero or immediately after birth.

Regardless of what the studies say, it is hard to deny that more information is better when it comes to the health of your baby. The ACOG therefore recommends "at least one" ultrasound for low-risk pregnancies, typically at 18 to 22 weeks. In many countries, the standard practice is to perform one ultrasound at approximately 12 weeks and another at approximately 20 weeks, in order to check that the baby is developing normally.

Beyond these standard milestones, the value of performing additional ultrasounds for low-risk pregnancies is questionable, and different doctors take different approaches. During the third trimester, there may be good reason to perform one or two additional scans to ensure the baby is growing at the proper rate. If growth slows dramatically (as a result of problems with the placenta, for example), doctors may consider inducing labor early. In rare cases, this can reduce the chance of stillbirth.[176] For this reason, experts typically recommend an ultrasound to check for growth restriction once or twice during the third trimester, often at around 32 to 36 weeks.

The total number of ultrasounds considered "medically useful" is therefore typically around three, with scans performed at approximately 12 weeks, 20 weeks, and 32 to 36 weeks. Some doctors, however, choose to perform an ultrasound at every checkup, throughout the pregnancy. This is unlikely to be harmful, but there is no evidence that it provides any benefit for the mother or baby. It is also at odds with the official recommendations. The ACOG's official position on this issue states:

> Currently, there is no evidence that ultrasound is harmful to a developing fetus. No links have been found between ultrasound and birth defects, childhood cancer, or developmental problems later in life. However, it is possible that effects could be identified in the future. For this reason, it is recommended that ultrasound exams be performed only for medical reasons by qualified health care professionals. Casual use of ultrasound during pregnancy should be avoided. [177]

Although the research to date suggests that the chance of ultrasounds causing any harm is extremely low, there is still a risk/benefit analysis to be made. As the FDA notes, "While ultrasound is generally considered to be safe with very low risks, the risks may increase with unnecessary prolonged exposure to ultrasound energy, or when untrained users operate the device."[178]

If an ultrasound will not give any useful medical information, then arguably there is no justification for taking any risk at all. The counterargument to this point is that regular ultrasounds can help relieve anxiety for many expectant mothers, and this is a benefit in and of itself.

In some cases, the reassurance from regular ultrasounds could indeed outweigh the incredibly small risk that these tests are somehow harmful in ways that are not yet understood. This is a personal decision to be made, based on how much you personally gain from seeing your growing baby on the ultrasound screen.

The most prudent approach is to follow the official recommendations that ultrasounds should only be performed to answer a medical question. Some doctors perform ultrasounds at every checkup out of habit, simply because many of their patients expect it. If you would prefer fewer ultrasounds, let your doctor know—they may be happy to skip ultrasounds at some appointments.

On the other hand, your doctor may have a good reason to perform scans more often in your particular case. If your pregnancy is considered "high-risk," whether due to carrying multiples, or a potential complication, the benefits of regular ultrasounds likely outweigh any possible risks, which remain theoretical and unlikely. As the FDA has noted, the weight of the evidence so far indicates that ultrasounds are very safe.[179]

The Temptation of Home Heartbeat Monitors

Another area where common practice often conflicts with the FDA guidance is the use of fetal doppler heartbeat monitors. Many women use these devices, which can be purchased inexpensively online, to listen to their baby's heartbeat on a daily basis, whether for fun or reassurance. Yet the FDA strongly recommends that these devices should only be used under medical supervision.

Unlike a stethoscope, which merely listens for sounds from the baby's heartbeat, doppler heartbeat monitors actually work like ultrasounds, emitting high frequency sound waves and then converting the reflected sound waves into a heartbeat. These devices are regarded as very safe and are typically used at every doctor's appointment but should not be used at home unless recommended by your doctor.

As noted by Dr. Shahram Vaezy, an FDA biomedical engineer, "when the product is purchased over the counter and used without consultation with a health care professional taking care of the pregnant woman, there is no oversight of how the device is used. Also, there is little or no medical benefit expected from the exposure.[180] Furthermore, the number of sessions or the length of a session in scanning a fetus is uncontrolled, and that increases the potential for harm to the fetus."

The potential for any harm from the sound waves is still extremely low, but there is also the concern that using a fetal heart monitor at home without medical guidance can sometimes give false reassurance. It takes training and experience to use the devices properly, and there have been reports of women who did not seek medical attention when they noticed their baby was not moving because they used a home heart monitor and were reassured by what they believed was their baby's heartbeat.

As *The New York Times* reported in an article on this problem, "it is difficult for an inexperienced person to distinguish between a baby's heartbeat and the whooshing sounds of a mother's own pulse or blood flow. And even when parents do find the fetal heartbeat, there is no way for them to know whether the baby is well or in distress."[181]

Dr. Abhijoy Chakladar of the Princess Royal Hospital in Britain told *The New York Times*, "this is something that comes only with experience. In hospital, fetal health is assessed by experienced midwives and doctors who take a team approach ..."[182] He advises that if a mother is concerned that something has changed with her baby's movement, she should consult her doctor instead of relying on a home fetal heart monitor. "On their own, these monitors are harmless; it is their improper use by parents to reassure themselves which can be dangerous," he says.

Points to Remember

- There is little evidence that prenatal ultrasounds increase the risk of autism or pose any other dangers.

- Even so, because of the possibility that problems could be discovered in the future, the official recommendation is that ultrasounds should only be used to answer a medical question, and then only for the shortest amount of time.

- If you would prefer to have limited ultrasounds, rather than a scan at every checkup, let your doctor know.

- For high-risk pregnancies, the benefits of regular ultrasounds likely outweigh the potential risks.

- Doppler heartbeat monitors are likely safe but should not be used at home unless recommended by your doctor. There are still uncertain risks from excessive use and these devices may give false reassurance, particularly to those who are untrained in how to properly use them.

Chapter 10

Baby Steps to a Cleaner, Greener Home

When we look at what has changed most in the world around us since our grandparents' generation, a time when autism, ADHD, and other developmental disabilities were very rare, one clear trend is an increase in chemicals that can interfere with hormones. These so-called "endocrine disruptors" can now be found throughout the home, lurking in plastic, highly processed food, and just about anything fragranced.

By learning about these chemicals and how to avoid the major sources of them, you can create a much less toxic home, which will have profound benefits for your baby's brain. Doing so is particularly useful while you are pregnant, but it is also important even if your baby is already here, because the same chemicals can likely impact brain health throughout early childhood.

How Do Chemicals Reach Babies in Utero?

During pregnancy, the umbilical cord not only transports oxygen and other nutrients from the mother's blood but also potentially harmful substances. We know this from studies examining the cord blood of newborn babies, with several groups of researchers finding that babies are often exposed to a cocktail of different chemicals during pregnancy.

In one of the studies demonstrating this effect, The Environmental Working Group (EWG) analyzed the cord blood of ten newborns and found 287 different industrial chemicals.[183] Babies each had an average of 200 chemicals, including mercury, flame retardants, and pesticides. The study noted that the vast majority of these chemicals are known to be toxic to the brain and nervous system.

Before we let this research drag us into a pit of despair, we have to remember that just because potentially dangerous chemicals are reaching babies even before they are born, it does not mean the concentration is high enough to cause harm. The fact is that toxin exposure is nearly universal in the modern world. Certain pesticides, flame retardants, nonstick chemicals, and phthalates have been detected in 99 percent of pregnant women.[184]

That is both good and bad news. On the one hand, it indicates the widespread nature of these chemicals and the scope of the problem for parents who want to protect their children. On the other hand, it also shows that the chemicals do not necessarily have dire consequences.

Common toxins may raise the risk of various health problems, such as asthma, language delay, autism, and ADHD, but these conditions still only impact a minority of children. From a statistical standpoint, even if you make no changes at all, chances are your baby will still be perfectly healthy.

That is an important point to keep in mind, because there will always be chemical sources beyond our control. As we learn about potential toxins in the world around us, it is easy to become anxious and feel like the challenge is simply too immense. The antidote to this natural anxiety is to remember that all babies are exposed to these chemicals and that just by reducing the worst offenders we are already making huge progress toward giving our own baby a healthier start in life.

This chapter will walk you through simple steps to minimize the top five toxins, listed in the box below. These chemicals all have one thing in common: they are so-called "endocrine disruptors," meaning they can interfere with hormones.

Top 5 Chemicals of Concern During Pregnancy and Early Childhood and Their Most Common Sources

1. **Pesticides:** home and garden insect sprays; heavily sprayed fruits, vegetables, and grains.
2. **Bisphenols:** hard plastic kitchenware, highly processed and fast food, paper receipts.
3. **Phthalates:** highly processed and fast food, fragrance, nail polish, fabric softener.
4. **Flame retardants:** house dust from furniture and electronics.
5. **Nonstick chemicals:** nonstick pots and pans.

Endocrine disruptors may either mimic or block the effects of any number of natural hormones, such as testosterone, estrogen, or progesterone. Because hormones carefully orchestrate development during pregnancy and early infancy, anything that alters their activity can easily disrupt a baby's growth and brain development.

As explained by Dr. Leonardo Trasande, professor in pediatrics, environmental medicine, and population health at the NYU School of Medicine, "chemicals that affect the endocrine system, for example, can have lasting effects on a child since hormones coordinate complex functions throughout the body."[185] As a result, "even small disruptions at key moments during development can have life-long consequences."

For this reason, it is especially helpful to reduce the level of endocrine-disrupting chemicals in your home while you are pregnant or caring for a newborn. As noted by Dr. Alan Greene, a veteran pediatrician and author of *Raising Baby Green: The Earth-Friendly Guide to Pregnancy, Childbirth, and Baby Care*, "At no other time in your child's life will you have this degree of control over the way her environment influences her development."[186]

The Problem with Pesticides

When it comes to creating a less toxic home, one of the best places to start is by tackling pesticides—all those chemicals used to control unwanted insects, weeds, or other living organisms. Pesticides are sprayed on crops, gardens, pets, and inside homes, in alarming quantities. Each year in the United States, farmers apply more than 1 billion pounds of pesticides.[187]

Pesticides are by their very nature intended to be toxic. They are primarily toxic to the insects and other pests they target, but when the concentration is high enough, they are also toxic to humans. A range of health problems, including an increased risk of asthma and certain cancers, have now been linked to the common pesticides used in homes and food production.[188]

When babies are exposed to these chemicals during critical windows of development, there is also a significant risk to brain development. A growing body of evidence now points to a link between prenatal exposure to pesticides and lower IQ in children, along with an increased risk of autism and ADHD.[189]

This link has even been recognized by the American Academy of Pediatrics (AAP). In an official policy statement, the AAP stated: "Epidemiologic evidence demonstrates associations between early life exposure to pesticides and pediatric cancers, decreased cognitive function, and behavioral problems."[190]

The policy statement goes on to state that studies link pesticides to many other adverse outcomes too, including preterm birth and asthma, but that "the evidence base is most robust" for problems with brain development. More specifically, the AAP notes that "studies link early-life exposure to organophosphate insecticides with reductions in IQ and abnormal behaviors associated with attention-deficit/hyperactivity disorder and autism." [191]

This link is particularly concerning given that organophosphates are currently the most heavily used insecticides in the world. Originally developed as human nerve gas agents during World War II, some were later adapted as insecticides at lower doses. They are now widely used in agriculture, as well as in home and garden insect sprays.

In 2018 a group of leading researchers came together to prepare policy recommendations on the dangers posed by these pesticides, stating that "Compelling evidence indicates that prenatal exposure at low levels is putting children at risk for cognitive and behavioral deficits and for neurodevelopmental disorders."[192] The researchers also noted that specific outcomes linked to pesticide exposure during pregnancy include

- mental and motor delays among preschoolers;
- reduction in working and visual memory, processing speed, verbal comprehension, perceptual reasoning, and IQ among elementary school–age children; and
- elevated risks for symptoms or diagnoses of attention-deficit/hyperactivity disorder (ADHD) and autism spectrum disorder (ASD).

On this last point, the evidence linking pesticide exposure to autism is indeed quite troubling.[193] The link is clearest in studies of pregnant women who live in agricultural areas. One such study in California found that living within a mile of fields treated with organophosphate pesticides during pregnancy increased the risk of autism by 60 percent.[194] Living close to farms applying other classes of pesticides, such as pyrethroids, was also found to dramatically increase the risk of autism and developmental delays.

These studies represent a unique scenario, in which pregnant women are exposed to particularly high levels of pesticides. Perhaps the more important issue is the impact of other possible sources of pesticide exposure, sources we are more likely to encounter in daily life.

On this point, the research is more limited, but troubling nonetheless. For example, a 2017 study found detectable levels of pyrethroid insecticides in up to 30 percent of pregnant women living on the Upper East Side of Manhattan, clearly a long way from agricultural land.[195] One likely culprit: home insect sprays and flea treatments for pets.

Even the trace amounts the New York women were exposed to appeared to harm infant brain development. The researchers found that when women had detectable levels of pyrethroids in their urine during pregnancy, their children were more likely to have problems with a range of executive functions, including emotional control and behavioral regulation.

To minimize exposure to these types of pesticides, it is better to use oral tablets or natural methods for flea control for pets, rather than topical treatments. To control insects in your house or garden, bait stations are much safer than sprays.

We also have to remember that all those chemicals that increased autism rates in the California families living near farms were being sprayed on *food*. Even if you live thousands of miles from any farm and don't use pesticides in your home or garden, you are likely consuming trace amounts of pesticide residues on fresh fruit and vegetables.

The evidence is not clear that these trace amounts pose a problem for brain development, but if budget permits and you live in an area where organic produce is available, it is reasonable to err on the side of caution and buy more organic foods when possible. This is particularly worthwhile for those fruits and vegetables known to carry higher levels of pesticide residues, namely

- berries
- grapes
- peaches
- apples
- pears

- spinach
- peppers
- tomatoes
- potatoes
- kale

An entirely organic diet is not practical for most families but is likely not necessary either. There are many other ways to reduce pesticide levels, such as by relying more heavily on fruits and vegetables that typically have low levels of pesticides. These include

- papaya
- mango
- honeydew
- kiwi
- cantaloupe
- pineapple
- avocado

- onion
- peas
- cabbage
- broccoli
- asparagus
- cauliflower

Peeling nonorganic fruit and vegetables is also a good cautionary step, especially in the case of apples and pears, which are among the most heavily contaminated.

For nonorganic berries and greens, you can also significantly reduce pesticide residues by soaking them in a dilute baking soda solution. A recent study found that soaking fruit for 15 minutes in one teaspoon of baking soda and two cups of water could reduce pesticides much more effectively than other washing methods.[196]

Going Beyond Organic Fruit and Vegetables

Although discussion of pesticides in food typically focuses on fresh produce, it may be even more important to choose organic when it comes to grains, which can be heavily contaminated with the pesticide glyphosate.

This particular pesticide, the main ingredient in Monsanto's weed killer Roundup, has seen a dramatic rise in use over the past several decades, as crops have been genetically engineered to withstand higher levels of the pesticide. In 1987, between six and eight million pounds of glyphosate were applied by US farmers.[197] Now, farmers are spraying crops with more than 200 million pounds each year.[198]

Tests show that this pesticide eventually ends up in the food we eat, with especially high levels in corn, soy, oats, and wheat.[199] The fact that our food has become more heavily laced with glyphosate over the same time period that has seen a rise in developmental disabilities raises a red flag for some researchers.[200] But there has still been very little investigation of the issue. At the moment, all we have is animal studies reporting that glyphosate can compromise brain development.[201]

Even though more research is clearly needed on how glyphosate exposure during pregnancy and early childhood could impact the brain, it does appear that this pesticide is problematic in other ways.[202] Most notably, the World Health Organization categorizes it as a likely carcinogen.[203] That is probably reason enough to start reducing your intake of nonorganic corn, soy, oats, and wheat, to the extent you can.

Choosing organic is especially worthwhile for foods made from oats and wheat, because nonorganic growers typically spray these crops with the herbicide immediately before harvest, to dry the crop.

This process leads to particularly high levels of glyphosate on the final grain.[204]

In 2018, the EWG commissioned laboratory tests on a range of popular oat products and found glyphosate in almost all products made with conventionally grown oats.[205] Almost three-fourths of samples had glyphosate levels higher than what EWG scientists consider safe. In comparison, none of the organic oats contained glyphosate levels above this benchmark.

After finding out about the results of those tests, I, like thousands of other parents, had an immediate wave of guilt for not being more careful with the foods I was feeding my young children. (I give them oatmeal or granola every single day and was not particularly diligent about buying organic.) But I have to remind myself that this guilt is not productive. All we can do is keep learning, and when we know better, we do better. Now, I choose organic oats whenever I have the option.

You may decide to go even further and choose organic meats and dairy too, and doing so is likely to have advantages, but here the balance between the potential health benefits versus higher cost is not as clear. Organic beef, in particular, is vastly more expensive than conventional, and it probably has fewer health benefits than choosing organic fruit, vegetables, and grains.

So while buying organic food is generally preferred, it is not something you need to be hypervigilant about. You can dramatically reduce pesticide exposure simply by choosing more of the low-pesticide fruit and vegetables and choosing organic for heavily contaminated foods such as oats.

In addition, it is helpful to take a step back and remember that the studies so far have only implicated the more concentrated sources of pesticides, such as home and garden insect and weed sprays, or living near agricultural fields, as potential contributors to autism. There is currently no clear evidence implicating the small amount of pesticide residues on food.

It is also important to bear in mind that pesticides are just one small piece of the overall risk puzzle. As explained by Dr. Irva Hertz-Picciotto, who has led key research investigating the links between pesticides and autism and is the director of the University of California's Children's Center for Environmental Health:

> *In any child who develops autism, a combination of genetic and environmental factors are at work. There's an accumulation of insults to the system. What we're seeing is that pesticides may be one more factor that for some kids may push them over the edge.*[206]

What this means at a practical level is that if you are already taking the other steps discussed in this book to help protect your baby's developing brain, any minor exposure to pesticides will likely have less impact.

Is BPA-Free Plastic in the Clear?

Bisphenol-A, or BPA for short, is now one of the most well-known chemicals that can disrupt the function of our hormones. In recent years, many companies that produce plastic kitchenware and canned food have phased out the use of this chemical, with a vast array of products now proudly claiming to be "BPA-free." But we are not yet living in a BPA-free world. It is still present in a variety of places, and many manufacturers are simply replacing BPA with closely related compounds that appear to act in much the same way.

Reducing exposure to these chemicals while trying to conceive has dramatic benefits for fertility, as discussed in my first book, *It Starts with the Egg*. But the payoff also continues once you are pregnant or caring for a newborn, particularly when it comes to supporting your baby's developing brain.

We know this from the research of Dr. Joseph Braun, an environmental health scientist at Brown University. Braun was one of the first to reveal that exposure to high levels of BPA during pregnancy can harm children's brain development.

Braun took a somewhat unusual career path for a public health researcher, first working as a school nurse in two inner-city elementary schools. "The number of children I saw who were diagnosed with either ADHD or autism was quite staggering," he says. Troubled by what he observed, Braun went on to complete a master's degree in public health and a PhD in epidemiology, before joining Harvard as a postdoctoral fellow. Braun has now spent more than a decade investigating chemical pollutants that may be affecting infant brain development and thereby contributing to autism or ADHD.

His research on this topic began in 2006, when he started tracking a group of women in their second trimester of pregnancy. He and his team tested their urine for BPA and followed their children for five years to see how prenatal BPA exposure affected childhood behavior.

What they uncovered was troubling. "We have found that the daughters of women with higher BPA exposure during pregnancy tend to have more ADHD-like and anxious behaviors. They also have difficulty with emotional and behavioral regulation—problems with what we refer to as executive function."[207] The girls exposed to more BPA in utero "exhibit more behavior like hyperactivity, aggression and depression," said Braun.

Many other studies have since confirmed the association between BPA exposure during pregnancy and adverse behavioral outcomes in children, including in boys.[208] Infants appear to be most vulnerable to the harmful effects of BPA during pregnancy, when their brains are growing most rapidly. But there is some evidence suggesting that continued exposure during childhood is also problematic for behavior.

Specifically, several studies have linked higher BPA levels during childhood to an increase in ADHD behaviors, aggression, and learning problems.[209] From a practical standpoint, this means that the steps you take now to start replacing items in your kitchen will have continued benefits for years to come, by reducing the amount of BPA your child is exposed to during early childhood.

It is important to find some balance in this process though. You do not have to replace every item of plastic in your home or try to avoid BPA completely. Instead, the goal is to ensure you do not have an unusually high level of BPA exposure, by avoiding the worst offenders. These are:

- Paper receipts and other thermal paper
- Canned food
- Old and damaged plastic kitchenware
- Plastic that comes into contact with hot food or liquids

In one of Braun's studies, the two most significant risk factors for having very high levels of BPA were working as a cashier (and therefore handling receipts) and consuming more canned food.[210] Other researchers have reported similar patterns.[211]

The fact that paper receipts are coated with BPA or closely related alternatives often comes as a surprise but should not be a source of anxiety every time you are handed a receipt. It is true that cashiers often have high levels of BPA or other similar chemicals in their bodies, but they are in contact with paper receipts for many hours each day, which is an entirely different scenario from occasionally handling a receipt while shopping. (If you are a cashier, it may be worth wearing cotton gloves or rubber fingertip protectors at work, if possible.)

For most people, receipts probably make only a very small contribution to overall BPA exposure. Nevertheless, it is likely still helpful to wash your hands when you return home after shopping.

Interestingly, canned food still appears to be one of the major sources of BPA exposure, despite the fact that many companies have phased out its use.[212] While it is now easier to find canned goods labeled as "BPA-free," many companies continue to use this chemical. To add to the problem, some of the replacement chemicals that are used in place of BPA are likely just as harmful. The best strategy, it seems, is to minimize the use of canned food and to look for safer alternatives.

This is particularly worthwhile for canned tomatoes, because the acidity increases the leaching of chemicals from the can lining and also requires manufacturers to use more harmful materials.[213] Buying tomato products packaged in glass is a much better alternative.

Canned beans are less problematic than tomatoes, but it is still better to buy dried or frozen beans when you can. Otherwise, look for a BPA-free brand such as Eden Organics, which uses an enamel lining for its canned beans.

For canned fish such as salmon and sardines, the benefit to your baby of consuming the omega-3 fats during pregnancy likely outweighs the risks from the can lining, especially with safer brands such as Wild Planet and Vital Choice. Even so, the best option is to rely on fresh or frozen fish more often, if you can.

The next major strategy for reducing your exposure to BPA and similar chemicals is to begin replacing reusable plastic food storage containers, travel coffee mugs, and reusable water bottles with stainless steel or glass. This is not something you have to do all at once, but it is most helpful for items that will be in contact with hot foods or liquids, because heat causes more chemicals to leach from plastic.

For this reason, tea kettles and coffee makers with plastic internal parts are high priorities to replace during pregnancy. The safest way to make coffee is with a metal pour-over filter or a traditional French press made from stainless steel or glass, without plastic components. (The research also suggests limiting caffeinated coffee to one cup per day, particularly during the first trimester, to reduce the risk of pregnancy loss.)[214]

To some extent, using plastic in the kitchen is unavoidable. It is difficult to find high-performance blenders and water filters without plastic, for example. For these and other items, the key is to wash by hand in cold water and replace any container that is old and scratched. (Blender manufacturers will often provide replacement containers on request.)

Currently, most high-end blender makers use a type of plastic called Tritan™ copolyester for their containers. Although it does not contain BPA and is relatively safe for cool or room temperature ingredients, it has been found to leach another harmful chemical, called fluorene-9-bisphenol, when in contact with hot liquids.[215] For blending hot soups and making baby food purées with hot ingredients, a better option is to use a stainless-steel immersion blender or a blender with a glass container.

For food storage containers, it is helpful to replace any old or damaged plastic items with stainless steel or glass. If you find that you do need to use plastic food storage containers for some reason, one of the better types of plastic is high-density polyethylene (HDPE). It is less likely to release significant amounts of hormone-disrupting chemicals, when compared to other types of plastic. Another relatively good choice is polypropylene, often used for cutting boards and storage containers.

Plastic baby bottles are now typically made from one of these safer types of plastics (HDPE or polyethylene), because many countries have banned the use of BPA. However, as with the other products mentioned above, these plastics can still potentially leach chemicals when damaged or in contact with hot liquids. For more specific advice on baby bottles, see chapter 12.

The types of plastic used for food packaging and single-use water bottles typically do not contain BPA, although it is still best to drink water from glass bottles when you have the option, as will be discussed later in this chapter.

Silicone is also a generally safe material, although silicone baking trays and liners are best avoided because this material can leach chemicals called siloxanes at high temperatures.[216] Little is known about the long-term safety of siloxanes, so it is better to avoid unnecessary exposure.

Although the process of reducing plastics in your kitchen can be daunting at first, it is worth reminding yourself that the goal is not to completely avoid BPA and similar chemicals, but to start reducing your overall exposure. This means making a few changes to items that make the most difference, such as avoiding canned tomatoes and plastic containers that will come into contact with hot foods or liquids. Just these small changes may be enough to make a significant difference to your BPA level and help support healthy brain development for your baby.

Safer Cookware

One last item to consider replacing in your kitchen is your nonstick pan. Research published in 2017 and 2018 indicates that pregnant women with higher exposure to nonstick chemicals are more likely to have babies who are born premature or with a low birth weight.[217] In another recent study, researchers measured the level of these chemicals in newborn blood samples and found that higher levels were associated with increased odds of behavioral difficulties at age seven.[218]

Nonstick pans pose the greatest problem when they become old and damaged or when heated to very high temperatures. Just replacing an old and damaged nonstick pan with a newer one and cooking at moderate temperatures is a worthwhile step. Choosing a nonstick pan that is labeled "PFOA free" and "PTFE free" is also a vastly better choice than standard Teflon.

You can further reduce your exposure to nonstick chemicals by using this type of cookware only when needed, and doing most of your cooking with even safer options. The best materials include cast iron, glass, and stainless steel.

For baking trays and sheet pans, once you are avoiding nonstick coatings, most other options will be made from aluminum. There is some controversy over this metal, which is suspected of compromising brain health.[219] Overall, aluminum is probably better than nonstick chemicals, since most aluminum we ingest is never absorbed into the body.[220] An even better strategy, though, is to use stainless steel sheet pans. These are not as common as aluminum, but they can be found online. For recommended brands, see brainhealthfrombirth.com/cookware.

Our Phthalate-Filled World

The final group of chemicals to reduce in order to protect your baby's growing brain is phthalates. These chemicals are typically found in more than 90 percent of people surveyed, which is perhaps unsurprising given that they are used in a wide array of products, such as soft plastic, skin care products, nail polish, and perfumes.

From these items, phthalates can be absorbed through the skin or released into the air and inhaled. Another common way phthalates get into the body is from food, especially highly processed and fast food. This is likely due to contact with plastic equipment during processing.

Amidst all the popular theories on why so many children today are affected by ADHD and other developmental and behavioral problems, all signs point to phthalates as one of the true culprits. Phthalates were relatively rare in our grandparents' generation, but we are now inundated with these chemicals, from PVC plastic, highly processed foods, and the dozens of heavily fragranced products found in almost every home.

The ubiquitous nature of phthalates is troubling because these compounds can mimic estrogen, while blocking testosterone and thyroid hormones. This has a negative impact on fertility but can also be harmful during pregnancy and early childhood, when these hormones play a key role in development.

The first startling discovery about the impact of phthalates during pregnancy was made more than fifteen years ago by Dr. Shanna Swan, Professor of Preventive Medicine at Mount Sinai Hospital in New York. Her groundbreaking research found a clear link between a mother's exposure to phthalates during pregnancy and changes in the ways that baby boys' genitals develop.[221] The higher the phthalate levels, the more likely boys were to show features of "demasculinization," such as smaller penis volume and incomplete descent of the testes. Scientists now understand this occurs because phthalates suppress the production of testosterone by male fetuses during pregnancy.[222]

This discovery garnered much attention, but it overshadowed another worrying trend that other researchers were discovering at approximately the same time: a link between phthalates and premature birth.[223] One explanation for the link is that these chemicals increase inflammation, which raises the risk of earlier labor.[224] It is also plausible that phthalates may contribute to preterm birth by lowering the levels of estrogen and progesterone in the uterus.[225]

The role of phthalates in contributing to genital malformations and premature birth is unfortunately not the end of the story. For the past decade, researchers have been investigating yet another problem: the link between phthalate exposure during pregnancy and altered brain development and behavior.

In one recent study in New York, researchers measured phthalate levels in each mother's system during pregnancy.[226] Three years later, the researchers assessed the toddlers' mental development and motor skills, noting any behavioral problems.

The results were disconcerting: children whose mothers had higher levels of phthalates in their system while pregnant scored significantly lower on measures of mental, motor, and behavioral development.

This finding was unfortunately not new.[227] More than a dozen studies have now found a link between exposure to phthalates in pregnancy and negative impacts on behavior or cognitive function in children. The higher the level of phthalates, the more likely children are to show attention deficits, hyperactivity, and withdrawn or aggressive behavior.[228] These effects seem to be much worse in boys, where increased aggressive behavior is still noticeable even at 6 to 10 years old.[229]

Phthalates also appear to have a harmful effect on language development. In 2018, two large studies tracked phthalate levels in pregnant women and then measured the language skills of their children.[230] Both studies found that children who were exposed to higher levels of phthalates in utero had a much greater chance of language delay.

Now for the good news. Governments have finally recognized the harms posed by these compounds and have started to limit their use. In many countries, including the United States, Canada, Europe, and Australia, specific phthalates are now banned in a variety of products intended for young children. These bans typically cover items such as toys, pacifiers, teethers, and baby bottles.

More recently, these bans have started to apply beyond children's products to include consumer products more generally. The European Union has banned certain phthalates from cosmetics and plastic items, for example, and the scope of these bans continues to expand. In the United States, consumer demand has also driven a reduction in the use of phthalates in cosmetics and plastic, with many more products now labeled as "phthalate-free."

Researchers can see that all of these changes are having some effect on the amount of phthalate levels in our bodies. Lab tests of thousands of individuals show that over the past 10 years, there has been a steady decline in the concentrations of certain phthalates, including the most common type found in vinyl/PVC plastic.[231]

This goes to show that change is possible, but it is still too soon to become complacent. Many pregnant women and young children are still being exposed to high levels of phthalates, likely contributing to problems with attention, behavior, and language development. This is a widespread problem impacting a whole generation of children.

The solution to this problem is information: by learning what factors contribute most to the overall level of phthalate exposure, we can make huge strides toward reducing phthalate levels.

Practical Steps to Minimize Phthalates

As the harmful effects of phthalates are becoming more widely known, much of the practical advice has focused on plastic and personal care items, overlooking one major source: food. It is now becoming clear that food is in fact a major source of phthalates, particularly the specific type found in vinyl/PVC plastic. In studies where participants simply stopped eating for 24 hours, the level of these phthalates in the body dropped by five to 10-fold—overnight.[232]

The lesson from this is not that we should stop eating altogether, but that we can make a huge difference to phthalate levels by minimizing the foods that are most likely to be contaminated.

Fortunately, we now also have research guiding us on how to do this, with studies finding that the main culprits are highly processed food and fast food.[233] In one of the largest studies on this issue, involving almost nine thousand people, researchers found that people who ate at least one fast-food meal per week had much higher phthalate levels.[234] In a similar vein, another study found that the powder in boxed mac and cheese can have phthalate levels four times higher than that made with natural cheese.[235]

As a result, one of the best ways to avoid phthalates is to limit highly processed foods and instead rely more heavily on foods made at home using whole, natural ingredients, as advised by Dr. Sheela Sathyanarayana, associate professor of pediatrics at the University of Washington in Seattle, who studies phthalates. "Avoid anything you find in a box that could sit around for many years," says Sathyanarayana. "There are so many steps to get to that boxed product, and every step along the way, there's usually plastic involved."[236]

Other research further confirms that preparing and storing meals without plastic, and using fresh ingredients, can dramatically lower phthalate levels in just a few days. That was the result of a study of five families in San Francisco, where participants had meals prepared for them from organic and unprocessed ingredients. The meals were made and stored without plastic utensils or containers, and the participants were only allowed to drink coffee made in a French press rather than a coffee machine with plastic parts. After only a couple of days, the families' levels of many phthalates fell by over 50 percent.[237]

This study also tried to reduce the use of ingredients that were packaged in plastic, but we know from further studies that the final packaging of most unprocessed, natural ingredients is not the major concern. As one example, researchers in Canada measured phthalates in more than 100 samples of meat, fish, and cheese, packaged mostly in cling films. Phthalates were not detected in the packaging.[238] The only food with measurable phthalate levels was cheese (likely from processing) and even then, the level was relatively low.

Additional studies have also found that packaging makes a relatively small contribution to the total amount of phthalates in food. Another study comparing a variety of processed and unprocessed foods concluded that "processing—and not packaging—was the most important contamination source."[239] This makes a lot of sense, given that the manufacturing process often uses plastic containers and equipment, much of which is likely sterilized with scalding hot water.

That is not to say that food packaging is completely in the clear. Although the main food sources of phthalates are fast food and highly processed foods, there are a couple of circumstances in which it may make sense to avoid plastic packaging when you can.

Researchers have found, for example, that milk has much lower phthalate levels when packaged in glass rather than in plastic.[240] As a more general principle, for phthalates to leach from the container into food, the main risk factors are heat, acid, fat, or liquid, all of which facilitate the release of phthalates from plastic. As a result, it is preferable to buy milk, oil, drinks, and condiments in glass bottles or other alternatives to plastic when possible.

It is also advisable to buy water in plastic bottles only when necessary, because researchers have consistently found that water packaged in these plastic bottles contains much higher phthalate levels than water packaged in glass bottles.[241] For making up baby formula, it is best to use water in glass bottles or filtered tap water. (See the water filter guide at brainhealthfrombirth.com/water)

It probably goes without saying that we should also try to avoid hot foods in plastic containers. If you frequently rely on takeout, this may mean choosing more sandwiches, salads, or dishes that are served in cardboard trays instead.

For the most part, however, you should feel comfortable buying food in plastic containers or bags, as long as you are placing more emphasis on natural ingredients, such as nuts, legumes, unprocessed grains, meat, eggs, fish, fruit, and vegetables. The more these foods contribute to your overall diet, and the more you prepare meals yourself at home, the better.

Apart from processed food, the other major way we are exposed to phthalates is through personal care products, such as hairspray, perfume, and nail polish. Other products with strong fragrances, such as air fresheners and fabric softeners, can also be significant sources.[242] The phthalates in these products can be readily absorbed through the skin or inhaled from the air.[243]

Phthalates are used in hairsprays and nail polish to give structure and flexibility to the product, similar to using eggs in baking. As a result, these items can have a particularly high concentration of these phthalates. These chemicals are also added to many other products to make fragrances stronger and more long-lasting. This means that anything fragranced is a potential culprit, providing good reason to move toward a fragrance-free home or buying only those products labeled as phthalate-free.

But this can be a gradual process. The best place to start is by eliminating the worst offenders: nail polish, perfume, hairspray, air freshener, and fabric softener. Replacing your body lotion with one that is either fragrance free or phthalate-free is also a good step, since it is applied over a larger surface area and so provides more opportunity for the chemicals to be absorbed through the skin. A safe and inexpensive alternative to conventional body lotion is natural jojoba oil, which is absorbed more quickly than other oils.

How much further you choose to go in replacing your cosmetics and cleaning products is up to you, but every little bit helps. Additional items to consider replacing include PVC shower curtains and yoga mats. Look for a shower curtain made from nylon, cotton, or polyester, and a yoga mat labeled "PVC free" or "phthalate free." To replace fabric softener, vinegar or wool dryer balls are good alternatives.

Other Skincare Ingredients to Minimize During Pregnancy

- **Parabens** are commonly used preservatives typically found in lotions, sunscreens, and other personal-care products. For many years it has been known that parabens disrupt hormones and fertility, but new research indicates that exposure to parabens during pregnancy may also compromise infant brain development.[244]

- **Triclosan** is an antimicrobial chemical often found in antibacterial hand soap and some brands of toothpaste, such as Colgate Total. It has now been recognized as a potent endocrine disruptor, causing disturbances to thyroid hormone levels during pregnancy.[245]

- **Chemical sunscreens** can also act as hormone disruptors. The worst is oxybenzone, which is added to the majority of nonmineral sunscreens and has been found to lower testosterone levels, reduce pregnancy duration, and alter birth weights.[246] Safer sunscreen ingredients include zinc and titanium dioxide.

- **Retinols** are vitamin A derivatives that are often added to antiaging skin care products. High doses can potentially interfere with fetal development and lead to birth defects, so pregnant women are typically advised to avoid skin care products containing retinol and other similar derivatives such as retin-A and retinoic acid.

- **Salicylic acid** is a chemical exfoliant often included in acne treatments, but it can also be found in cleansers and moisturizers. Pregnant women are usually advised to avoid salicylic acid because it can be absorbed through the skin and has aspirin-like effects. Some doctors advise that up to 2 percent salicylic acid is safe to treat acne during pregnancy, but azelaic acid or topical antibiotics such as erythromycin and clindamycin are considered better options.[247]

Points to Remember

Pesticides

- Avoid using chemical pesticides in your home, garden, or on pets.

- Emphasize fruits and vegetables with lower pesticide levels, typically those with a tough outer peel.

- For fruits and vegetables with higher pesticide levels, choose organic, wash in a baking soda solution, or remove peel where possible.

- Choose organic grains where possible, especially when buying foods made from corn, soy, wheat, or oats.

Bisphenols

- For food storage, use glass or stainless steel instead of plastic where possible.

- When you need to use plastic in the kitchen, choose HDPE or polyethylene and avoid heat.

- In place of canned food, choose options that are dried, fresh, frozen, or packaged in glass jars.

- Safer Cookware

- Replace any old and damaged nonstick pans, preferably with a brand labeled "PFOA and PTFE free."

- Even better, rely on cast iron, stainless steel, and glass whenever practical.

Phthalates

- Avoid highly processed food and instead emphasize whole foods such as fruit, vegetables, grains, meat, nuts, and eggs.

- Avoid wearing perfume, nail polish, and hair spray.

- Stop using air freshener and fabric softener.

- As budget permits, start moving toward skin care, cleaning, and laundry products that are labeled fragrance free or phthalate free. For recommendations, see brainhealthfrom-birth.com

This is a lot to work on, but you can choose where to focus your efforts and make changes gradually over time. In an ideal world, you will be able to make at least some of these changes during pregnancy, a time when relatively minor steps can have lasting benefits for your baby's health. But it is never too late to start. The same steps will also have payoffs even after your baby arrives, by shielding your little one from chemicals that can compromise brain development during early childhood.

PART 4

Protecting Brain Health During the First Year

Chapter 11

The Natural Nursery

Setting up a nursery for your new baby can be a joyous yet somewhat daunting project. There are so many choices to make and more "necessary" items than one could ever imagine. Now armed with the knowledge that plastics and fragrances can release chemicals that compromise infant brain development, you are likely to approach this process somewhat differently, with the hope of choosing products that are as safe as possible.

This is fortunately becoming an easier task. As awareness grows that we should be minimizing harmful chemicals around babies and young children, manufacturers are taking notice. A visit to a baby store will reveal organic options for just about everything imaginable, including clothing, sheets, and even crib mattresses and baby carriers.

While this is a welcome trend, choosing organic cotton versus conventional cotton is actually a relatively low priority, as you will learn later in this chapter. The more important mission is to avoid certain man-made materials that are likely to contain harmful chemicals, such as phthalates and flame retardants.

In the end, setting up a nontoxic nursery should not require a much greater investment of time or money than buying standard products. It simply requires a few smarter choices for the items that matter most, starting with the crib.

Cribs and Crib Mattresses

One item where it is worth spending a little more to get the safest option is the crib mattress. In the first two years, your little one will spend up to 14 hours a day sleeping, so you want to make sure she isn't inhaling chemicals from a plastic-coated mattress during that time.

This is a problem that has gained significant government attention in recent years. In 2017, the United States Consumer Product Safety Commission (CPSC) finally banned certain phthalates in crib mattresses and waterproof mattress pads.

The problem is that many manufacturers have just switched to closely related compounds to make plastic coatings soft and flexible. These compounds, known collectively as "plasticizers," include less common phthalates that are not technically banned, but only because they have not yet been studied.

We know that exposure to high levels of phthalates during pregnancy compromises brain development, but babies are also vulnerable to the effects of these chemicals after they are born. Studies have reported that children with higher levels of phthalates in their bodies tend to have lower IQ scores and a higher risk of asthma and allergy.[248] Researchers have also linked higher phthalate exposure in early life to a greater risk of autism.[249] Therefore, it is worth doing what we can to protect babies and young children from phthalates and their closely related chemical cousins.

To that end, the most important step is avoiding crib mattresses or mattress covers made from vinyl or PVC. This type of plastic is suspect even if labeled as non-toxic or phthalate free, because other similar chemicals may still be present.

One of the safest alternative materials for crib mattresses is food-grade polyethylene. Although this is a type of plastic, it is soft and flexible by nature, so manufacturers do not have to add phthalates or similar "plasticizer" compounds. Several brands now produce crib mattresses and changing pads using this material as the waterproof layer, including Naturepedic.

The major limitation with polyethylene is that it does not withstand frequent washing, so it is only found in durable items such as mattresses, not washable covers. When choosing a separate cover, the best material is cotton with a thin polyurethane waterproofing layer. Polyurethane is generally considered non-toxic when used in this way, although there is some variation in safety depending on the manufacturing process. As a result, for waterproof mattress pads it is best to choose a brand that carries Greenguard certification, such as Naturepedic.

In addition to choosing a crib mattress and cover wisely, it is important to look for safer materials when buying the crib itself. Although cribs are stringently regulated in most countries and almost all manufacturers claim to use nontoxic paints and finishes, a crib could still have glues and adhesives that release chemicals such as formaldehyde. This is more of a concern for cribs made from particleboard (also known as MDF or wood composite) rather than solid wood.

The finishes on cribs can also be problematic, particularly for items made in countries with lower regulatory standards. In 2015, more than 4,000 cribs were recalled in the United States because they contained excessive levels of lead paint,[250] which can cause significant intellectual impairment in children.

The cribs in question were manufactured in Chile, but there have been similar violations for cribs manufactured in Asia. For this reason, it is best to buy from a company that manufactures in Europe, the United States, Canada, or another country with strong regulatory oversight.

Another way to avoid the potential dangers in paints and finishes is to buy a crib made from unfinished wood. Good options include the cribs made by Green Cradle, a company based in California, and Ikea's Sniglar crib, which is made from unfinished solid beech wood and costs less than $100, which goes to show that safer products aren't always more expensive. (I personally bought and loved the Sniglar crib.)

If you would prefer a varnished or painted crib, the best way to ensure that the one you are buying meets the most stringent chemical standards is to choose a brand that is Greenguard certified. This means the crib has been independently tested for thousands of different chemicals, including formaldehyde, phthalates, lead, and flame retardants. Popular brands that carry this certification include Oeuf, Stokke, and certain models at Crate & Barrel and Pottery Barn Kids.

It is also helpful to look for Greenguard certification for other furniture you may need for the nursery, such as a recliner, changing table, or dresser. If you are on a tight budget, buying these items from Ikea is a reasonable alternative. Although they will likely not be Greenguard certified, Ikea holds its products to Europe's much more stringent standards for chemicals such as formaldehyde.

Used furniture is also a very good option, because furniture is most likely to release chemicals when new. This illustrates the general principle that setting up a nontoxic nursery is often about choosing wisely, rather than buying the most expensive option. The exceptions to this principle may be your baby's crib mattress and changing pad, where it may be worth investing a little more to ensure safer materials.

Car Seats and Flame Retardants

Car seats are one area where it may cost a little more to avoid potential toxins. The main concern is chemical flame retardants, which are typically added to the foams and fabrics of car seats as a cheap way to comply with an outdated—and illogical—rule.

In 1971, at a time when cigarette smoking was the norm, the U.S. agency responsible for traffic safety introduced a requirement that the material inside vehicles should not burn or transmit a flame "at a rate of more than four inches per minute." This rule also applies to car seats for infants and children, so manufacturers started spraying chemical flame retardants on the seats' foam and coverings. Doing so was easier and less costly than switching to materials that were more naturally flame resistant.

There is, however, no evidence that the use of chemical flame retardants has accomplished anything in terms of fire safety. The agency that introduced the rule has reportedly said that it was "unaware of any records, data, or studies that indicate the current flammability standard is relevant or provides any fire safety benefit in a child's car seat."[251]

To the contrary, the evidence indicates that chemical flame retardants may actually make a fire more dangerous. One study found that when foam treated with a certain flame retardant burned, it produced twice as much smoke, seven times as much carbon monoxide, and 70 times as much soot as untreated foam.[252]

Perhaps just as troubling is the fact that, over time, flame-retardant chemicals are released into the air and dust inside vehicles and find their way into children's bodies. This is concerning because this class of chemicals includes known carcinogens and hormone disruptors.[253]

Research has also confirmed that exposure to flame retardants early in life can have long-lasting effects on the brain. In animal studies, this is reflected in increased hyperactivity and poor performance in learning and memory tests.[254] In humans, research has found that exposure to certain flame retardants in utero or in early childhood is linked to poorer attention and fine motor coordination and lower IQ.[255]

Fortunately, the flame retardants that seem to pose the clearest threat to brain development are being phased out. We do not yet know if the newer flame retardants more commonly used today pose similar risks, or if the amount of flame retardants in children's car seats makes a significant difference to the overall level of exposure.

Flame retardants are, after all, used in a variety of other places, including other surfaces in car interiors and home electronics. For many years, flame retardants were also added to upholstered

BRAIN HEALTH FROM BIRTH

furniture in the United States, in order to meet California's flammability standards.

In 2015, the situation changed for the better, with California no longer requiring flame retardant to be added to foam used in furniture and instead requiring labeling warning of the presence of these chemicals. In 2018, the state went further and outright banned the use of flame retardants in furniture, stating that they "do not provide a meaningful fire safety benefit," and it is "senseless to allow these toxic chemicals to continue being used."[256]

Although these rules technically only applied in California, the result was a nationwide shift away from flame retardants. Most major furniture manufacturers have now phased out their use.

The problem persists for car seats, however, because manufacturers must still comply with federal flammability standards for car interiors. Fortunately, consumer demand has inspired some car seat manufacturers to find a creative way to comply with these standards without using chemical flame retardants. The solution, it turned out, was surprisingly simple: merino wool.

Wool is a naturally flame-resistant material. When used to cover the foam of car seats, it is possible to meet federal flammability standards without any flame-retardant chemicals at all. The first manufacturer to do this was UPPAbaby, with the release of their Mesa infant car seat. UPPAbaby has now been joined by at least two other companies adopting the same strategy.

As of 2019, the car seats that are entirely free of flame retardants and rely on the natural flame resistance of merino wool include

- UPPAbaby Mesa (Henry or Jordan models)
- Nuna Pipa Lite
- Clek (Fllo, Foonf, and Liing models)

Of these brands, the car seat with the highest rating from Consumer Reports (which evaluates crash protection, ease of use, and installation) is the UPPAbaby Mesa. The potential drawbacks are that it is somewhat heavy, relatively expensive, and suitable only for infants, meaning your baby will outgrow the seat when they are a little over a year old. If you would prefer a car seat that can convert to a forward-facing seat for an older child, Clek may be a better option.

Beyond these brands, we can also look to the car seat ratings by The Ecology Center, a nonprofit organization that tests a variety of car seats each year for the presence of flame-retardant compounds. Their tests show that the brands listed above are the best choices, but Britax and Maxi-Cosi also score fairly well. The brands receiving a "high concern" rating by the Ecology Institute, indicating the presence of more harmful flame retardants, include Chicco, Evenflo, and Graco.

Britax is a particularly good choice because the company has not only eliminated the most concerning flame retardants, but the three similar Britax ClickTight models are also the three highest-rated convertible car seats by Consumer Reports, with the top scores on crash protection and ease of use. A convertible car seat means it can convert from a rear-facing infant seat for a brand-new baby to a forward-facing seat for an older child. Your baby will likely be able to continue using one of these models until they are at least three years old.

For more information on choosing the right car seat for you, see brainhealthfrombirth.com/carseats.

If you have already purchased a car seat that is rated as "high concern" in terms of flame retardants, is it worth replacing it? This is an area where reasonable minds differ, and the answer ultimately depends on your budget and priorities.

I have to admit that I am one of the many parents who read the data on flame retardants in car seats only after buying one of the worst possible brands. I have not yet replaced the car seat in question but feel that I probably should. My lingering guilt over not doing my homework is somewhat lessened by the knowledge that I am already doing so many other things to protect my children from chemicals.

Although it makes sense to take flame retardants into account if you are still in the process of choosing a car seat, it is also worth noting that car seats are probably not the single most important source of flame retardants for our children. There are several other strategies to minimize exposure to these chemicals—strategies that may actually have even more impact.

Other Ways to Avoid Flame Retardants

The best opportunity to minimize your child's exposure to flame retardants comes from tackling a surprising source: household dust.

Before flame retardants get into our bodies, they first get into dust. As explained by the Environmental Protection Agency (EPA), "Flame retardant chemicals escape from products into the air and they can attach to dust. Dust is in the air we breathe and can also be transported via our hands and our food and into our mouths."[257] This happens in our cars, due to the chemicals added to car interiors, as well as in our homes, where flame retardants can be found in older upholstered furniture, electronics, and possibly other items such as rugs and window coverings.

By vacuuming regularly and dusting surfaces with a damp cloth, you can dramatically reduce your exposure to flame retardants.[258] In a recent intervention study of mother-and-child pairs, more frequent vacuuming and dusting with a damp cloth reduced flame retardant levels by more than half in just one week.[259] Keeping dust under control is particularly important when you have a crawling baby, because dust from the floor and furniture quickly ends up in their mouth.

To further reduce exposure to flame retardants, the intervention study also found that more frequent hand washing, particularly before eating, could also reduce flame retardant levels by more than 50 percent.

An optional extra step to consider if budget permits is to buy a home air filter. This will remove dust carrying flame retardants and other potentially harmful chemicals released from items in your home. A good quality air filter will also help remove particles from external air pollution, such as vehicle exhaust.

Recent studies point to heavy exposure to vehicle exhaust during pregnancy as a possible risk factor for autism, miscarriage, low birth weight, and preterm birth.[260] This is likely because air pollution increases inflammation.[261] Studies also show that for people living in polluted areas, using a home air filter can significantly reduce this inflammation.[262] Recommended brands include Austin Air and Blueair. (For up-to-date advice on choosing an air filter, visit brain-healthfrombirth.com/airfilters.)

Strollers

From a chemical standpoint, strollers are generally low risk. Flame retardants are unlikely to be found in strollers, but there is a chance that some manufacturers may use phthalates (in PVC/vinyl) or stain-proofing chemicals, some of which appear to act as endocrine disruptors.

Recommended stroller brands that do not use any of these chemicals include Baby Jogger City Mini and UPPAbaby. The City Mini is a very popular stroller and works well for many parents, but it is not compatible with any of the car seats made without flame retardants and does not have the option of turning the seat around so your baby can face you (except when using a car seat).

In contrast, UPPAbaby's Cruz and Vista strollers are compatible with their Mesa infant car seat. This means you can unclick the car seat from the base attachment in the car and transfer the car seat to the stroller frame, perhaps complete with sleeping baby. Both the Cruz and Vista can also be configured to either have the baby face you or the world at large. They also have the option for a bassinet attachment for young babies. (For more information, see brainhealthfrombirth.com/strollers.)

Clothing, Bedding, and Baby Carriers

While it is generally worth spending a little more on a nontoxic crib mattress, car seat, and stroller, it is not necessary to buy expensive organic clothing and bedding. Although growing conventional cotton uses a tremendous amount of pesticides, by the time cotton is incorporated into fabric, the pesticides are long gone, according to author and environmental expert Debra Lynn Dadd.[263]

As long as you are buying baby clothes and bedding made from natural fibers, such as cotton, there is little reason to worry about chemical contamination. Although fabric items can be treated with chemicals after processing, washing several times and using vinegar in a rinse cycle can typically remove these chemicals.

That said, there are still some advantages to buying organic cotton if budget permits. From an environmental perspective, organic cotton is clearly better. Items made from organic cotton are also typically higher quality, so the fabric will be smoother and last longer. (This is more relevant for crib sheets than clothing, which your little one will quickly outgrow.) In addition, buying organic is not necessarily that much more expensive, with the rise of affordable brands such as Burt's Bees. Another good way to reduce costs and benefit the environment is to use secondhand baby clothes where possible.

Because they are typically not treated with chemicals such as flame retardants, baby carriers are another item where there is little reason to worry about toxic chemicals. Although there are several organic brands available, you could also choose from one of the many brands of baby carriers made from 100 percent cotton.

All models of BabyBjorn carriers are certified by Oeko-Tex, an independent testing and certification system that tests for the presence of harmful chemicals in textile-based products. Oeko-Tex certification means the products have been independently verified to be free of harmful dyes, phthalates, formaldehyde, pesticides, heavy metals, and flame retardants, giving additional peace of mind. (For specific recommendations for other products such as play mats and travel cribs see brainhealthfrombirth.com/gear.)

Rugs, Window Coverings, and Wallpaper

When it comes to decorating your baby's nursery, the general philosophy is to keep it simple and choose natural fibers such as wool and cotton as much as possible. This will help reduce the overall level of chemicals in the room and create cleaner and healthier air for your little one to breathe.

Choosing natural materials makes the most difference for large items such as rugs and window coverings, which can pollute a room with chemicals if not chosen wisely. For rugs, wool is the best material because it is naturally flame- and stain-resistant. Wool rugs are therefore much less likely to be treated with toxic chemicals than rugs made from other materials. For added reassurance, look for the "Green Label Plus" certification by the Carpet and Rug Institute.

For window coverings, the main problem occurs when blinds or window shades are made from vinyl or PVC, which can release phthalates into the air. Several large manufacturers of blinds and roller shades now carry Greenguard certification, which means the products have been tested and found to meet specific limits for chemical emissions. Normally this should give sufficient peace of mind, but there is some question over the value of this certification in the case of window coverings. It has been reported that the Greenguard testing does not adequately take into account the effect of high heat and direct sunlight on chemical release from blinds, so blinds may be an anomaly where we cannot rely on Greenguard certification.

There are some companies that go even further to ensure chemical safety, such as Earthshade blinds, but these brands can be quite expensive. Other good options include drapes or roman blinds made from cotton, ideally with a cotton lining layer, rather than a synthetic blackout coating. Inexpensive pleated paper blackout shades are also typically safe.

Choosing the right rugs and window coverings can make a big difference to the air quality in your baby's room, but there is one more potential hazard that is good to avoid: wallpaper.

Typically made from vinyl, wallpaper is one of the worst offenders when it comes to phthalates. In a 2010 study by The Ecology Center, most samples of wallpaper contained banned phthalates, along with other hazardous chemicals such as lead and cadmium.[264] The adhesives used to install wallpaper can also release potentially toxic compounds.

If you have already installed wallpaper, let your nose be your guide on whether it is worth removing. If there is any chemical smell in the room, I would vote to remove it. The same applies to wall decals and large decorative wall stickers, which are often made of vinyl and should be removed if they have any chemical smell.

A much safer alternative is to paint nursery walls, ideally using a brand of paint that is specifically designed to emit fewer chemicals as it dries, such as Benjamin Moore Natura or AFM Safecoat. (If you have already painted, the brand is not important—existing paint that has already dried will not release chemicals.)

If painting the nursery is still on your to-do list, bear in mind that even with one of the safer brands, The American Pregnancy Association recommends minimizing exposure to any fumes while pregnant. It is therefore best to have someone else do the actual painting and ensure good ventilation while it dries. The paint should also be given at least a week to dry before your baby moves into her new room.

Points to Remember

- Look for a crib mattress that uses polyethylene as the waterproof layer, such as one made by Naturepedic.

- When choosing a crib, natural unfinished wood is a good choice. For finished wood and other furniture, look for Greenguard certification.

- Car seats can be treated with toxic flame-retardant chemicals. UPPAbaby and several other brands now use merino wool instead of chemicals to meet flammability standards. Britax also scores well on flame retardants and is the top convertible car seat in crash tests.

- To further reduce flame retardants, minimize household dust by vacuuming and dusting regularly with a damp cloth.

- Although strollers do not typically have toxic chemicals, Baby Jogger City Mini and UPPAbaby are particularly safe, non-toxic options.

- For clothing, bedding, and baby carriers, look for 100 percent cotton. Choosing organic cotton is not essential.

- When decorating your baby's nursery, choose natural fibers where possible for rugs and window coverings, and choose paint instead of wallpaper.

Chapter 12

Clean and Green Baby Care

After setting up a nontoxic nursery, the next step is buying the products you will use for day-to-day baby care, such as baby bottles, diapers, pacifiers, lotion, and shampoo. If you take the standard approach to buying baby supplies, this means bringing home a vast number of items that are either made of plastic or heavily fragranced, both potential risks for chemicals such as phthalates.

In our grandparents' generation, baby care looked very different. Cloth diapers, breastfeeding, and glass baby bottles were the norm, and there was little to no plastic involved. In that time, the modern plagues of autism, ADHD, asthma, and allergies were also extremely rare. How closely these factors are linked remains to be seen, but as chapter 10 discussed, there is good quality evidence that certain chemicals in plastic, such as BPA and phthalates, are contributing to health problems and damaging young minds.

In Europe, the United States, Canada, and Australia, this concern has finally led to government action. BPA, along with several common phthalates, have now been banned in most items intended for babies. Yet companies are often free to replace these specific chemicals with other similar compounds that have not yet been studied for safety.

Taking the "nuclear option" and returning to the old ways of caring for a baby with minimal plastic is an admirable strategy for those parents who can make it work. This approach is getting easier, with the advent of prefolded cloth diapers, diaper services, lactation consultants, and a booming industry of plastic-free baby items. We now have ready access to everything imaginable made from wood, stainless steel, and other safer materials, including sippy cups, bowls, toys, and teeters.

But for the parents without the time, financial resources, or motivation to eschew plastic completely, there is a happy medium. By learning which baby products are best avoided and which modern conveniences you can take advantage of without guilt, you can get the best of both worlds.

Diapers

One of the best examples of a modern convenience with a bad reputation is the disposable diaper. Although they are still used by the vast majority of parents today, over the past decade there has been a gradual rise in the number of parents who are instead opting for washable cloth diapers.

Consumer demand in this area has led to the creation of many new forms of reusable diapers, which are typically much simpler and easier to use than the cloth diapers of previous generations.

The parents who use these diapers are often motivated by environmental concerns, with the desire to avoid the pollution involved in producing and disposing of single-use diapers. But the environmental benefit of reusable diapers is actually not so clear cut.

Growing cotton to make cloth diapers takes a tremendous amount of environmental resources, while the energy involved in washing the diapers in hot water on a daily basis likely creates as much pollution as the manufacturing and disposal of single-use diapers.[265]

There are other much more effective ways to reduce the overall environmental impact of caring for your baby, starting with simply buying fewer clothes, toys, and other items. The manufacturing of baby clothes and other textiles leaves a major environmental footprint, which can be lessened by only buying as much as you really need or, better yet, buying secondhand items.

If the environmental reasons for using cloth diapers are not entirely persuasive, what about the potential health benefits. Do the materials in disposable diapers pose any hazards?

Answering this question is somewhat challenging because most manufacturers do not disclose full details about the materials they use. But we do know that disposable diapers are usually made from a combination of paper, thin plastic such as polypropylene, and an inner core polymer material that absorbs liquids and forms a gel. These materials are generally safe and nontoxic.[266]

For the absorbent gel-forming layer, the exact same material is used by both conventional brands and eco-friendly brands. As noted by an engineer for Seventh Generation, one of the largest eco-friendly brands: "All of the diaper suppliers do a great job of making sure that their diaper designs are safe for babies," he said. "That's not really where they differ. They differ in how responsible their ingredients are."[267]

More specifically, the main difference between conventional and eco-friendly diaper brands is whether they use bleached or unbleached paper. Chlorine bleaching is potentially harmful to the environment, but likely not harmful to your baby. Trace amounts of chemicals called dioxins may be present in chlorine-bleached diapers, but dioxins are ubiquitous in the world around us. The amount in diapers is infinitesimally small, making bleached paper simply not worth worrying about from a health perspective. If you would prefer chlorine-free diapers for environmental reasons, good options include Seventh Generation and Naty.

From a health standpoint, the biggest problem with disposable diapers is the fragrance that is added to certain brands, such as

Pampers and Luvs (at the time of writing). If a diaper has a synthetic fragrance added, that means your little one will be inhaling a cocktail of unnecessary chemicals, potentially including phthalates. Recent tests have found phthalates in several unnamed diaper brands.[268] Although the amounts were generally small, we can likely reduce the chance of phthalate exposure from diapers by choosing a fragrance-free brand such as Huggies.

You may of course choose to go further and use an eco-friendly brand that provides even greater reassurance when it comes to phthalates and other chemicals. Naty diapers, for example, have been independently certified to be free of harmful substances such as phthalates. I personally used Naty for the newborn stage but switched to Huggies when my babies were sleeping for longer periods of time and needed a diaper that kept them dry longer. Eco-friendly diapers may be marginally better from an environmental and chemical standpoint, but sometimes we have to make compromises and prioritize other factors.

Baby Shampoos, Lotions, Sunscreen, and Other Products

In years past, baby lotions and powders were a major source of phthalate exposure. The more of these types of products a mother used on her baby, the higher the levels of phthalates.[269] This pattern may be shifting now, with progress on banning certain phthalates, especially in Europe. But it still remains important to pay attention to ingredients in products that come into contact with your baby's skin, either directly or indirectly. This includes baby soaps, shampoos, lotions, wipes, and laundry detergents.

For these products, avoiding phthalates is unfortunately not simply a matter of checking for the word "phthalates" on the list of ingredients. These chemicals can be hidden in anything fragranced, so it is best to choose products that are specifically labeled as fragrance free or phthalate free. Natural fragrances from essential oils are likely not a problem with respect to phthalates, but they can be irritating for new-borns with sensitive skin so are best avoided during the early months.

Parabens, which are preservatives added to many products in order to inhibit microbial growth, are another potentially harmful ingredient to watch out for, especially in baby lotions and wipes. Just like phthalates, parabens can act as hormone disruptors, so it is a good idea to minimize your baby's exposure. If a product is not labeled as "paraben free," check the ingredients list for chemicals such as methylparaben, ethylparaben, or propylparaben.

Going beyond phthalates and parabens, it is also preferable to choose products with mostly natural ingredients where possible. This helps avoid the numerous other chemicals that may not necessarily be harmful but are worthy of suspicion. Specific chemicals in this category include

- polyethylene glycol (PEG)
- cocamidopropyl betaine
- sodium laureth sulfate
- sodium benzoate
- limonene
- linalool
- geraniol
- phenoxyethanol

For recommended brands without these chemicals, see brainhealthfrombirth.com/babyproducts

Pacifiers

After learning about the potential dangers of phthalates, which are often found in soft and flexible plastic, the idea of giving your newborn a pacifier can be somewhat alarming. It shouldn't be.

First of all, manufacturers have been banned from using BPA and phthalates in pacifiers for many years. In the United States, the Consumer Products Safety Commission actually asked manufacturers to remove phthalates from pacifiers twenty years ago, long before the broader uprising against these chemicals.

There is of course a danger that manufacturers will flout these rules, but most pacifiers are made of medical grade silicone, which is unlikely to contain large amounts of BPA or phthalates to begin with. Some studies have found small amounts of phthalates and other chemicals in silicone, but overall the risk is very low, especially with a good-quality pacifier brand such as Phillips Avent.

Another alternative is to choose a pacifier made from natural rubber, which does not contain phthalates or other endocrine disruptors. But here the brand is important. Natural rubber can contain chemicals known as nitrosamines, which are known to be carcinogenic. The quantity of nitrosamines in rubber depends on exactly how it was made, so if you plan to use this type of pacifier, choose a brand that carefully controls the manufacturing process and tests for the presence of nitrosamines. One such brand is Natursutten, which manufactures natural rubber pacifiers and bottle nipples in Italy. The company regularly has its products tested for nitrosamines at an independent laboratory.[270]

The popular teething toy Sophie the Giraffe is also made from natural rubber, which led to a flurry of controversy several years ago over whether the toy exceeded the stringent European standards for nitrosamines. The manufacturer reports that its production process is now controlled even more tightly, with every batch independently tested for nitrosamines. The net result is that this ubiquitous toy is probably one of the safest options for a teething baby.

Apart from the presence of chemicals in pacifiers, some parents are also concerned that a pacifier may interfere with breastfeeding. For precisely this reason, the World Health Organization's pro-breast-feeding guidelines formerly instructed hospitals not to give pacifiers to breastfeeding babies.

There is some support for this concern in observational studies, which simply look for patterns in populations. Several studies per-formed in the late 1990s and early 2000s reported that mothers who gave their infants pacifiers in the first month were less likely to be exclusively breastfeeding at six months.[271] But that does not mean that giving the pacifiers actually *caused* the difference in breast-feeding duration. To answer that question, a randomized controlled study would be needed to see what happens when mothers are ran-domly assigned to either use a pacifier or not.

Fortunately, such a study has now been done—five times. In all but one of the randomized, controlled trials, it is clear that pacifier use has no significant impact on the proportion of infants who are still exclusively breastfeeding at three or six months.[272]

Far from compromising breastfeeding, pacifiers may in fact help, by giving mothers another tool to soothe their baby before resorting to formula. When a hospital in Oregon restricted access to pacifiers and effectively banned nurses from giving them to breastfeeding mothers, there was actually a drop in the number of mothers who were able to exclusively breastfeed.[273]

Another study found that for mothers at high risk of postpartum depression, receiving a pacifier in the hospital was linked to a much higher chance of continued breastfeeding at three months.[274] This suggests that pacifiers really do make life easier for new mothers, allowing them to continue with breastfeeding during difficult times.

Hospital policies that discourage pacifiers are not only futile when it comes to supporting breastfeeding, they may actually be doing real harm in other ways. As three pediatricians wrote in the prestigious journal *JAMA Pediatrics*, "there is strong evidence that pacifiers may have a protective effect against sudden infant death syndrome (SIDS)."[275]

This strong evidence comes from more than a dozen studies investigating the link between pacifier use and SIDS.[276] The answer is clear and consistent: putting a baby to bed with a pacifier reduces the risk of SIDS by approximately 30 to 50 percent.

No one is quite sure why this is so, but it could be because the baby does not drift into quite such a deep sleep. Interestingly, it does not seem to matter if the pacifier falls out of the baby's mouth soon after they go to sleep. A policy statement from the American Academy of Pediatrics SIDS task force notes "the protective effect of the pacifier is observed even if the pacifier falls out of the infant's mouth… It does not need to be reinserted once the infant falls asleep."[277]

The policy statement also advises that "for breastfed infants, pacifier introduction should be delayed until breastfeeding is firmly established." On this last point, it seems that the policy is not supported by the most current evidence, which shows that pacifiers do not actually compromise breastfeeding. Several pediatricians have therefore described the AAP's suggestion to delay pacifier use as "difficult to defend."[278]

The new data indicating that pacifiers can help prevent SIDS without interfering with breastfeeding should be welcome news for any new parent, since pacifiers can be truly sanity saving during the first few months. As noted by Dr. Sydney Spiesel, a pediatrician with more than forty years of experience, the new research "reinforces my long-standing support for pacifiers. I've never believed that they interfere with breastfeeding, and I generally favor any practice that makes a child happy. It's nice to have my indulgent instincts acquire authoritative support."[279]

Baby Bottles

Plastic baby bottles have a come a long way over the past 10 years, with manufacturers abandoning BPA-containing polycarbonate in favor of safer alternatives such as polypropylene. This is definitely a step in the right direction, but studies have found that even BPA-free plastic baby bottles can still leach other endocrine-disrupting chemicals.[280] Since bottles are typically sterilized or washed in very hot water each day for newborns, we do not even have the option of treating the plastic carefully to minimize leaching.

For peace of mind, the best solution is to avoid plastic entirely in favor of bottles made from glass. Although there is some concern with glass bottles breaking when dropped, many brands use glass that is tougher than you might expect and can sometimes survive a drop to hard floors. The type of glass is typically borosilicate, which is also designed to withstand rapid changes in temperature without cracking. Glass bottles have the added advantages of being much more durable and easier to clean than plastic.

The main disadvantage of glass bottles is that your older baby will not be able to hold the bottle themselves, both due to concerns about breakage and the simple fact that it may be too heavy for them to hold comfortably. One good solution is to use stainless-steel baby bottles instead, such as those made by Pura. These bottles can also be converted to sippy bottles as your baby grows, by replacing the infant nipple with a sipper spout. The disadvantage is that stainless steel can't be transferred from fridge to microwave for easy heating, and it is harder to see how much milk or formula remains. For these reasons, glass bottles are typically easier for the newborn stage.

Whether you use glass or stainless-steel baby bottles, there will typically still be some plastic parts. This is nothing to worry about, since the rings that hold nipples in place do not come into contact with the milk, and the nipples themselves are usually medical-grade silicone. Alternatively, you can buy glass baby bottles with natural rubber nipples, such as those sold by Natursutten.

Some specialized baby bottles do have plastic parts that come in contact with the milk, such as anti-colic bottles with large plastic internal tubes to vent air bubbles. This is claimed to reduce how much air a baby swallows and therefore reduce gas pain and reflux. Whether the benefit of this feature is worth the use of plastic is difficult to know. In the end, the answer probably depends on how much your own baby benefits from this venting feature. If you find that your baby really does much better with this type of bottle, then it is probably not worth worrying about the small amount of plastic, especially if the milk or formula is not stored in the bottle for a long period of time before feedings.

Once your baby moves on to solid food and starts drinking from a cup, it is still useful to look for alternatives to plastic. At this point, stainless steel will likely become a fixture in your kitchen. It has the unparalleled advantage of being simultaneously lightweight, unbreakable, and nontoxic, making it the best material for toddler cups, bowls, plates, water bottles, and travel food containers.

Fortunately, it is now becoming easier than ever to find stainless-steel versions of all these products, which illustrates how much consumer demand is driving change in the industry. As awareness grows that plastic contains potentially harmful chemicals, manufacturers are taking note and giving us better alternatives. A similar process is happening with many different baby products, with safer options for baby shampoos, lotions, and a myriad of other baby-care items, giving us the opportunity to avoid toxins without a great deal of effort or expense.

Points to Remember

- The environmental advantages of cloth diapers are not as clear cut as we might expect.

- The materials used in disposable diapers are generally safe, but it pays to avoid brands that are fragranced.

- It is also best to avoid fragrance in other baby-care products, including lotions, shampoo, and baby wipes.

- Ideally, baby skin care products should be phthalate free and paraben free.

- The evidence suggests that pacifiers can help reduce the risk of SIDS, without posing a threat to successful breastfeeding.

- Pacifiers made from medical-grade silicone are likely safe, but another good option is natural rubber, if manufactured by a company that tests for nitrosamines.

- From a chemical standpoint, glass baby bottles are a better choice than plastic.

- For older babies, stainless steel bottles may be better because they are lightweight and unbreakable.

- Stainless steel is also an excellent choice for toddler bowls, cups, snack containers, and water bottles.

- For specific product recommendations, see brainhealthfrombirth.com/babyproducts

Chapter 13

Breastfeeding and the Formula Wars

There is no doubt that breast milk is the best source of nutrition for babies. But the messaging to new mothers on this topic often overshadows some critical points, such as the dangers of insisting on exclusive breastfeeding when milk supply is significantly delayed.

If a newborn gets little to no breast milk in the first days of life, but a mother is told to avoid formula at all costs, the baby can quickly become dehydrated and develop dangerously low blood sugar. This can have a long-term impact on brain development that is much greater than the difference between formula and breastfeeding, as this chapter explains.

It is clear that breastfeeding should be supported, but there is also a time and place for formula. If you do need to give your baby formula, the real question is how to choose a formula that best mimics the benefits of breast milk.

Before delving into those important issues, it is helpful to understand the broader context, to know what the research says on just how much better breastfeeding really is and why.

The Evidence on Breastfeeding

The purported benefits of breastfeeding include lower rates of asthma, eczema, allergy, obesity, and infections, along with higher IQ scores. But when we look at all the evidence, it appears that these benefits are somewhat exaggerated, causing unnecessary guilt for the many mothers who are unable to breastfeed or find they need to supplement with formula.

As Courtney Jung wrote in an opinion piece in the *New York Times*, "Oddly, the fervor of breast-feeding advocacy has ramped up even as medical research—published in *The Journal of the American Medical Association, BMJ* in Britain and *The American Journal of Clinical Nutrition*—has begun to report that the effects of breast-feeding are probably 'modest.'"[281]

One such study is Dr. Michael Kramer's PROBIT trial, which studied the degree and duration of breastfeeding among 14,000 mother-infant pairs. Kramer found that breastfeeding did not reduce the risk of respiratory infections, asthma, allergies, or attention-deficit hyperactivity disorder.[282] It did however slightly reduce gastrointestinal infections and improve cognitive development.

These two specific benefits—to the brain and the GI system—are the most consistent findings among the many other studies evaluating breastfeeding versus formula feeding. In another example, researchers compared various health outcomes and vocabulary scores among 500 sibling pairs where only one sibling was breastfed.[283] On respiratory infections, asthma, and allergies, the researchers found that breastfeeding made little difference. For the most part, the "long-term effects of breast feeding have been overstated," they wrote.

Yet the children who were breastfed scored higher on vocabulary tests, indicating that breast milk provides unique support for cognitive development. This finding is consistent with more than a dozen other studies finding higher cognitive scores in breastfed infants, with even greater benefits with longer duration of breastfeeding.[284]

Through the sea of conflicting information in this area, there is one other relatively consistent finding: a slight reduction in gastrointestinal infections.[285] When it comes to other types of infections, the benefits of breastfeeding are often exaggerated, based on a common misconception about how the human immune system works.

Many people believe that breastfeeding offers powerful immune benefits because antibodies are transferred through colostrum and milk from mother to baby. That is not actually true, as explained by Dr. Sydney Spiesel, a pediatrician and clinical professor at Yale University's School of Medicine:

> *When you ask a bunch of doctors about how breast-feeding prevents infection, they get it wrong—I know they do, because I've asked the question. Doctors tell you that colostrum (produced in the first three days or so after a baby is born) and breast milk are full of maternal antibodies. Next, doctors say that these maternal antibodies are absorbed into the infant's blood circulation and thus serve to protect infants from disease.*[286]

That's true for most mammals, but not humans. Breast milk is rich in antibodies, but babies cannot absorb these antibodies into the bloodstream in any significant amount.[287] The antibodies instead remain in the gastrointestinal tract, where they do help prevent some infections, but this is far from the protective force field many people imagine.

That does not mean a newborn is left defenseless. Unlike other animals, humans are actually *born* with the powerful protection of their mother's antibodies: during the third trimester, these antibodies are transferred across the placenta into the infant's bloodstream.[288] There, they remain and provide protection from birth until the baby's own immune system develops during the first few months of life. "That's why we don't need to absorb maternal anti-bodies from colostrum. And it's why formula-fed babies are not at a disadvantage, compared with breast-fed babies, in their supply of cir-culating maternal antibodies," Spiesel notes.[289]

Early studies finding reduced rates of ear infections and upper respiratory infections in breastfed infants were likely plagued by a problem known as "confounding." In plain English, this means that some additional factor other than breastfeeding was the true cause of lower infection rates in breastfed infants.

This pattern was shown in a recent study that categorized mothers by whether they *intended* to breastfeed or not. The mothers who had every intention of nursing had children with fewer infections, even if the mother did not actually end up breastfeeding. The study authors com-mented that "the same characteristics that lead a mother to breastfeed may also lead to an infant having improved health."[290] As explained by Dr. Amy Tuteur, obstetrician and author of *Push Back: Guilt in the Age of Natural Parenting*, "It is the differences between mothers that are responsible for the differences in outcome, not breastfeeding."[291]

Another often-cited benefit of breastfeeding is a more balanced immune system, evident from reduced rates of asthma, eczema, and allergies. The evidence on this point is somewhat inconsistent. In one review of dozens of studies, researchers reported that less than half the studies found that breastfeeding reduced the risk of asthma, eczema, and food allergy. In the rest of the studies, breastfeeding made little to no difference.[292] A more recent systematic review concluded that "There is some evidence that breastfeeding is protective for asthma ... There is weaker evidence for a protective effect for eczema."[293]

If breastfeeding does indeed help prevent these conditions, it is likely by way of supporting the population of beneficial microbes in the gastrointestinal tract, known as the microbiome. We know that breast milk helps "seed" a baby's microbiome with beneficial bacteria such as Lactobacilli and Bifidobacteria, microbes that play a critical role in educating the immune system.

We also know that breast milk contains a wide variety of indigestible carbohydrates, also known as *prebiotics*, which are present solely to nurture gut microbes. The net result is that babies who are breastfed typically have a more robust population of beneficial microbes and fewer harmful ones.[294] This in turn appears to reduce the rates of allergy and eczema in breastfed babies.[295]

Yet the major studies in this area were performed before formula-manufacturers began adding prebiotics in an effort to mimic the beneficial effects of breast milk on the microbiome. As discussed in more detail in chapter 17, by choosing a formula containing prebiotics, and supplementing with the right probiotics, we can build a microbiome that is very similar to that of a breastfed infant, resulting in similar rates of food allergy, eczema, and other immune conditions. [296]

Supporting the microbiome in this way also appears to reduce the number of gastrointestinal infections, mimicking another potential advantage of breastfeeding. By building a healthier population of beneficial species using probiotics and prebiotics, the harmful species that cause gastrointestinal infections have less opportunity to take hold.

Breastfeeding still has a clear advantage over formula when it comes to cognitive development, but here too recent developments in formula development are starting to close the gap.

Breast Milk vs. Formula for Brain Development

Initially, it was thought that breast milk was so advantageous for brain development because it contained a higher proportion of omega-3 fatty acids, particularly DHA. For this reason, manufacturers have been adding DHA to infant formula for many years now, but the benefits in terms of cognitive development have been somewhat disappointing. To be sure, as discussed in chapter 4, a steady supply of DHA during pregnancy is important for brain development. Breastfed infants also typically show higher levels of DHA than formula-fed infants, as long as the mother has adequate intake.[297] But the addition of DHA to formula does not seem to lessen the gap between formula and breast milk when it comes to supporting brain development.[298]

More recently, formula manufacturers have developed a new way to replicate some of the brain-boosting effects of breast milk, by adding a component of milk known as milk fat globule membrane, or MFGM for short. This is a combination of lipids and proteins that forms a membrane around fat droplets in breast milk. MFGM is also present in cow's milk, but it has historically been discarded along with the milk fat in the manufacturing of infant formula. That changed when researchers discovered that MFGM actually contains several components that could be helpful for brain development, including sialic acid, gangliosides, sphingomyelin, and choline.

In 2014, researchers in Sweden performed a randomized study where a group of infants were given formula supplemented with MFGM from cow's milk. [299] Surprisingly, when the babies were 12 months old, their cognitive scores were similar to breastfed babies. The study's authors concluded, "this nutritional intervention eradicated the gap in cognitive performance between breastfed and formula-fed infants at 12 months of age."

Other studies have since confirmed the brain-building benefits of MFGM, along with an apparent reduction in infections.[300] As a result, MFGM is now added to several brands of infant formula, as discussed in more detail in chapter 14.

Taking a step back, the fact remains that breast milk is still the best choice for nourishing babies. But formula is getting closer than ever and the benefits of breastfeeding are less extreme than suggested by many experts. This is important to recognize because many mothers are not able to breastfeed at all, or for as long as they would like, or may need to supplement with formula.

The World Health Organization recommends exclusive breastfeeding for six months, but in the United States, only a quarter of mothers manage that extraordinary feat.[301] Most women stop breastfeeding earlier than they would like, due to factors such as illnesses requiring medication, unsupportive work policies, and lack of parental leave.

If you are one of the 75 percent of mothers who need to feed your baby formula, take comfort in the knowledge that you are still providing a perfectly good source of nutrition. This important message is often lost among the cacophony of advice about the superiority of breastfeeding.

In an opinion piece in *The New York Times*, professor of political science Courtney Jung argued that many pro-breastfeeding campaigners have been focusing on the wrong issue. "There is a difference between supporting a woman's decision to breast-feed through policy changes like improved maternity leave, flexible work schedules and on-site day care facilities, and compelling women to breast-feed by demonizing formula."[302]

Formula, Guilt, and Hospital Policies

Demonizing formula has unfortunately become commonplace in many U.S. hospitals, based on attempts to implement the World Health Organization's pro-breastfeeding guidelines. The guidelines set forth 10 steps for hospitals to follow to encourage breastfeeding. Hospitals that implement these steps can be accredited by the Baby-Friendly Hospitals Initiative, a global program founded by the World Health Organization with independent accrediting bodies in various countries.

This initiative has now been widely criticized. In 2016 several pediatricians at the prestigious Massachusetts General Hospital raised concerns about the initiative and it insistence on the "10 steps," noting that "Unfortunately, there is now emerging evidence that full compliance with the 10 steps of the initiative may inadvertently be promoting potentially hazardous practices and/or having counterproductive outcomes."[303]

Another opponent of the Baby-Friendly Initiative is Dr. Amy Tuteur, an obstetrician gynecologist who runs the popular blog The Skeptical OB. She argues that the initiative is "unfriendly to mothers, dangerous to babies, and contemptuous of scientific evidence."[304]

The facts seem to bear this out. In a recent survey of patients at one Baby-Friendly hospital, 26 percent of formula-feeding mothers felt shamed regarding their decision.[305]

Perhaps even more troubling is the fact that the guidelines promote a single-minded focus on breastfeeding so extreme that it puts babies at risk in other ways.

As just one example, for over a decade the guidelines instructed hospitals not to give pacifiers to breastfeeding infants. The rationale for this was that pacifiers could cause "nipple confusion" and make it more difficult for newborns to learn to breastfeed. (There is actually no evidence for this.)

The problem with this policy is that, as mentioned in chapter 12, pacifiers have been shown to reduce the risk of sudden infant death syndrome (SIDS). The guidelines were effectively ranking breastfeeding as a higher priority than preventing SIDS. In the most recent version of the guidelines, the wording of the pacifier ban has now been watered down to instead instruct hospitals to "educate on the risks" of pacifier use. Yet other rules remain that similarly rank breastfeeding as a higher priority than safety.

Another example is the rule stating that hospitals should encourage 24-hour rooming-in, which is when the baby remains in the mother's hospital room at all times, rather than going to a nursery for periods of time while the mother sleeps or recovers from surgery. Many experts have criticized this policy as carrying risks to the infant when a new mother is sedated by pain medication and trying to nurse alone at night. This scenario raises the possibility that the mother may accidentally fall asleep with the baby in the hospital bed, which could lead to suffocation or falls.

Fortunately, hospital policies discouraging pacifiers and encouraging rooming-in are typically enforced quite loosely. If a new mother firmly requests a pacifier or help with the baby so she can sleep or recover from a C-section, hospital staff will often comply. There is, however, one other guideline in the Baby-Friendly Hospital Initiative that is enforced more strictly in many hospitals, with potentially dire consequences.

The rule in question states that hospitals should "not provide breastfed newborns any food or fluids other than breast milk, unless medically indicated." The difficulty lies in the assessment of what is "medically indicated." If a mother's milk supply is delayed by several days, some hospitals take the view that supplementing with formula still isn't needed and that the baby can wait until milk supply is fully established. The latest research suggests that in some cases that is a huge mistake.

Early Formula Supplementation and the Fed Is Best Campaign

Significant delays in milk supply are surprisingly common, with up to 15 percent of first-time mothers not producing enough milk to meet their baby's nutritional needs, particularly in the first few days after birth.[306] Risk factors include Cesarean delivery, severe bleeding after birth, diabetes, obesity, thyroid conditions, and prolonged bed rest during pregnancy.[307]

Unfortunately, the problem of delayed milk supply does not get taken seriously enough, out of fear of interfering with the delicate process of nursing. Many hospitals and health professionals are eager to encourage breastfeeding at all costs, with the result that they may advise against supplementing with formula even when infants truly need it.

This can be quite dangerous. If a mother is trying to exclusively breastfeed but there is an unusual delay in her milk production, a newborn can quickly become dehydrated and experience severely low blood glucose levels. In extreme cases, this can result in long-term brain damage. Severe low blood sugar in newborns, known as "neonatal hypoglycemia," is in fact the most common preventable cause of brain damage in infancy.

This important topic has recently been brought to light by the work of the Fed is Best Foundation, a nonprofit started by Dr. Christie del Castillo-Hegyi, an emergency physician, former NIH scientist, and newborn brain injury researcher, who is also the mother of a 6-year-old child who is neurologically disabled. Her story is anxiety provoking, but important to know:

> *My child fell victim to newborn jaundice, hypoglycemia and severe dehydration due to insufficient milk intake from exclusive breastfeeding in the first days of life. As an expectant mom, I read all the guidelines on breastfeeding my first-born child. Unfortunately, following the guidelines and our pediatrician's advice resulted in my child going 4 days with absolutely no milk intake, requiring ICU care. He was subsequently diagnosed with multiple neurodevelopmental disabilities. Being a physician and scientist, I sought out peer-reviewed journals to explain why this happened. I found that there is ample evidence showing the links between neonatal jaundice, dehydration, hypoglycemia and developmental disabilities.[308]*

This heartbreaking story is unfortunately not unique. There have been many other reports of exclusively breastfed babies who developed severe low blood glucose levels between the second and fifth day of life from insufficient milk intake.[309]

Del Castillo-Hegyi reports that she knows dozens of other parents whose children have experienced long-term neurodevelopmental impairments from insufficient feeding at birth. One such parent is Molly Christine Blake, who shares her story to help prevent other babies from suffering the same fate.

My Feeding Story, by Molly Christine Blake

I wish I had known about the Fed Is Best Foundation before my 1st son was born. I felt enormous pressure to exclusively breastfeed at my hospital. My son was born at 37 weeks, weighing 5 pounds, 13 ounces and he struggled to latch-on and breastfeed at each feeding. When I told the midwife, she came back with a leaflet, which described how to hand express. She told me to express 1 mL of colostrum into a syringe and feed that to my baby whenever he struggled to latch. I asked her if 1 mL was enough and she said it was because his tummy was very small and this amount would be fine until my milk came in. Note: 1 teaspoon equals 5 ml.

I was discharged hours later not feeling confident my baby was getting enough colostrum. A midwife came out to see me at home on day 3 because I said I was worried about his feeding. By this time, he had become extremely jaundiced and lethargic, would let out random high pitch screams, slept all of the time, and never wanted to feed. He would also have random body spasms, which doctors shrugged off as normal baby reflexes (later we found out different). The midwife said I could wait and see how he did overnight or go to the hospital. I chose the hospital. When arriving, we found that he had lost 12% of his body weight and his blood sugars levels dropped dangerously low.

When my son turned 7 months old, he started having seizures and was diagnosed with infantile spasms epilepsy. The cause was confirmed to be hypoglycemia when he was a few days old, from poor feeding advice.

According to Dr. Tuteur, the driving force behind the problem of newborn hypoglycemia and dehydration causing brain injury is the policy of encouraging breastfeeding at all costs. "Breastfeeding has risks as well as benefits. Aggressive efforts to increase breastfeeding rates have led to tens of thousands of neonatal hospital readmissions for dehydration and jaundice, some of which have culminated in infant brain injuries and deaths."

Del Castillo-Hegyi is now working to spread this message to parents, hospitals, pediatricians, and government policy makers. "I advocate for mothers to be informed of the possibility that her child can become dehydrated, jaundiced and hypoglycemic from insufficient breast milk intake and that these conditions can cause developmental and neurological disability."

Her most important message: "Safely meeting an infant's full nutritional need is more important than exclusively breastfeeding."

Del Castillo-Hegyi also notes that, in her experience, it is the mothers that are most determined to breastfeed that are at highest risk. "The mothers that are most educated in breastfeeding are the ones who have been taught that offering even a single bottle will ruin her breastfeeding and potentially harm her child."

On the other side of the debate are the doctors and lactation consultants expressing concern that jumping in with formula too soon will make it more difficult to successfully breastfeed, a legitimate concern.

In some cases it may be a very close call as to whether a newborn needs to be supplemented with formula. But the studies do not support the common view that supplementing will harm the chance of success with breastfeeding. In fact, as with the studies on pacifiers, the opposite may be true.

A randomized study led by Dr. Valerie Flaherman at the University of California, San Francisco found that supplementing with formula after each breastfeeding from the first day after birth until the mother's milk supply is established did not have any negative impact on the likelihood of successful breastfeeding at three months.[310]

A follow-up study published in 2019 found that this "early, limited feeding" program had no impact on breastfeeding rates at six months, but there was a slight decline in breastfeeding in the formula-supplemented group by 12 months.[311]

According to Flaherman, "The results suggest that using early, limited formula may not have a negative impact on infants, but it may alter maternal attitudes toward breastfeeding." In other words, while giving small amounts of formula did not cause nipple confusion or any other problem with breastfeeding over the first three to six months, "it's possible that supplementation reduced commitment, by the mother or other family members, to avoid it later in infancy," she said.

This seems to be a relatively minor risk. If you are hoping to breastfeed for as long as possible, supplementing with formula before your milk supply is established does not have to harm your chances. It is a matter of your own mindset and determination.

The slight risk of giving up on breastfeeding sooner is also clearly outweighed by the potential benefits. Apart from reducing the risk of dehydration and low blood sugar causing harm to the developing brain, Flaherman's research also suggests that infants receiving supplemental formula in the first few days could be much less likely to be readmitted to hospital for conditions such as jaundice.[312]

In addition, supplementing with formula when breast milk is inadequate may also have more subtle benefits for brain development.[313] Even when low blood sugar is not severe enough to cause significant neurological impairment, there can be a negative impact on cognitive development.

Researchers have found that a baby who has very low blood glucose levels within the first 24 hours is five times more likely to have lower motor, cognitive, and language scores at 1 year of age. [314] These negative effects are still apparent many years later. Even at four years of age, the effects of low blood sugar in the first days of life are still evident, with these young children more likely to face problems with planning, memory, attention, problem-solving, and motor function.[315]

Although the vast majority of exclusively breastfed infants receive adequate nutrition and do not need to be supplemented with formula, it is helpful to be fully informed about what to watch for so you can act quickly if it becomes clear there is a problem with early milk supply.

This is particularly important if you have one of the risk factors for insufficient milk supply, namely[316]

- delivery by C-section
- hypothyroidism
- polycystic ovarian syndrome
- minimal growth of breast tissue during pregnancy
- history of infertility
- advanced maternal age
- autoimmune disease
- retained placenta

The main warning signs of insufficient milk supply are when a newborn wants to nurse constantly, cries inconsolably, or is very lethargic, limp, or jaundiced. The baby may also have a reduced number of wet diapers, but this is not a reliable measure of adequate milk intake because a baby may still produce urine even if they are not getting enough milk.

The Fed is Best Foundation also recommends the following steps to prevent and detect hypoglycemia before it becomes a serious problem:

- Manually expressing to confirm the presence of milk
- Twice daily weighing of exclusively breastfed newborns for the first few days. More than a 7 percent weight loss signals the need to supplement with formula.
- Checking blood glucose levels of newborns in the hospital and taking action if the level is below 47 milligrams per decilter (mg/dL)

- Weighing the baby before and after breastfeeding to determine how much milk is being transferred. Newborns need approximately two ounces every three hours.

- Babies who are crying inconsolably at home, especially before full milk production is established, should be supplemented with formula after nursing until their glucose level can be checked.

If you find that you do need to supplement with formula in the first few days after your baby is born, rest assured that this is not likely to undermine your chance of successfully breastfeeding.[317] In Flaherman's studies demonstrating that point, the following protocol was used: when newborns had lost more weight than usual by their second or third day, mothers were instructed to syringe-feed 10 mL of hypoallergenic formula immediately after each breastfeeding session. The mothers were advised to stop supplementing once their milk supply was established, which typically occurs by around day five.

This strategy has very little downside, but the potential benefits are immense. By ensuring that babies are getting enough milk in the first few days, we can easily prevent newborn hypoglycemia and dehydration, which pose serious threats to brain development.

The bottom line, according to the Fed is Best Foundation, is to trust your maternal instincts: "Even brand-new mothers know when something is wrong. Remember that formula feeding is not failure. Fed is best."

Points to Remember

- Some of the purported benefits of breast milk have been exaggerated, but breastfeeding does seem to have a slight edge when it comes to supporting babies' cognitive development and gastrointestinal health.

- To the extent breastfeeding reduces asthma, allergies, and eczema, this likely occurs by supporting a healthy microbiome, an effect we can mimic with prebiotics and probiotics (see chapters 14 and 17).

- Breastfeeding is not essential for protecting your baby from infection—your antibodies will be transferred through the placenta during pregnancy to provide some immunity for the first few months.

- If milk supply is significantly delayed, newborns can quickly become dehydrated and develop dangerously low blood sugar, which can cause long-term harm to the brain.

- It is therefore important to monitor for sufficient milk supply in the first few days of life, such as by weighing your baby before and after feedings.

- If your baby is not getting enough nutrition from nursing, supplementing with formula can help protect her brain development without undermining breastfeeding success.

Chapter 14

Choosing a Formula

Determining which formula is the healthiest for your newborn can be overwhelming, given the vast array of choices and confusing marketing messages. We can simplify the process by starting with the overarching principle of choosing a formula with ingredients that most closely resemble those in breast milk. This chapter will help you do just that, by building a wish list of preferred ingredients.

The second general principle to keep in mind is that no one formula is the best for every baby. It is a matter of weighing priorities to choose your baby's first formula and then seeing how they respond.

You are the expert on your own baby. If you notice that she is thriving on a particular formula, then that is the right one for her and there is no need to second-guess. On the other hand, if you select what you consider to be the best possible formula but your baby simply does not tolerate it, then you may have to compromise some of the items on your formula wish-list to find a brand that works.

Formula Ingredients to Look For

1. Whey Protein or Partially Hydrolyzed Whey Protein

The single most important factor that determines how well your baby will tolerate a specific formula is the type of protein present. Cow's milk formulas are typically a better starting point than soy or goat milk, but even among cow's milk formulas there can be differences in the specific types of proteins used.

In both human breast milk and cow's milk, the two main types of protein are casein and whey. When milk is exposed to stomach acid, the casein forms small curds, similar to cottage cheese, whereas whey protein remains suspended in liquid. As a result, whey is digested much more rapidly, while casein remains in the stomach for a longer period of time. Casein is also considered more "reactive" from an allergy perspective.

In human breast milk, whey is the dominant protein. In the first few weeks after birth it makes up 80 percent of the total protein. After several months, the percentage shifts to approximately 60 percent whey, 40 percent casein. This is quite different to cow's milk, which has more than 80 percent casein.

If the ingredients list for a particular formula states "nonfat milk protein" and there is no whey protein separately listed in the ingredients, that means it will have 80 percent casein. To balance out the ratio and more closely mimic breast milk, some formula brands now add additional whey protein or use whey as the sole protein source. These formulas are usually a better starting point for newborns.

In practical terms, having a greater percentage of whey makes formula easier to digest and less allergenic. Because whey-based formulas leave the stomach more quickly, a 100 percent whey formula can reduce spitting up and acid reflux.[318] Whey also produces softer stools, which eases stomach pain for many babies. Finally, whey-based formulas appear to be better for supporting the growth of beneficial microbes such as Bifidobacteria.[319]

For babies with either a family history of allergy or eczema, or symptoms of colic or reflux, it is helpful to go one step further and choose a formula made from "partially hydrolyzed whey," at least for the first few months. This term refers to a manufacturing process in which the proteins are partially broken down, making them easier to digest and less likely to trigger allergies. Studies have confirmed that partially hydrolyzed formulas give long-term reductions in the risk of eczema and allergies in high-risk babies.[320]

Unfortunately, it is still possible for a baby to have an allergic reaction to a partially hydrolyzed formula, but such cases are very rare. Dr. Harvey Marcovitch, of the Royal College of Pediatrics and Child Health in England, says that parents are often too quick to abandon cows' milk formulas. "Less than five percent of babies are allergic to cows' milk proteins—and there are carefully designed formulas for such cases." These formulas include extensively hydrolyzed formulas, where the proteins are almost entirely broken down, or soy formula. The general advice is that these alternative formulas should only be used as a last resort and when recommended by your pediatrician.

Another option to consider before moving to one of these last resorts is formula made from goat's milk, the proteins of which are said to be easier to digest and less allergenic than cow's milk, although the evidence for this claim is relatively weak. It is also clear that some babies who are allergic to cow's milk are also allergic to goat's milk. Nevertheless, some babies who have difficulty with standard formula tolerate goat's milk formula very well, so this is an alternative worth considering if your baby seems to have trouble with standard formulas.

2. Lactose as the Primary Carbohydrate Source

The preferred carbohydrate source to look for in baby formula is lactose, because this is the main carbohydrate found in breast milk. Although babies can also do well on other carbohydrate sources, such as corn syrup or maltodextrin, the metabolism of a typical baby is designed to use lactose, so it makes sense to stay as close to nature as possible.

The main driver behind the use of alternative sugars in baby formula is profit: corn syrup, maltodextrin, and sucrose are much cheaper to produce than lactose. These alternative sugars are also sweeter, which increases the chance that a baby will willingly take a new formula.

Some companies may also use corn syrup or other sugars in order to cater to parents' concerns over lactose intolerance. Yet very few babies have genuine difficulty with lactose.[321] Problems digesting the protein component of cow's milk formula are actually far more common. In studies of babies with colic, switching to a lactose-free formula can occasionally help, but more often it makes no difference.[322]

A better strategy for dealing with colic is to choose a partially hydrolyzed whey formula with prebiotics and to supplement with probiotics, as discussed in more detail in chapter 17. A formula containing lactose is actually more likely to help babies build a healthy microbiome, which may prevent colic.[323]

Although our starting point should be choosing a formula that contains lactose as the main carbohydrate source, there is no specific evidence that corn syrup, maltodextrin, or other sugars in formula are harmful. Corn syrup and maltodextrin are easily digestible forms of glucose, produced by breaking down cornstarch. In hydrolyzed formulas in particular, these other sugars may be needed to disguise the bitter taste from the broken-down proteins.

Corn syrup and maltodextrin may sound like poor choices for your baby's nutrition, but they are much better than sucrose, which contains a high proportion of fructose. Babies are not designed to metabolize fructose and it is likely that large amounts of this sugar would place too much burden on the liver. It is therefore best to avoid formulas that have sucrose appearing early in the list of ingredients, indicating that it is one of the main sources of carbohydrates.

If a formula meets all your other requirements but contains corn syrup or maltodextrin as the carbohydrate, this should not be a deal breaker. We would just prefer to have lactose as the main carbohydrate to more closely approximate breast milk.

3. Prebiotics

Prebiotics are indigestible carbohydrates that serve to nourish beneficial gut microbes. Breast milk actually contains hundreds of different prebiotics, in quite large amounts. Collectively, these prebiotics are known as human milk oligosaccharides or HMOs.

The oligosaccharides in breast milk seem to be tailor-made to feed only beneficial species, such as Bifidobacteria. This is thought to be the main reason why breastfed babies seem to have a healthier balance of species in their gut microbiome.

Since the late 2000s, formula manufacturers have tried to mimic this extraordinary property by adding other prebiotics that are also good at nourishing the beneficial bacteria typically found in infants. The evidence shows that this strategy is actually effective when it comes to building a healthier microbiome in formula-fed babies.

The most common prebiotic added to formula is known as GOS, which stands for galactooligosaccharides. Researchers have found that a baby receiving formula with GOS will have a similar level of beneficial Bifidobacteria and lactobacilli as a breastfed infant.[324]

Infant formula supplemented with a combination of GOS and another type of prebiotic, called fructooligosaccharides (FOS), has also been studied in numerous randomized, double-blind, placebo-controlled studies, with very promising results.

These studies have found that giving prebiotics to formula-fed infants significantly lowers the risk of respiratory infections, gastrointestinal infections, and allergic conditions such as asthma and eczema.[325] In one study, where infants were given either breast milk, prebiotic formula, or standard formula, the prebiotic formula was found to reduce the risk of food allergy in much the same way as breast milk.[326] (17 percent of children in the standard formula group had food allergies by 18 months, compared to 4 percent of breastfed infants and 5 percent of infants given the prebiotic formula.)

After reviewing all the studies in this area, the World Allergy Organization recently issued guidelines recommending prebiotic supplementation for formula-fed infants, in order to reduce the risk of developing asthma, eczema, and food allergy.[327]

Most of the successful studies of prebiotics in infant formula used a combination of GOS and FOS, a combination that can be found in Happy Baby Organic Infant Formula. Another prebiotic combination used in infant formula is GOS and polydextrose, which is found in Enfamil Reguline and has been proven to be effective in supporting important beneficial species in infants.[328]

In just the past few years, formula makers have found a way to mimic the prebiotics found in breast milk even more closely, by adding a lactose derivative known as 2'-fucosyllactose (2'-FL). This is actually the most abundant prebiotic in most mothers' breast milk. It can now be produced in the laboratory by fermentation (similar to how many vitamins are made), resulting in a prebiotic that is structurally identical to that found in breast milk.

This prebiotic is now included in several premium formula brands, where it is listed in the ingredients as 2'-FL HMO (Human Milk Oligosaccharide). At the time of writing, formulas containing this prebiotic include Gerber Good Start and Similac Pro Advance.

4. Milk Fat Globule Membrane (MFGM)

For decades, formula manufacturers have been trying to figure out exactly why breastfed babies perform better on IQ and vocabulary tests. The difference in scores is relatively minor once you control for the fact that breastfeeding mothers typically have a higher IQ and education level, but there is a difference, nevertheless, suggesting that some important ingredient for brain building is missing in formula. In just the past couple of years, a new suspect has emerged: milk fat globule membrane (MFGM).

In both human milk and cow's milk, the fat globules are surrounded by a membrane containing many different components, such as proteins, lipids, and cholesterol. Researchers have now discovered that one or more of these components must be essential to brain development.

As mentioned in the previous chapter, when babies are given formula containing MFGM, they have similar cognitive scores to breastfed babies.[329] Research also indicates that MFGM helps protect against harmful microbes and intestinal inflammation, which are likely the major causes of colic.[330] Knowing all this, MFGM should be a fairly high priority ingredient when choosing a formula for exclusively formula-fed babies. (Breastfed babies who are merely supplemented with formula will probably already be getting enough MFGM when nursing.)

At the time of writing, formulas containing MFGM include Enfamil NeuroPro varieties and Enfamil Enspire. The main difference between these two formulas is that Enspire has the added benefit of containing lactoferrin, one of the whey proteins found in breast milk. A whey-based cow's milk formula already contains some lactoferrin, but adding more, so as to get closer to the amount found in breast milk, may slightly reduce the number of gastrointestinal infections, although this benefit is modest.[331]

What about DHA and Other Fats?

For many parents, one of the common sticking points in choosing a formula is concern over so-called "hexane extraction" of docosahexaenoic acid (DHA), an omega-3 fatty acid commonly added to formula because it is thought to be important to brain and eye development. DHA is often added alongside arachidonic acid (ARA), an omega-6 fatty acid.

DHA is typically extracted from algae and fish oil using hexane as the solvent—which raises a red flag for many because hexane is quite toxic. However, the hexane is removed long before the DHA is added to baby formula,[332] so this concern is probably unfounded.

On the other hand, manufacturer claims over the benefits of DHA are also probably exaggerated. It is true that DHA is essential to neurological development and one of the two most prominent fatty acids in the brain. Babies definitely need DHA. But they build up a store of it during the third trimester of pregnancy and can also convert other oils found in formula into DHA.

Preterm babies may be the exception here, because they can miss out on DHA in both ways: they have less opportunity to build up DHA during the end of pregnancy and are less able to convert other fats into DHA. In these situations, your pediatrician may recommend giving a formula that contains DHA. But for other babies, whether or not a formula contains this fatty acid probably makes little difference either way.

If you would like to give your baby a source of DHA but remain troubled by hexane extraction, you have two potential options. One is to use Baby's Only Formula with DHA, which contains DHA from egg yolk that is extracted without hexane. Another option is to add a stand-alone DHA supplement from fish oil, such as Nordic Naturals Infant DHA.

When it comes to the other fats present in formula, the differences between brands are not particularly important. Most formulas will include a combination of safflower, palm, soy, or coconut oil, to replicate the range of fats present in breast milk.

All of these oils are good fat sources for babies and the precise combination of oils probably does not matter much. There is some concern that palm oil can cause constipation for some babies, because it forms soap-like compounds with calcium. If you run into this problem, you may want to consider a formula without palm oil. For other babies, the type of oil present should not be a major consideration in choosing a formula. Instead, it is more important to look for some or all of the preferred ingredients discussed above:

1. Whey protein or partially hydrolyzed whey

2. Lactose as the primary carbohydrate

3. Prebiotics such as GOS or 2'-FL

4. Milk fat globule membrane (MFGM)

Optional Extras and Personal Preferences

One pitfall of finding a formula with the preferred ingredients is that you may not have the option of buying organic. Many parents feel that organic formula is a high priority, based on concerns that nonorganic varieties may contain traces of pesticides or antibiotics.

The problem is that insisting on organic typically means giving up ingredients that have been found to be incredibly beneficial for growing babies, such as MFGM. It is also difficult to find an organic formula that is based on hydrolyzed whey and contains prebiotics (see brainhealthfrombirth.com/formula for some options).

The decision of organic versus nonorganic is ultimately a matter of personal preference and weighing priorities, but my personal view is that it is more important to focus on giving your baby the beneficial nutrients they need to thrive rather than choosing an organic formula.

Part of the reason for this is that even if pesticides are present in conventional milk, that does not necessarily mean they will find their way into infant formula made from that milk, given the degree of processing that occurs. If a formula manufacturer takes only highly purified whey protein and lactose from milk, many of the pesticides and other contaminants will be left behind.

In one study of more than 300 samples of conventional milk and infant formulas, pesticide residues were found in the milk but not in the formulas.[333] Other researchers have either reported the same finding or found extremely low levels of pesticides in only a small minority of formulas.[334]

Overall, it seems that the risk of exposure to pesticides from standard formula is very low and on a par with breast milk, given that mothers consume pesticides through food and pass it on to their baby via breastfeeding. One study found that the level of pesticide residues was actually *higher* in human breast milk than in formula.[335]

All of this suggests that it is not critical for infant formula to be organic and that we should instead prioritize the beneficial ingredients that are not typically found in organic formulas.

Separate from concerns over pesticide contamination in nonorganic formulas, there is also a growing trend among American parents of ordering organic baby formulas directly from Europe, based on several online articles that describe these formulas as "cleaner" because they do not contain synthetic nutrients.

It is true that the label of an American baby formula will typically show a long list of chemical names, whereas an organic European formula is more likely to have a shorter list of recognizable ingredients. When shopping for food, health-conscious consumers have been trained to look for short ingredients lists and to avoid chemical additives, so this approach naturally leads parents to assume that the European formulas are superior. But baby formula is different.

The chemical-sounding ingredients in American formulas are typically just the full names for important vitamins, added to make up for deficits in cow's milk and to more closely match the nutrient profile of breast milk. Some of these nutrients are present in both American and European formulas—they just go by different names. For example, a

European formula may list "vitamin B6," whereas an American formula will list "pyridoxine hydrochloride." The two are exactly the same thing. We should not be fooled into believing the American formula is somehow harmful because it lists unfamiliar ingredients.

On the contrary, American formulas are in some ways even better because they often contain additional helpful nutrients, such as taurine. Alarmist bloggers advise parents to choose European formulas precisely to avoid these added nutrients, because they are produced "synthetically." But there is no evidence that the method of production poses any harm. There is, however, clear evidence that many optional extra nutrients added to formulas in the United States are highly beneficial.

For instance, taurine—one of the most abundant amino acids found in breast milk—is also found in high concentrations in the brain and is likely quite important for brain development.[336] Humans can produce taurine from other amino acids, but preterm babies and some newborns may not be able to do so efficiently, so a formula that contains added taurine can be beneficial in the early stages.[337]

Advice to choose European formulas without taurine in order to stay closer to nature is misplaced. We stay closer to human breast milk by choosing a formula that contains the same nutrients, regardless of how they were produced. This comes back to the overarching point that it is likely more important to choose a formula with high-priority ingredients, such as prebiotics and MFGM, rather than an organic formula.

Yet there are circumstances where other factors may be even more important than prebiotics or MFGM. For a newborn with a family history of allergy or eczema, symptoms of colic or reflux, or other problems digesting their existing formula, choosing a partially hydrolyzed whey formula should be the highest priority.

At the time of writing, Enfamil NeuroPro Gentlease is the only partially hydrolyzed formula that also contains MFGM. Yet it has some potential downsides. Rather than being entirely whey-based, it contains some casein, which is more likely to trigger allergies and can also delay stomach emptying in babies with reflux. It also contains corn syrup rather than lactose and lacks prebiotics.

Gerber Good Start Gentle may be a better choice for allergy-prone or colicky babies because it has lactose as the primary carbohydrate and is 100 percent whey-based. It also contains the preferred prebiotic 2'-FL, which can further reduce the chance of allergies. Yet Gerber does not contain MFGM, so it is a matter of choosing where you are willing to compromise based on your own priorities and your baby's unique circumstances. For a detailed comparison of currently available formulas and specific brand recommendations, see brainhealthfrombirth.com/formula.

Points to Remember

- To more closely replicate breast milk, look for a formula that contains

    1. Whey protein or partially hydrolyzed whey

    2. Lactose as the primary carbohydrate

    3. Prebiotics such as GOS or 2'-FL

    4. Milk fat globule membrane (MFGM)

- DHA is a lower-priority ingredient but may be beneficial for brain and eye development. Hexane extraction of DHA is not a great concern.

- Choosing a formula with the nutrients your baby needs is likely more important that buying organic, since infant formula has been found to have little or no pesticide residues.

- For babies with allergies, colic, or reflux, a partially hydrolyzed, 100 percent whey-based formula is usually the highest priority.

Chapter 15

Pain & Fever Relief for Babies

Acetaminophen, also known as paracetamol, Tylenol, or Panadol, is generally regarded as one of the safest medications to treat pain and fever. But emerging science suggests that it could leave a lasting impact on a baby's developing brain.

There are two time points at which the potential harm could happen. The first is during pregnancy, when the mother takes acetaminophen to treat chronic pain or fever. The second is during infancy, when the medication is given directly to babies to treat pain and fevers.

On the first point, chapter 7 explained that acetaminophen use during pregnancy might increase the risk of autism, ADHD, and language delay. Yet the increase in risk is quite small and seems to only occur when the medication is taken for weeks at a time; occasional use during pregnancy appears to be safe.

This chapter focuses on the second time point, exploring whether it is safe to give acetaminophen directly to newborn babies.

One would think the safety of acetaminophen had already been thoroughly tested, since Tylenol is available over the counter and routinely given to infants to treat pain and fever. This practice often starts in the very first week of life, when many hospitals give baby boys acetaminophen before and after circumcision. But, perhaps somewhat surprisingly, the long-term safety of giving this medicine to babies has never been tested.

In the 1980s, there was a sudden switch from aspirin to acetaminophen as the pain and fever medicine of choice for young children, without any thorough safety assessment. This switch was prompted by concerns that aspirin could be contributing to Reye's syndrome, an extremely rare but potentially fatal condition that can occur after infections. (The link between aspirin and Reye's syndrome has since been seriously questioned.[338])

The practical result of the backlash against aspirin was a sudden rise in the use of acetaminophen beginning in the mid-1980s. Acetaminophen became even more widely used in very young infants through the 1990s, as awareness grew that newborns actually do experience significant pain from procedures such as circumcision.[339]

The timing of the switch from aspirin to acetaminophen and the gradual increase in acetaminophen use over the following decade is troubling, since it parallels the dramatic rise in the number of children diagnosed with autism. Naturally, this overlap in timing raises the question of whether acetaminophen could be a contributing factor to the autism epidemic.

Dr. Stephen Schultz published one of the earliest papers flagging this question in 2008. As a parent of a child with autism, Schultz suspected that some factor associated with vaccines could be causing autism in some cases. Compelled to investigate the issue, he retired from his career as a dentist and enrolled in graduate school.

In the course of his research, Schultz's focus eventually shifted from vaccines themselves to acetaminophen, which is often given immediately after vaccines to treat the resulting pain and fever. In a small study based on parent surveys, Schultz reported a higher prevalence of autism in children who received acetaminophen at 12 to 18 months than those who did not.[340] The 2008 study was not designed to definitively prove a link between acetaminophen and autism, but it was among the first to raise the possibility that a link exists.

Now, more than a decade later, research on this issue is only just beginning. We still have little direct evidence from controlled human studies, just a collection of lower-quality data that together paints a troubling picture.

Animal studies, for example, have shown direct toxicity to the brain.[341] One such study found that giving acetaminophen to 10-day-old mice caused permanent changes to behavior and cognitive function.[342] Dr. William Parker, a researcher at Duke University who is concerned about a potential link between acetaminophen and autism, told me in an interview that if those animal studies had been available earlier, acetaminophen would never have been approved as an over-the-counter medication. "It has effectively slipped through the cracks of our regulatory regime."[343]

Another small study based on parental surveys also reported a substantially higher risk of autism in children who had received more than 64 doses of acetaminophen by their second birthday.[344] In comparison, children who had not received any acetaminophen in their first two years had a much lower than average risk.

As another data point, some researchers have suggested that part of the reason why boys are more likely to develop autism is that they are routinely given acetaminophen as newborns to relieve pain from circumcision. In a Danish study of more than 300,000 boys, researchers found that the overall risk of autism was 46 percent higher in boys who were circumcised.[345] Yet this study did not investigate the reason for the link, with lead author Dr. Morten Frisch commenting that "All we can say at this point is that there is a statistical association between circumcision and autism."

Frisch's study has been criticized based on some inconsistencies in the data,[346] but it fits with an earlier study finding a correlation between the rates of autism in various different populations and the rate of circumcision.[347] For every 10 percent increase in the proportion of boys who are circumcised in a particular country, researchers found an additional two in 1,000 boys with autism.

Importantly, the correlation was only seen for boys born after 1995, when doctors started routinely giving acetaminophen after circumcisions. Before then, circumcision rates seemed to have little relationship to autism rates. This pattern suggests that, if there actually is a link between circumcision and autism (which remains uncertain), a plausible explanation is that circumcised boys are given multiple doses of acetaminophen during their first few days of life, when their brain is most vulnerable.

Another interesting observation supporting the acetaminophen-autism link comes from temporary dips in acetaminophen use in 1982 and 1986, as a result of product tampering. Researchers noted that when acetaminophen use briefly dropped, so did the rate of autism.[348]

Even when we piece all of these data points together, there is still not enough evidence to know for sure whether giving this medication to newborns really does contribute to autism. We urgently need large controlled studies, where infants are randomized to receive acetaminophen or not, and are followed for several years to track rates of autism, ADHD, and other measures of brain development.

Unfortunately, no one wants to fund studies on the possible link between acetaminophen and autism. Parker comments that "We cannot find anyone at the Federal level interested in funding that research....I think this could be the biggest medical mistake in modern history. And no one wants to look at it."[349]

Parker suspects that the impact of acetaminophen on brain development may actually be much worse when the medication is given to newborns as compared to use during pregnancy. As he explains:

The use of acetaminophen in babies and young children may be much more strongly associated with autism than its use during pregnancy, perhaps because of well-known deficiencies in the metabolic breakdown of pharmaceuticals during early development. ... This view mandates extreme urgency in probing the long-term effects of acetaminophen use in babies and the possibility that many cases of infantile autism may actually be induced by acetaminophen exposure shortly after birth. [350]

Parker also comments that:

Although more research must be conducted to prove a definitive link, the evidence already gathered justifies careful consideration before administering acetaminophen to infants and to children younger than about 6 years of age.[351]

There is unfortunately no easy alternative to using acetaminophen in young children, because other medications have their own potential risks. Ibuprofen, the active ingredient in Advil, Motrin, and Nurofen, is the main alternative, but it can potentially damage the gastrointestinal tract, with prolonged use causing bleeding and ulcers.[352]

Doctors and parents are therefore left with no choice but to balance the potential benefits and risks of using acetaminophen or ibuprofen on a case-by-case basis. At the moment, this risk/benefit analysis probably leans in favor of ibuprofen for occasional use in the first months of life, because acetaminophen is more likely to impact the developing brain. But the fact is that we have very little solid data to guide the decision.

This gaping hole in our knowledge is at least becoming more widely recognized, which will hopefully lead to more answers soon. A recent review called for long-term studies following brain development of newborns given acetaminophen, "in view of concerns raised regarding neurodevelopmental outcomes following prenatal and postnatal exposure."[353] The review concluded that this medication cannot be recommended for newborns until more research is done.

Based on what is currently known, the best solution is probably to give babies either acetaminophen or ibuprofen only when absolutely necessary, especially during the first six months. To that end, it is useful to keep in mind two important points:

First, acetaminophen is not actually that effective for pain relief in babies.[354] This means that if you are giving Tylenol only to relieve pain, the benefit may not outweigh the potential risks.

In a double-blind study of newborns randomized to receive acetaminophen or a placebo for two hours before and 24 hours after circumcision, babies in both groups showed signs of pain during circumcision, with no difference between the groups.[355] Acetaminophen only became somewhat helpful at about six hours after the procedure, when local numbing medications probably wore off. Other studies have reported similarly disappointing pain relief from acetaminophen in babies, with a review concluding that "trials of oral acetaminophen … to reduce circumcision pain did not prove effective."[356]

Given these results, it may be better to give your baby ibuprofen starting six hours after circumcision, with your pediatrician's approval. It is important to note, however, that this medication should not be given *before* the procedure because it can increase bleeding.

The second point to keep in mind is that although acetaminophen may be moderately effective when it comes to bringing down a fever, fever actually serves an important purpose and, as such, does not always need to be treated with medication.

The American Academy of Pediatrics (AAP) has long cautioned against administering fever-reducing medicine for low-grade fevers, noting, "there is no evidence that fever itself worsens the course of an illness or that it causes long-term neurologic complications."[357]

Fever is a valuable mechanism that plays a role in fighting infection.

Allowing a child to run a mild fever may help that child fight off the infection more quickly. As a result, the AAP emphasizes that "the primary goal should be to help the child feel more comfortable, rather than to maintain a 'normal' temperature ... Parents should focus on the general well-being of the child, his/her activity, observing the child for signs of serious illness and maintaining appropriate fluid intake."[358]

In babies less than three months old, fevers are taken quite seriously, but only because they can signal the possibility of a serious infection. Dr. Justin Smith, a pediatrician at Cook Children's Hospital in Texas, advises that parents should call their doctor for any temperature over 100 degrees in a baby younger than three months. That is because lab tests may be needed to investigate the cause, not because the fever itself is dangerous.

Smith also notes that although febrile seizures can sometimes occur from very rapidly rising fevers, it is a myth that higher temperatures can leave lasting effects on the brain. "Temperatures that the body is generating on their own as a response to illness will not cause brain damage or any of the other things that your grandmother/ neighbor/best friend said they would."[359]

It is also important to keep in mind that medication is not the only way to soothe a child with a fever. You can often reduce body temperature with a cool wet cloth or giving a shallow bath slightly below body temperature. The bath water should not be too cold, however, because this can cause shivering, which can worsen the fever. (Take your child out of the bath if they start to shiver.)

If these measures are not enough and fever is making your child so uncomfortable that they are not drinking water or sleeping, it may be worth using either acetaminophen or ibuprofen. Since there is no clear data on which medication is safer long term, for my own children I typically alternate between the two, with the hope that this reduces the overall risk of side effects.

I also choose to believe that by taking so many other steps to reduce the burden of other toxins on my children's bodies, there will be more leeway for medications such as acetaminophen. In other words, by my focusing on the factors more within my control, such as limiting exposure to pesticides and phthalates, and ensuring adequate nutrients, my children will hopefully have more capacity to detoxify necessary medications, without suffering any harm.

This may be wishful thinking on my part, but it is supported by the views of several experts.[360] When caring for a sick child in the middle of the night, and giving medication with uncertain risks, it always helps for parents to remember that they are doing the best they can based on the information currently available.

Points to Remember

- Preliminary research has raised the possibility of a connection between acetaminophen use in babies and an increased risk of autism.

- This link could explain observations of higher rates of autism in circumcised boys, due to acetaminophen use for pain relief in the first days of life, although great uncertainty remains.

- Until large randomized and controlled trials are done, we should use acetaminophen only when truly needed.

- Acetaminophen is not particularly effective for pain relief for babies, including pain from circumcision.

- Ibuprofen is likely more effective but can potentially harm the gastrointestinal system when used often.

- It is not always necessary to treat a fever with medication; fever serves an important role in fighting infection and can help your child recover more quickly.

- The main reason to medicate a fever is to allow your child to feel well enough to stay hydrated.

Chapter 16

Infant Vaccines

Ever since I was a young child, when my father led immunization campaigns for the government in Australia, I have marveled at the apparent magic of vaccines. Even now, having studied advanced-level immunology and learned in detail about exactly how vaccines generate a lasting immune response, I am still in awe of the fact that it is possible for one little shot to protect us from life-threatening illness for many years to come.

Yet my general pro-vaccine stance does not mean that I have unshakeable faith in every element of the current vaccine schedule. My own children are fully vaccinated, but I chose to spread the recommended vaccines over additional doctor's visits, so they were not receiving quite as many at one time. This decision was not based on any specific evidence of harm, but rather a glimmer of uncertainty and my own instinct that it is better to err on the side of caution.

To me, beginning to question the safety of the current vaccine schedule felt like crossing over to the dark side—turning my back on evidence-based medicine and accepting anecdotes in place of hard science. But I know there is a reasonable and scientifically minded middle ground, where we can get the protective benefits of vaccines while still taking steps to protect our children from the remote possibility that giving too many too soon is putting their developing brains at risk.

Casting doubt on the safety of the overall U.S. vaccine schedule also seems more reasonable once you become aware of just how much the schedule has expanded in recent years, how much it differs from the recommendations in other countries, and how little research has been done on the aggregate effect of so many vaccines.

The Potential Problems with Current Vaccine Schedules

In the 1980s, a young child would receive only three vaccines: DTP, polio, and MMR. Today, a child receives those as well as vaccines against another seven diseases, typically with three doses for each additional vaccine, along with annual flu vaccines.

All told, this represents a fivefold increase in the total number of inoculations we give to children over the course of their infancy and childhood. In some respects, this is a positive development because it means our children are better protected from a range of serious diseases, but we do have to question the cumulative effect of so many vaccines.

The dramatic expansion in the number of immunizations given to young children also happens to have occurred over roughly the same time period that autism rates have increased, raising concerns for many parents. Yet there is no clear evidence of a causal link; many other factors have also come into play over the same time frame, such as an increased use of acetaminophen and certain pesticides. The combination of these other factors is a more likely culprit than vaccines.

Those who believe that the increased number of vaccines is to blame for the autism epidemic often pointed to the cumulative amount of mercury, which used to be present in many vaccines in the form of the preservative thimerosal. According to CDC estimates, the safe limit of exposure to mercury is 0.3 micrograms per kilogram per day. The amount given to young children in the early 2000s was much greater: at that time, a two-month-old following the vaccine schedule might have received 12 micrograms per kilogram, or 40 times the CDC's safety limit.

It was never proven that mercury contributed to autism, but vaccine manufacturers nevertheless largely phased out thimerosal in the mid-2000s. Since then, the cumulative amount of mercury in vaccines has been negligible, while autism rates have continued to increase, further eroding the potential of a link between mercury and autism.

More recently, suspicions have turned to another ingredient that is still used in many vaccines: aluminum. This metal is added to encourage the immune system to respond more aggressively. This extra boost was not needed in the vaccines developed many decades ago, which typically used a weakened strain of a live virus or a solution of heat-killed bacteria. The immune system readily recognizes such ingredients as foreign invaders and launches a vigorous immune response.

It is a different story for more recently developed immunizations. In the 1980s, scientists figured out how to produce highly purified vaccines with only a small component of an organism, such as a single toxin or a few surface proteins. In the 1990s, the pertussis vaccine switched over to this newer form. Instead of including a whole bacterial cell, the new formula contained only a small number of molecules from the bacteria, with the hope that this would be sufficient to trick the immune system into acting.

The problem is, tricking the immune system in this way requires a little help in the form of an adjuvant, a substance used to increase the immune response. Typically, the adjuvant is aluminum, which causes a burst of inflammation so as to put our immune cells on high alert.[361] Many second-generation vaccines include a small amount of aluminum adjuvant to ensure that the vaccine stimulates enough of an immune response to provide long-term protection.

In recent years, the number of vaccines containing aluminum

has increased exponentially, without thorough investigation into the cumulative effect. In the U.S. vaccine schedule as it existed in 2002, the only vaccines that included aluminum were Diphtheria-Pertussis-Tetanus and Hepatitis B. Now, the schedule contains five aluminum-containing vaccines, which are given multiple times during the first two years of life, namely:

- Hepatitis B
- Diphtheria, Tetanus, acellular Pertussis (DTaP)
- Haemophilus influenza B (HiB)
- Hepatitis A
- Pneumococcal

Some have argued that this surge in aluminum exposure is putting children at greater risk of developing autism.[362] Proponents of this theory claim there are two troubling patterns in population-based data:

1. Autism prevalence in the United States has increased over exactly the same time frame as aluminum-containing vaccines have become more common.

2. Children from countries with the highest exposure to aluminum from vaccines (such as the United States and United Kingdom) also have the highest autism rates.[363]

The World Health Organization has specifically criticized two studies reporting these patterns, describing the reports as seriously flawed because of incorrect assumptions and questions over the accuracy of the underlying data.[364]

Yet even if we overlook these concerns and accept for the sake of argument that there is a correlation between aluminum exposure from vaccines and autism rates in the overall population, that still does not establish that aluminum causes autism—it simply raises suspicions. The next question is whether there is a biological explanation for the link.

To answer that, it is helpful to understand some background on aluminum. For decades, we have known that this metal is harmful to the brain if the exposure level is high enough.[365] Although this was first witnessed in animal experiments as early as 1877, the effect of excessive aluminum on the brain became more apparent in the 1970s, with the phenomena of "dialysis dementia."

This condition occurred when patients on long-term dialysis treatment for kidney disease accumulated extremely high levels of aluminum in the brain, as a result of aluminum present in intravenous (IV) fluids. The symptoms began with slurred speech and memory problems and often progressed to movement problems, seizures, and ultimately death.[366]

This problem is now uncommon because aluminum is removed from water used for dialysis, but a similar condition can also occur in patients with kidney problems who take aluminum-containing drugs long term.[367] The fact that aluminum is toxic to the brain in large doses is therefore beyond controversy. The question is whether the small amount found in vaccines poses any significant risk. That is an issue on which the pro- and antivaccine camps part ways. And it is ultimately an issue on which we have very little reliable research.

Animal studies purportedly showing harm from the amount of aluminum in vaccines have been thoroughly criticized and, in some cases retracted, with accusations of scientific fraud.[368] Human studies reporting a supposed link between aluminum adjuvants and autoimmune disease have also been seriously questioned, with a group of researchers from Australia's premiere research institutions reviewing 80 publications on this issue and concluding "there is currently a lack of reproducible evidence for any consistent relationship between [vaccine] adjuvant and autoimmune conditions."[369]

Within this sea of controversy, there are some things scientists can generally agree on. One is the fact that aluminum adjuvants trigger inflammation—that is precisely why they are added to vaccines.[370] Another point of agreement is that several of the known risk factors for autism also involve inflammation (such as a mother's serious infection or autoimmunity during pregnancy).[371] Finally, we know that in large amounts, injected aluminum does harm the brain. The unresolved question is how these facts intersect: whether the small amount of aluminum in vaccines, and the resulting inflammation, is significant enough to affect the brain.

Answering this question in laboratory animals is hard. Figuring out the answer in newborn babies is harder still. Those in the pro-vaccine camp point out that aluminum is everywhere, and babies are likely to get more aluminum from breast milk or formula than vaccines. As stated by the Children's Hospital of Philadelphia:

> While infants receive about 4.4 milligrams of aluminum in the first six months of life from vaccines, they receive more than that in their diet. Breast-fed infants ingest about 7 milligrams, formula-fed infants ingest about 38 milligrams, and infants who are fed soy formula ingest almost 117 milligrams of aluminum during the first six months of life.[372]

But that is not a fair comparison, because most ingested aluminum is never absorbed: it passes right through the digestive system and is excreted in stool. This is an entirely different scenario to vaccines, where all of the aluminum is injected directly into the body. When injected, aluminum eventually finds its way into the bloodstream and other areas, including the brain.[373]

For this reason, the FDA places strict limits on the amount of aluminum in intravenous fluids. U.S. federal regulations also require the following labeling, to caution about the potential toxic effects on the nervous system:

> WARNING: *This product contains aluminum that may be toxic. Aluminum may reach toxic levels with prolonged parenteral administration if kidney function is impaired. Premature neonates [babies] are particularly at risk because their kidneys are immature, and they require large amounts of calcium and phosphate solutions, which contain aluminum.*
>
> *Research indicates that patients with impaired kidney function, including premature neonates, who receive parenteral levels of aluminum at greater than 4 to 5 micrograms per kilogram per day accumulate aluminum at levels associated with central nervous system and bone toxicity.* [374]

In other words, the regulation requires a specific warning that giving aluminum to premature babies can be toxic to the brain. The regulation was prompted by research published in 1997, which showed that the amount of aluminum present in standard intravenous feeding solution for premature infants compromised brain development and contributed to developmental delay.[375]

Newborns are particularly sensitive to aluminum not only because they are in a delicate stage of development, but also because they have immature kidneys and are therefore not capable of excreting aluminum efficiently.[376]

This is a key concern because for almost all babies, aluminum exposure from vaccines begins the day they are born. According to the standard vaccine schedule in many countries, infants are given the hepatitis B vaccine within 24 hours of birth. This is intended to prevent infection from a mother with hepatitis B, but it involves injecting babies with a significant amount of aluminum, at a time when they are at their most vulnerable. The current hepatitis B vaccine contains 250 milligrams of aluminum. For a four-kilogram newborn, this exceeds the limit that the FDA sets for intravenous fluids by about 15 times.

If we do not know beyond all possible doubt that this is harmless for an infant's developing brain, there should be a very good justification for giving the vaccine to newborns. As will be discussed further below, if tests confirm that a mother does not have hepatitis B, the benefit of giving the shot immediately after birth is questionable and delaying by even a couple of weeks could be a better option.

The hepatitis B vaccine is not the only issue, however. A baby will actually get vastly more aluminum from the vaccines given at two, four, and six months of age. At each of these doctor's visits, a baby typically receives five vaccines:

- Diphtheria, Tetanus, acellular Pertussis (DTaP)
- Haemophilus influenza B (Hib)
- Pneumococcal conjugate (PCV)
- Rotavirus
- Polio

Of these, the first three contain substantial amounts of aluminum. Depending on the brands chosen, giving these vaccines according to the CDC schedule could result in a combined dose of around 1,000 micrograms of aluminum at a time. The best evidence we have so far indicates that this amount is safe for a two-month old baby, but not everyone is convinced.[377]

Until we know more, a conservative approach is to make smart choices when it comes to the timing and brands of vaccines, to minimize the theoretical risk of aluminum, while still protecting our children from serious illness.

In the United States, one such strategy is to give Pentacel and Prevnar at 2, 4, and 6 months, rather than Pediarix and Prevnar. Doing so will protect against whooping cough, Hib, polio, and pneumococcal on the same timeline as the recommended schedule, but with less than 500 mg of aluminum per visit. In contrast, the combination of Pediarix and Prevnar protects against a similar set of diseases (swapping hepatitis B for Hib), but contains almost 1000 mg of aluminum.

You can further minimize the total dose of aluminum at any one time if you are willing to spread vaccines over additional doctor's visits. You may, for example, choose to separate the whooping cough and pneumococcal vaccines, so that Pentacel is given at 2, 4, and 6 months, while Prevnar is given at 3, 5, and 7 months. (Other non-aluminum containing vaccines such as rotavirus and influenza could also be given at the same time as Pentacel).

The main downside to this approach is the added burden of additional appointments and the fact that it is easy to fall behind. It also potentially leaves your child vulnerable to pneumococcal infection for slightly longer. I personally chose to spread out vaccines in this way, but it is by no means necessary and many pediatricians understandably advise against it.

Aluminum Content in Selected Infant Vaccines

Vaccine	Brand Name	Aluminum per dosage (micrograms)
DTaP	Daptacel	330
DTaP	Infanrix	625
DTaP, HepB, polio	Pediarix	850
DTaP, Hib, polio	Pentacel	330
Hib	ActHIB	0
Hib	PedvaxHIB	225
Pneumoccocal	Prevnar, Prevnar-13	125

Timing the Hepatitis B Vaccine

According to the CDC schedule, infants should receive the hepatitis B vaccine at birth and then again at one month and six months. If you test negative for hepatitis B and decide not to give your baby this vaccine while in the hospital, how long you should wait depends on your personal circumstances and perspective.

Hepatitis B is a virus that can occasionally cause long-term liver damage, particularly when young babies contract it. Preventing this infection is no doubt worthwhile, but because hepatitis B is transmitted only by blood, the chances of a child coming into contact with it are slim.

The vaccine was originally reserved for high-risk cases, such as mothers from countries where the virus is common or with a history of injection drug use. However, in 1991, the American vaccine schedule was changed to recommend the hepatitis B vaccine for all newborns, because hospitals were not catching enough of the high-risk cases.

This is no longer a great concern, as obstetricians now routinely test pregnant women for hepatitis B. If your results are negative, the possibility of your baby catching the virus in the first few months of life is remote. He would probably have to come into contact with a surface contaminated with blood from an infected person. This is possible, such as on a playground where another child scraped their knee, but it is very unlikely for the youngest babies.

As a result, some pediatricians now advise against giving the vaccine to newborns. Others maintain that an infant should receive the vaccine before leaving the hospital, because there is still a risk that the mother's lab results are inaccurate. Because of these complexities, the right answer may ultimately differ between families, depending on the risk of the mother or another family member having an infection that was missed during lab testing, and depending on the age at which the baby will start interacting with the world and attending daycare.

In the United States and most other countries, you will be required to bring your baby up to date with hepatitis B vaccines before he or she attends day care. If your baby will start attending day care at two months old, for example, it may make sense to give the vaccine at the two-week check-up and again at six weeks.

The Hepatitis A Vaccine

Hepatitis A is another aluminum-containing vaccine, protecting against a virus that is relatively rare in the developed world. In countries where the virus is more common, it can be easily spread by contaminated food or water. In the United States there are only occasional small outbreaks, typically involving inadequate hand washing by an infected restaurant worker or food packager.

In teens and adults, the virus can cause fatigue, stomach pain, and nausea for several months, but children will typically have no symptoms at all, or just a mild fever and nausea. Given the mildness of the illness in children, and the fact that the virus is uncommon in developed countries, this vaccine is not included in the infant vaccine schedule in the United Kingdom, Australia, or Canada. Instead, it is given only before travel to countries where the virus is more common.

In the United States, however, the hepatitis A vaccine is included on the official schedule and is required for childcare or school attendance in many states. Given that this vaccine is a relatively low priority and contains a significant amount of aluminum, some critics of the CDC schedule advise delaying the Hepatitis A vaccine until a child is much older—or skipping it entirely, as they do in other countries. On the other hand, there is less reason to alter the schedule for this vaccine, since it is normally given as two doses between a child's first and second birthday, a time when few other aluminum-containing vaccines are given.

The MMR Controversy

Aluminum is the main focus of the current debate on brain health and vaccines, but the other long-standing area of controversy is the MMR vaccine. This combination vaccine, which protects against measles, mumps, and rubella, is typically given when children are 12 to 18 months old.

Suspicions about its role in autism first arose from parents who reported that their child was developing normally and then suddenly regressed into autism shortly after receiving the vaccine. Many parents claimed this occurred alongside a consistent set of other symptoms following the vaccine, such as a high fever and severe diarrhea.

The possibility of a link between MMR and autism has now been studied for many years, with massive population-based studies concluding that this vaccine does not raise the risk of autism.[378] As just one example, in 2019, a study that followed more than 600,000 children in Denmark for many years reported no increased rate of autism associated with the MMR vaccine.[379]

Another large study noted that parents with an older child with autism were more likely to leave their younger children unvaccinated, but that skipping the MMR vaccine did not reduce the odds of autism for the younger siblings.[380]

Even so, some vaccine critics argue that these large historical studies are not sufficient—the only way to know that any given vaccine is safe is with a head-to-head clinical trial where children are randomized to receive the vaccine or not. In the absence of this kind of clinical trial, the controversy rages on.

This controversy will likely continue simply because so many parents report that their child developed regressive autism shortly after receiving the MMR vaccine. Up to half of all parents of children with autism suspect vaccines as an underlying cause of their child's condition.[381]

Another factor that has stoked the fire of the MMR controversy is the recent debate on whether the CDC hid data showing a higher rate of autism in some children who received the MMR vaccine. This issue first came to light in 2014, when William Thompson, a senior scientist from the CDC, became a whistleblower. He contacted Dr. Brian Hooker, an outside researcher, and encouraged him to submit a freedom of information request to the CDC to obtain their raw data on MMR and autism. Hooker then published a study claiming that the CDC data shows a higher rate of autism associated with early vaccination with MMR.[382]

Specifically, the paper alleged that African American boys who received the vaccine on schedule had a higher rate of autism compared to those who received the vaccine when they were older. Whether the newly revealed data truly shows that trend is far from settled. Hooker's publication was quickly retracted because of "concerns about the validity of the methods and statistical analysis." The paper is also at odds with the CDC's own interpretation of the data, along with prior studies finding no link between age of vaccination and the likelihood of a child developing autism.[383]

Another area of controversy centers on whether there is a small subset of children who are uniquely vulnerable to developing autism after MMR, perhaps because of an underlying medical condition or the cumulative effect of many different risk factors. The argument is that such a rare effect may be missed in general population-based studies.

Dr. Richard Halvorsen, a pediatrician who is generally pro-vaccine and runs a vaccination clinic in London, takes the view that when we consider all the evidence, including reports from parents, "The MMR vaccine can almost certainly cause or trigger autism in a small number of susceptible children."

If that is true, the number does seem to be incredibly small. One way to gauge this is by looking at the number of claims for monetary compensation by parents who believe their child was harmed by the vaccine.

In the 1980s, a special legal process was set up to take liability away from vaccine manufacturers and make the U.S. government responsible for compensating for serious health effects from vaccines. Between 2006 and 2017, a total of 246 claims were filed alleging harm from the MMR vaccine. Many of those claims were dismissed, but 120 were compensated.[384] That may sound like a high number, and the fact that even one child could have been harmed by a vaccine is distressing, but over the same time period, more than 100 million doses of the vaccine were given.[385] This suggests that adverse reactions are in fact very rare.

In some of the cases where the vaccine court did grant compensation to children who developed autism, the argument was made that the child was uniquely vulnerable to harm from the vaccine because of an underlying condition.

One such case involved Hannah Poling, the daughter of neurologist Dr. Jon Poling. Hannah was described as a happy and precocious child for her first 18 months. Then, after falling behind on her vaccines due to recurrent ear infections, she received five vaccines against nine diseases in one doctor's visit. Soon after, she developed high fevers, stopped eating, and started showing signs of autism.

Hannah's family filed a claim for compensation, alleging that she developed autism as a result of the vaccines. In 2008, the U.S. government settled the case, awarding compensation expected to reach $20 million over the course of Hannah's lifetime. In awarding these damages, the vaccine court noted that she suffered brain injury from vaccines (which manifested as autism), but this was due to an underlying predisposition.[386]

If some children really are uniquely vulnerable to harm from vaccines such as MMR, the hope is that one day we may be able to identify these children before vaccines are given. Until then, it is up to parents and doctors to weigh the benefits of giving the vaccine against what appears to be an extremely low risk of potential harm.

Weighing in favor of giving the MMR vaccine at the recommended age of 12 to 18 months is the fact that measles is becoming more prevalent and can sometimes be a serious disease. In one in 1,000 cases it can lead to a potentially life-threatening brain infection. If the vaccine is delayed, the child is at a greater risk of catching this infection in the intervening time, and potentially passing it to a younger sibling who is too young to be vaccinated.

On the other hand, delaying the vaccine could be justified if a child has a severe and active inflammatory condition, such as asthma, eczema, gastrointestinal problems, or a history of recent illness or antibiotic use. One of the common patterns among the children reportedly developing autism after the MMR vaccine is being vaccinated soon after a major illness or many courses of antibiotics, as in the case of Hannah Poling.

If the MMR vaccine really can cause harm to the brain in some rare cases, it is probably the cumulative effect of many different assaults on a child's immune system that is the real culprit, rather than the vaccine itself.

My own view of the evidence is that for the vast majority of children, the MMR vaccine is safe and worth giving at 12 months, since it protects from a potentially fatal illness that is becoming more common with each passing year. Yet there remains a possibility that a small subset of children is uniquely vulnerable to developing autism after MMR, perhaps because of an underlying condition, recent illness, or the cumulative effect of many different risk factors.

The best way to deal with this problem is likely to address the other contributing factors—to be careful with vaccine timing and support a healthy brain and immune system from birth, so we can make vaccines as safe as possible.

Points to Remember

- There has been a dramatic expansion in the total number of vaccines given to children since the 1980s, with a corresponding increase in exposure to aluminum.

- There is no clear evidence that the amount of aluminum in vaccines is harmful, but it is possible to minimize exposure by splitting the recommended vaccines across additional doctor visits and choosing the lowest-aluminum brands of vaccines where available.

- If you test negative for the hepatitis B virus, you may also consider delaying the hepatitis B vaccine, rather than giving it soon after birth.

- Adverse reactions to the MMR vaccine appear to be exceedingly rare. Even so, it may make sense to err on the side of caution and delay the vaccine if your child has been ill recently.

Chapter 17

Safeguarding the Microbiome

As research continues into the various factors that can impact children's brain health, the next big frontier is the microbiome—the vast community of microbes living in our gastrointestinal system. We are only just beginning to discover the many different ways these microbes can influence the brain, but some of the recent studies in this area have produced dramatic results.

In one particularly bold experiment, children with autism had their entire population of gut bacteria replaced, by way of "fecal microbiota transfer."[387] After being given powerful antibiotics to clear away their existing gut bacteria, the children received daily doses of a purified set of approximately 1,000 bacterial species obtained from the stool of healthy individuals.

At the end of the two-month treatment, the children saw an 80 percent reduction in gastrointestinal problems, which often go hand-in-hand with autism. There was also a significant improvement in behavioral symptoms. But the real surprise came when the researchers followed up with the children two years later. It turned out the beneficial microbes were still present long after the treatment ended and both gastrointestinal and autism symptoms had continued to steadily improve.[388]

At the two-year point, the improvements in neurological and behavioral symptoms were particularly impressive. Before treatment, professional evaluators rated 83 percent of the children as in the severe autism category. Two years after the microbiome transfer, only 17 percent were rated as severe and 44 percent of children no longer met the criteria for an autism diagnosis. As noted by Professor Thomas Borody, an early pioneer of fecal microbiota transfer who helped with the initial treatment, "I would call it the highest improvement in a cohort that anyone has achieved for autism symptoms."[389]

While this clearly represents a promising strategy for children already diagnosed with autism, the real value of this study is showing just how much influence gut bacteria can have on brain health. The key question, then, is how to take advantage of this knowledge to help our babies build healthier brains from day one. The answer to that starts with an understanding of how exactly the microbiome "talks" to the brain.

How the Microbiome Influences Brain Health

The sheer number of microbes residing within every human on the planet is staggering. In total, the bacterial cells in our gut outnumber the human cells in our entire body—by ten to one.

We have evolved in concert with these microbes over hundreds of thousands of years to have a mutually beneficial relationship. Humans provide nutrients and a safe environment; the bacteria in return help produce vitamins, hormones, and other compounds that regulate a variety of systems in our body, including the brain and immune system.

Compounds produced with the help of our gut bacteria include important neurotransmitters such as serotonin, typically known as the happiness hormone because it regulates mood and social behavior. Although some serotonin is made in the brain, it turns out that even more is made in the gut, with assistance from the microbiome. The cells lining the intestines actually pump out serotonin when they receive certain signals from beneficial gut microbes.[390]

The extent to which serotonin made in the gut actually reaches the brain and alters our mood and behavior is an open question, but it is likely that the gut microbes can also influence the brain in other ways.[391]

For example, some species of gut bacteria may also produce compounds that negatively impact the brain. One of these compounds is propionate, also known as propionic acid. This short chain fatty acid is normally produced in small amounts by certain species of normal gut bacteria, but if these bacteria are present in unusually high numbers, they can produce more propionate than the body can handle. Some doctors and researchers have suggested that this could be linked to the development of autism. One such doctor is Patrick Nemechek, who has witnessed extraordinary improvements in autism symptoms by giving children the prebiotic inulin. He reports that this prebiotic can indirectly reduce the overgrowth of undesirable bacterial species in the gut, reducing the production of potentially harmful chemicals such as propionate.[392]

Another potential link between gut and brain health stems from the fact that certain microbes help calm the immune system and turn back the dial on inflammation. This is critical because inflammation seems to wreak havoc on the developing brain. As discussed in earlier chapters, the harmful effect of inflammation is most apparent when mothers are affected by serious infection or autoimmune disease during pregnancy, because these factors can increase the risk of developmental disorders. But inflammation is also the underlying explanation for how many other factors influence brain health, including vitamin D deficiency and toxin exposure.

Our beneficial gut microbes are one important line of defense against inflammation, because the right species secrete compounds that calm our immune system.[393] Unfortunately, there has been a decline in these beneficial microbes in Western populations in recent decades. This is likely due to the advent of antibiotics, pesticides, and diets emphasizing processed food and lacking fiber.

With the reduction in beneficial microbes, we not only lose a powerful mechanism that calms our immune system and reduces inflammation, but we also leave real estate available for harmful species.

The Battle Between Good and Bad Microbes

The gastrointestinal tract is a highly competitive environment, with hundreds of different species constantly vying for space and nutrients. If there are fewer of the beneficial species in place, harmful bacteria and yeast have less competition and more opportunity to take hold.

A diet low in fiber but rich in sugar and highly refined starches is one factor that tips the scale in favor of harmful species, which often thrive on these nutrients. Antibiotics are another major problem, because each time the beneficial species are killed off, others seize the opportunity to increase their numbers.

When that happens, there can be a long-term impact on our immune system. Rather than calming the immune system, certain opportunistic microbes can produce toxins that ignite the inflammatory response, causing unwanted immune activity throughout the body.

At the extreme end of the spectrum, this can likely result in autoimmune disease. In recent years there has been growing evidence that a disruption to the microbiome could be a driving factor behind the modern plague of autoimmunity. This topic is discussed in great detail in my book *The Keystone Approach*, which explains the marked disruptions to the microbiome that are seen in people with multiple sclerosis, lupus, psoriasis, Crohn's disease, ulcerative colitis, and various types of autoimmune arthritis.

These are all conditions that have become much more common in recent decades, at least in the developed world. They are also beginning to affect children at younger and younger ages, when previously most autoimmune diseases only occurred in adults. Interestingly, many autoimmune conditions are still virtually unheard of in traditional societies that lack access to processed food or antibiotics, the two main factors that appear to inflict the most damage on the microbiome.

It is clear that severe disruptions to the microbiome can likely lead to severe inflammatory conditions, but the connection between the microbiome and the immune system actually has much wider implications. A vast body of research now indicates that milder disruptions to the microbiome can likely contribute to the chronic low-grade inflammation that occurs routinely in modern populations.[394]

During pregnancy, this background of slightly elevated inflammation appears to be contributing to preterm birth,[395] preeclampsia,[396] ADHD,[397] autism,[398] and perhaps impaired cognitive development.[399] Lowering inflammation during pregnancy by supporting your microbiome could potentially reduce the risk of the whole array of downstream consequences, giving your child a better opportunity to build a healthy brain during this critical window of development.

Dr. John Lukens, an assistant professor of neuroscience at the University of Virginia who is researching links between a mother's microbiome and autism, notes that "the really important thing is to figure out what kind of things can be used to modulate the microbiome in the mother as effectively and safely as we can."

Those steps will be discussed in the section that follows, before turning to ways to support your baby's own microbiome after they are born.

Supporting an Anti-Inflammatory Microbiome During Pregnancy

So far, the safest and most effective tool we have to modulate the microbiome during pregnancy appears to be a healthy diet. Specifically, this means cutting back on sugar, which helps unwanted microbes thrive, and instead eating more foods in their whole, natural state.

High-fiber foods, such as lentils, beans, whole grains, nuts, seeds, and vegetables, are helpful for supporting our beneficial microbes because they contain a range of natural prebiotics. By eating more of these foods, you can build a healthy microbiome that reduces inflammation.[400]

We know that adopting a high-fiber diet while pregnant is worthwhile simply because it has been shown to reduce the risk of preeclampsia and gestational diabetes.[401] Eating more fiber-rich plant foods is also likely to reduce the risk of many other problems related to inflammation during pregnancy, including preterm birth and compromised brain development.

Another way to support a healthy microbiome is to start taking a probiotic supplement. Many studies have now reported that taking probiotics during pregnancy can reduce inflammation and help build a healthier balance of species in the microbiome.[402]

This step is not absolutely essential, since a high-fiber diet will likely make much more difference to your overall microbiome. Nevertheless, probiotics can be useful for those who have autoimmunity, gastrointestinal symptoms, or a history of antibiotic use or poor diet.

If you do decide to start taking a probiotic during pregnancy, any good- quality combination of lactobacilli and Bifidobacteria will probably suffice. One particular strain that has been proven to both reduce inflammation and rebalance the overall microbiome is *L. rhamnosus GG* (found in Culturelle and various other brands).

During the third trimester, it can be especially helpful to add two specialized lactobacillus strains that have been found to reduce the chance of needing antibiotics for group B streptococcus during delivery.

About 25 percent of women carry this bacterium in their gastrointestinal system and vagina. Although it generally causes no symptoms, it can be quite dangerous for babies who acquire it during birth. As a result, the CDC recommends screening pregnant women for group B strep at 35 to 37 weeks. For women who test positive, the CDC recommends IV antibiotics during labor, ideally every four hours until the baby is born.

Even this short-term treatment has been found to cause lasting changes to the microbiome of babies.[403] Nevertheless, the need to protect babies from serious infection takes precedence, as pediatrician Dr. Paul Thomas notes:

> *While I agree with the concept of avoiding antibiotics whenever possible, this is one situation where the risks posed by the antibiotics are low in comparison to the risks of a Group B strep infection.*[404]

If you test positive for group B strep shortly before delivery, antibiotics are basically inevitable. But here is the good news: with the right probiotics, you may be able to lower the odds of testing positive.

That was the finding of one recent study where researchers gave women who carried group B strep either a specific probiotic or a placebo, starting at 35 to 37 weeks.[405] Each woman was then tested again when they were admitted to hospital for delivery. At that point, more than 40 percent of the women taking the probiotic tested free of group B strep, compared to only 18 percent in the placebo group.

The specific probiotic used in this study contained two strains: *L. rhamnosus GR-1* and *L. reuteri RC-14*. Numerous studies over the past 25 years have found that these strains help maintain a healthier vaginal flora.[406] The combination is sold as Jarrow Fem-Dophilus, RepHresh Pro-B, and Metagenics UltraFlora Women's.

While further research in this area is needed, the information available to date suggests that adding one of these probiotics during the third trimester is a good way to reduce the odds of needing antibiotics during delivery.

Your Baby's Own Microbiome and Why It Matters

Supporting a healthy microbiome during pregnancy is important, but only half of the equation. After your baby is born, she has to build her own microbiome from the ground up. Protecting this process likely has countless benefits—not only supporting brain health, but also potentially reducing the risk of a range of conditions involving the immune system, such as asthma, eczema, and food allergy.

All of these conditions have become more common in recent decades, particularly in the case of life-threatening food allergy. They are also more likely to occur in babies who were delivered by C-section, exclusively formula fed from birth, or treated with multiple doses of antibiotics in early life, all factors that can compromise the microbiome.[407]

When we look at autism in particular, the connection between the development of this condition and a child's own microbiome has been a particularly hot area of research in recent years. One of the most consistent findings so far is that children with autism often have much lower levels of Bifidobacteria.[408]

These microbes, commonly found in probiotic supplements and yogurts, are normally the first to colonize the gastrointestinal system of newborn babies. They are also known to calm inflammation. A lack of these all-important Bifidobacteria is not the only problem seen in children with autism, however. Researchers have also found higher levels of certain bacteria that seem to trigger inflammation and could therefore be impacting the brain.[409]

We do not yet know if these disruptions to the gut microbiome are in fact a contributing cause of autism, but there are several data points supporting a link. We know, for example, that children with autism typically have chronic gastrointestinal symptoms that correlate with autism severity.[410] Many children with autism show temporary improvements in both their gastrointestinal function and brain function after being treated with antibiotics.[411]

This improvement is likely because the antibiotics temporarily suppress harmful species that drive inflammation. On its own, antibiotic treatment is not a long-term solution, though, because without any competition from beneficial species, the harmful species quickly multiply once antibiotics are stopped.

As discussed at the beginning of the chapter, a much more aggressive approach, which involves wiping out and then replacing the entire population of microbes with a fecal microbiota transfer, seems to be vastly more effective. In the recent study on this point, most children saw lasting and dramatic benefits, with a substantial proportion no longer qualifying as autistic.[412] Perhaps the most significant point to take away from this study is just how powerfully the microbiome can influence the brain.

If so, the best way to take advantage of this new knowledge, to support our children's brain health, is to prevent disruptions to the microbiome before they occur. To do so, we need to act in the critical window of time when children are first establishing their unique population of gut microbes.

Babies are born with a relatively blank slate when it comes to their microbiome. While new discoveries have found that the placenta and amniotic fluid actually do contain some beneficial microbes, few are transferred to the infant's gut.

Over the first few weeks of life, a baby begins to establish a diverse community of bacteria, with many coming from the mother during birth or via her breast milk. The balance of species changes rapidly over the following months and years, in response to diet and the surrounding environment. Researchers can see, for example, that young children with pets typically have a wider range of species present.[413] As a child grows and develops their own unique population of microbes, external factors begin to have less influence. At around age 3 the microbiome becomes a well-established, stable ecosystem.

From that point on, the balance of species typically remains much the same long-term.

It is clear that early influences on a child's microbiome can have a significant long-term impact, especially when it comes to the risk of developing food allergies and other immune problems. By taking full advantage of this important time frame, you may be able to significantly reduce the risk of a whole array of conditions that are now becoming all too common in young children.

Overcoming Modern Threats to the Microbiome

In an ideal world, a baby would be delivered naturally by a mother with a healthy balance of microbes, given at least some breast milk in the first few months, and never need antibiotics. But we do not live in a perfect world and many obstacles can get in the way of best-laid plans. Fortunately, the more we learn about the microbiome, the more strategies we have to overcome the major threats.

Formula, for instance, has come a long way in recent years. One of the main developments in this area takes advantage of the discovery that breast milk contains a significant concentration of *prebiotics*— specific types of carbohydrates that babies cannot metabolize themselves. These compounds instead serve to nourish beneficial bacteria in the newborn's gastrointestinal system.

Studies show that formula with added prebiotics can help support the important beneficial microbes in much the same way as breast milk, helping to reduce rates of eczema, asthma, and food allergy.[414]

The most common prebiotic added to formula is GOS, which can be found in basic Similac and Enfamil varieties. This type of prebiotic is good at supporting Bifidobacteria and is likely sufficient, but there are other prebiotics available that may be even more effective.

Many of the studies showing reduced rates of food allergy, asthma, and eczema used a combination of FOS and GOS, for example.[415]

Another type of prebiotic, which is a relative newcomer to the formula market, may be even better. Known as HMOs or 2'-FL, this is the same as the major prebiotic found naturally in breast milk.[416] It appears to be tailor-made to encourage the exact species babies need for a healthy immune system.[417] Gerber Good Start and Similac Pro Advance both contain 2'-FL.

Although choosing a formula with prebiotics can go a long way toward mimicking the beneficial effects of breastfeeding on the microbiome, breast milk also directly provides the beneficial bacteria babies need, such as lactobacilli and Bifidobacteria. For formula-fed babies, we can try to replicate this by giving an infant probiotic supplement. Doing so can actually be helpful for breastfed babies too, as the following section explains.

Using Probiotics to Support Your Baby's Microbiome

In adults, supplementing with probiotics has only a modest impact on the overall balance of species in the microbiome. This is likely because adults already have a well-established community of microbes in place—a community that is resistant to change.

In newborn babies, however, probiotics can be incredibly helpful for establishing a population of beneficial species. In addition, probiotics can help prevent colonization by harmful species, such as yeast, streptococci, and E. coli.[418]

Probiotics actually reduce these harmful species in two ways. First, the probiotic strains of bacteria take up real estate and compete for nutrients, providing less opportunity for harmful species to flourish. Second, certain probiotic strains produce powerful antimicrobial compounds to directly target and suppress pathogens.

As a result, many hospitals now routinely give probiotics to babies who are born premature.[419] These babies are especially vulnerable to serious gastrointestinal infections, which can be life threatening.

Preterm babies who survive these infections can also be left with long-term neurodevelopmental problems, likely as a result of inflammation triggered by the infection.[420] Preventing severe infections in preemies is therefore paramount, and certain probiotics have proven surprisingly effective.

Clinical studies have investigated a variety of different probiotics for this purpose, but one that stands out is *Lactobacillus rhamnosus GG (LGG)*.[421] This is commonly sold under the brand name Culturelle, but the strain is also found in other probiotic supplements.

Another highly effective species is *Bifidobacteria infantis (B. infantis)*. A variety of probiotic combinations all containing *B. infantis* have been found to significantly reduce the risk of serious infection in premature babies.[422]

B. infantis and *LGG* have also been studied extensively in older children and even adults, with many apparent benefits. Specifically, these probiotics have been found to be particularly good at supporting other beneficial species, suppressing pathogens, and calibrating the immune system.[423]

Researchers speculate that *B. infantis* may be especially important for the health of newborn babies. Interest in this species was sparked when researchers discovered that it is much better at metabolizing the prebiotics found in breast milk than all other species.[424] In other words, breast milk seems to be tailor-made to encourage *B. infantis* to thrive. This suggests that humans evolved alongside *B. infantis*, likely with major benefits for the baby.

One of these benefits is protection from harmful species. As Professor Bruce German of the University of California told *The New York Times*, "The central benefits of having a microbiota dominated by *B. infantis* is that it crowds all the other guys out—especially pathogenic bacteria, which can cause both acute illnesses and chronic inflammation that leads to disease."

Another important benefit of having enough Bifidobacteria during infancy is "education" of the immune system. As explained by Dr. Katri Korpela, an immunobiologist at the University of Helsinki, "the immune system is constantly talking with the microbes in the gut." Beneficial microbes help set the dial on the immune system, a process that is particularly critical during infancy, when "the long-term programming of the immune system happens." Without this education, the immune system may be more likely to overreact to food allergens, for example.

In recent decades, babies in the developed world have begun to lose these benefits of Bifidobacteria, with most babies no longer being colonized with *B. infantis* at birth.[425] This unfortunate development is thought to be caused by the increase in antibiotic use, C-sections, and formula feeding. In countries without these risk factors, such as Gambia and Bangladesh, *B. infantis* is still the dominant species in new babies.[426]

Research now suggests that giving *B. infantis* probiotics to newborns may restore this natural state of affairs, which may in turn reduce some of the afflictions that are becoming widespread in the developed world, such as food allergy, asthma, eczema, and neurodevelopmental disorders.[427]

Giving newborns the *LGG* probiotic also appears to produce many of these benefits. In a recent double-blind, placebo-controlled study, pregnant women and their newborn babies were given either a placebo or a specific probiotic combination containing *LGG* and a Bifidobacteria strain. In the group given the probiotics, the usual negative impact of C-sections and antibiotics on the baby's microbiome was either reduced or completely eliminated.[428] This in turn canceled out the increased risk of allergies normally seen in babies born by C-section.

The ability of probiotics to encourage the good species while suppressing the bad also appears to be useful for preventing and treating colic. For decades, the reason why some babies cry for many hours a day remained a mystery. With the advent of new technology to analyze the microbiome, researchers can see distinct changes in gut bacteria in these infants.

It is now believed that colic is most often caused by abdominal pain from an excess of inflammatory bacteria, which may have proliferated due to a lack of beneficial Bifidobacteria.[429] By suppressing these harmful species, probiotics can quickly alleviate colic for many babies. This has recently been demonstrated in several clinical trials, with particularly good evidence for one specific probiotic strain, known as *Lactobacillus reuteri DSM17938*. Originally obtained from the breast milk of a Peruvian mother, this strain is sold as BioGaia Protectis and Gerber Soothe probiotic drops.

In babies with colic, treatment with *L. reuteri DSM17938* significantly reduces crying time, while also reducing markers of gut inflammation.[430] In one study, babies who were given this probiotic for 30 days cried for half as much time each day as babies in the placebo group.[431]

Other studies have found that the more Bifidobacteria babies have, the less they cry during the first three months.[432] This suggests that we may be able to help prevent colic before it develops by giving babies a *B. infantis* probiotic together with either breastfeeding or a formula containing prebiotics.

In a survey of more than 400 mothers who gave their baby *B. infantis* (as the specific brand Evivo), nearly half reported that their baby's sleep was longer or more consistent within the first few weeks after starting the probiotic.[433] (For specific probiotic recommendations, see brainhealthfrombirth.com/probiotics.)

Other Strategies to Address Colic and Reflux, by Dr. Elisa Song, holistic pediatrician

When I graduated from my pediatrics residency in 2000 it was unheard of to use antacids in babies. Just a few years later, Zantac was approved for infants and suddenly it became a common treatment for fussiness and colic, based on the theory that the babies were in pain due to acid reflux.

In 2018, the tide began to shift again, with a study of almost 800,000 infants finding that early use of antacids doubled the risk of food allergy.[434] Dr. Edward Mitre, who led this study, commented that "Antibiotics and antacids might change the makeup of a baby's microbiome, perhaps enough to cause an overreaction in the immune system that shows up as an allergy."

In light of this study, pediatricians are now beginning to prescribe antacids more judiciously and looking for other approaches to help babies with abdominal pain and colic. Luckily there are so many other things we can do from an integrative and functional medicine standpoint.

The first thing to realize is that for most babies, reflux or colic is caused by inflammation in their gut. Often this is due to an imbalance in gut bacteria, so I recommend giving babies probiotics, specifically *L. reuteri* and an infant probiotic combination.

In other cases, babies have gut inflammation because they are reacting to either their formula or something in breast milk. For formula-fed babies, a partially hydrolyzed or hypoallergenic formula may help. For babies that are breastfeeding, I typically have moms follow an elimination diet for two weeks to exclude some of the biggest culprits, such as dairy, gluten, soy, eggs, and citrus. If you take out all those foods, many babies are much better within just a few days. We can then add the foods back one by one and see how the baby responds.

Herbal medicine can also be helpful. Many years ago, a study found that herbs such as chamomile, ginger, lemon balm, and fennel seed can help relieve colic symptoms.[435] These herbs are included in Gripe Water, which can be quite effective in calming a baby's digestive system.

If all these measures fail and a baby is still spitting up constantly, arching their back, and screaming after feedings, they may have reflux caused by an immature valve that keeps milk in the stomach. In these cases, feeding babies smaller amounts less often, with frequent burping during feedings, can be helpful. Holding your baby upright for half an hour after feedings can also reduce their symptoms. If your baby is still in great discomfort after all these measures, we might then consider an antacid as a last resort.

We also have to remember that sometimes fussiness is just a side effect of normal brain development. Starting at around two weeks old, babies begin to spend more time awake and become more aware of their surroundings. It is normal for babies to go through a fussy period at this time, with sensory overload from the day causing them to cry more than normal, particularly in the early evenings. This usually peaks at around 6-8 weeks, then improves as the baby's brain starts to mature and the social smile starts to develop, and babies are able to take in the world without getting overstimulated. Once the fussy stage passes, life gets better. If your baby is still in this difficult phase, understand that this is normal and use soothing and comforting techniques until it passes.

When your baby is miserable, it is natural to want to solve the problem as quickly as possible by going straight to medication. But now that we know antacids can have long-term impacts on baby's immune system, and even the developing brain, it makes sense to try other strategies first. The holistic, functional medicine approach to colic and reflux is a process, not a quick fix, but it will help your baby thrive so much better in the long run.

* * *

To learn more from Dr. Song, please visit www.healthykidshappykids.com. There you will find information about Dr. Song's Everyday Holistic Pediatrics course, an online video series that offers holistic solutions to common acute health concerns in children.

Minimizing the Harm from Antibiotics

Antibiotics are one of the major threats to a baby's microbiome, causing a drop in beneficial species and a rise in harmful species for many months after treatment ends. It is perhaps not surprising then that children who receive antibiotics in the first year of life are more likely to develop asthma, eczema, food allergies, and autoimmune conditions.[436]

In years past, up to one in five visits to the pediatrician for a new illness resulted in an antibiotic prescription, with ear infections as the number one trigger. But many pediatricians are now aware of the potential long-term ramifications of antibiotics and are prescribing these medications much less often.

One such pediatrician is Dr. Song, who notes that:

In the past 12 years that I've had my holistic integrative pediatric practice, I can probably count on the fingers of both hands how many times I've had to prescribe antibiotics for ear infections. Prior to that, in my conventional practice, it was probably a daily occurrence. Now we know that a significant percentage of earaches are caused by

> *viral infections, and even the bacterial infections can often*
> *resolve on their own.*

Song is not alone in this new hesitant approach to antibiotics. Official treatment guidelines from the American Academy of Pediatrics (AAP) and the U.K. National Health Service now recommend watchful waiting rather than immediate antibiotic prescriptions for common infections, including many ear infections in babies over six months.[437] Rather than prescribing antibiotics at the first sign of a fever and earache, the preferred strategy is to wait for several days to see if the infection starts getting better on its own, leaving antibiotics as a last resort.

Unfortunately, antibiotics will still be necessary in some cases, especially when babies are too young or too sick for the wait-and-see approach. If your child does end up needing antibiotics, it is not the end of the world. The right probiotics can significantly reduce the disruption to the microbiome and help your baby's population of beneficial microbes recover as quickly as possible.[438]

In clinical studies, the two probiotics found to have the most impact in this context are *S. boullardii* and *LGG*.[439] When given in combination with antibiotics, both prevent harmful species such as E.coli and yeasts from taking hold.[440] They also help the microbiome recover more rapidly after antibiotic treatment ends, allowing the beneficial species to bounce back.[441] In addition, both *S. boullardii* and *LGG* have a long track record of safety in clinical studies, including in premature babies.[442]

Balancing the Immune System with Vitamin D

Supporting your child's natural immunity against infections can also help avoid the potential harms of antibiotics, as Song explains: "In my practice, I focus on boosting children's immune systems throughout the year, to reduce the chance of any illness requiring antibiotics. One important element of this is maintaining good vitamin D levels."

Studies have shown that children supplemented with adequate levels of vitamin D3 during the cold and flu season have significantly lower rates of infection. As one example, pediatricians in Japan performed a randomized, double-blind study where they gave children vitamin D supplements throughout the winter and tracked the number of cases of influenza. In the vitamin D–supplemented group, just 11 percent developed flu, compared to 19 percent in the placebo group.[443] Such a clear reduction in infections is useful in itself but likely has the additional benefit of reducing the need for antibiotics. That is because flu-related congestion can often lead to secondary bacterial infections, such as pneumonia, bronchitis, or ear infections, which may end up requiring antibiotics.

Preventing infections is not the only reason to ensure your baby gets enough vitamin D. Studies suggest that it can also help prevent inappropriate immune activity, reducing the risk of autoimmune diseases such as type 1 diabetes, and possibly even autism.[444]

Given these important benefits, it is troubling that many babies still do not get enough. One study in Boston found that 40 percent of babies had suboptimal levels.[445] This widespread problem is recognized by the AAP, which recommends giving babies supplemental vitamin D starting soon after birth.

Initially, the AAP's recommendation applied only to breastfed babies, since it was thought that formula-fed babies were already getting enough vitamin D from the amount added to formula. But in 2010, researchers at the Centers for Disease Control (CDC) found that only a third of exclusively formula-fed babies were drinking enough formula each day to meet their vitamin D needs.[446] The problem was even worse for babies who were partially breastfed and supplemented with formula. The CDC researchers concluded that "most infants, not just those who are breastfed, may require an oral vitamin D supplement daily, beginning within their first few days of life."

The AAP's current recommendation states:

> Pediatricians should encourage parents of infants who are either breastfed or consuming less than 1 liter (just under 1 quart, or 33.8 ounces) of infant formula per day to give their infants an oral vitamin D supplement.[447]

The dose recommended by the AAP is 400 IU per day, which is typically one drop of an infant vitamin D supplement. Some infant probiotics already contain this amount, so a separate vitamin D supplement may not be needed.

Your baby will be ready to stop their daily vitamin D supplement when they can get sufficient vitamin D from other sources, typically through brief daily sun exposure once they are six months old, or regularly eating vitamin D–rich food, such as salmon. In colder climates, many children will continue to need a vitamin D supplement every winter in order to prevent a deficiency.

Points to Remember

- The beneficial species in our microbiome play many important roles, including stimulating the production of neurotransmitters, regulating the immune system, and out-competing harmful microbes.

- Disruptions to the microbiome during pregnancy could contribute to any one of the downstream consequences of inflammation, including preterm birth, preeclampsia, and possibly autism.

- To support a healthy microbiome during pregnancy, emphasize high-fiber whole foods, rather than highly processed starches and sugar, and consider adding a probiotic.

- After your baby is born, she will need to build her own microbiome from scratch, a process that is important for preventing food allergy, eczema, asthma, and autism.

- The main threats to a child's microbiome are antibiotics, C-section birth, and formula feeding.

- The right prebiotics and probiotics can often overcome these threats, especially when included right from the start.

- If you are formula feeding, look for formula containing prebiotics, particularly 2'-FL, which mimics one of the main prebiotics found in breast milk. See brainhealthfrombirth.com/formula.

- Recommended probiotics for infants include LGG, B. infantis, and L. reuteri DSM 17938. See brainhealthfrombirth.com/probiotics.

- The AAP recommends giving babies 400 IU of vitamin D per day, which is usually one drop of an infant vitamin D supplement.

Chapter 18

Putting It All Together

It is clear that something humans have been doing differently in the past thirty years is compromising our children's brain function. The most dramatic reflection of this is the rise in autism and ADHD, which will together affect nearly one in ten children born today. But the same external factors are probably producing more subtle changes in brain function for many more children, contributing to milder problems with IQ, attention span, language development, memory, and emotional regulation.

These and other cognitive functions are important not only for a child's academic success but also for the development of close social bonds. The better a child can communicate and regulate their own emotional state, the more likely they are to form positive relationships with friends and family. Studies suggest that these relationships are key drivers of lifelong happiness.

Supporting our children's cognitive development is therefore one of the most important goals we have as parents. One way of doing so is by giving children the right learning experiences after they are born. Language skills, for example, can be supported with frequent conversations and reading time, while self-regulation can be supported by teaching toddlers to recognize their own emotions. These steps are worthwhile, but they can only go so far.

We now have a vast body of research showing that a child's potential for language development, self-regulation, intelligence, and many other facets of cognitive function can be heavily influenced by environmental factors during pregnancy and early infancy. To truly support our children's development, we need to protect the delicate brain-building process that begins before a child is even born.

To do so, we need to address the factors associated with a higher risk of autism and ADHD, since these factors are also likely to compromise brain health more generally. The research in this area is in its infancy, but it has revealed a number of likely culprits we have the power to shift. This includes reducing the odds of preterm birth by ensuring adequate vitamin D, limiting exposure to pesticides and other toxins, and reducing inflammation by building a healthy microbiome.

The studies also point to many other ways to nurture your baby's brain during pregnancy. By getting adequate amounts of key nutrients such as folate, choline, iron, and omega-3 fats, you will give your baby the raw materials needed to produce new brain cells. This is no small matter—during pregnancy, a growing baby produces an average of 250,000 nerve cells *every minute*.

After your baby is born, her brain continues to grow at an astonishing pace, increasing in size by 1 percent per day. During this time, nutrients continue to matter. Breastfeeding may be the best source of nutrition to support a growing brain, but that does not mean that exclusive breastfeeding should take priority over all else. In the first few days of life, dehydration or low blood sugar can leave a lasting impact on the brain, so it is important to recognize that sometimes supplementing with formula is the best option.

Formula is also getting closer than ever to breast milk, as research reveals more about how exactly breast milk may support a baby's health and brain development. With the addition of prebiotics to nourish the microbiome, and other new specialty ingredients, formula makers are helping to give babies as many benefits of breast milk as possible.

In addition to providing a newborn with all the nutrients needed to support brain development, our other major goal is to protect babies from the potential impact of toxins after they are born. In doing so, one of the common themes to emerge is a return to child-rearing strategies of our grandparents' generation.

When we pay attention to the potential risks of chemicals, we end up parenting in much the same way humans have done for hundreds of years, before homes were filled with items made from plastic or synthetic fragrance, when food was prepared at home from natural ingredients, and fevers were treated with a cool wet cloth rather than heavy doses of medication.

But we do not have to completely turn our back on all of the modern conveniences that make parenting a little easier in modern times. There is really no reason to feel guilty about using pacifiers or disposable diapers, because the materials used to produce these products are safer than you might expect. When it comes to avoiding toxins, the key is knowing where to focus your efforts. Choosing a safer crib mattress and using glass or stainless-steel baby bottles matters, while buying only organic cotton baby clothes probably does not.

We are also fortunate that avoiding toxins is in some ways becoming a little easier today. With regulations limiting phthalates, and the growing range of baby products made from natural and nontoxic materials, it is actually easier to avoid certain toxins than it was a decade ago.

Other areas of child rearing are getting easier too. We know more about how to support babies with colic; to soothe their crying by alleviating stomach discomfort with probiotics. There is also much more awareness among doctors of the potential risks from medications such as antacids and antibiotics, so it's no longer such an uphill battle to protect your baby's microbiome.

I wish I'd had some of this information when I was struggling with my son's colic and reflux, but the reality is that all we can do as parents is try to learn as much as possible and make the best decisions we can with the information we have at the time. I wrote this book with the hope of supporting that process by giving you the latest information, so you can make the best decisions for your own child.

Although it takes a great deal of effort to help a child build a healthy brain, when you see your baby smile for the first time or hear her call you "mama," you will know it was all worth it.

References

1   Padilla, N., Eklöf, E., Mårtensson, G. E., Bölte, S., Lagercrantz,
     H., & Ådén, U. (2015). Poor brain growth in extremely preterm
     neonates long before the onset of autism spectrum disorder
     symptoms. *Cerebral Cortex*, bhv300.

2   De-Regil, L. M., Palacios, C., Lombardo, L. K., & Peña-Rosas, J. P.
     (2016). Vitamin D supplementation for women during pregnancy.
     Sao Paulo Medical Journal, 134(3), 274–275.

3   Cull-Candy, Stuart, and Jonathan Ashmore. Paul Fatt 1924–2014.
     Nature Neuroscience (2014): 1634.

4   Xu, G., Strathearn, L., Liu, B., & Bao, W. (2018). Prevalence of
     autism spectrum disorder among US children and adolescents,
     2014–2016. *Jama, 319*(1), 81-82.

5   Holder, M. D., & Coleman, B. (2009). The contribution of social
     relationships to children's happiness. *Journal of Happiness
     Studies, 10*(3), 329–349.
     Goswami, H. (2012). Social relationships and children's subjective
     well-being. *Social Indicators Research, 107*(3), 575–588.
     Demır, M., & Weitekamp, L. A. (2007). I am so happy 'cause
     today I found my friend: Friendship and personality as predictors
     of happiness. *Journal of Happiness Studies, 8*(2), 181–211.

6   Reviewed in Medina, J. (2014). *Brain rules for baby: How to raise
     a smart and happy child from zero to five*. Pear Press.

7   Parker, W., Hornik, C. D., Bilbo, S., Holzknecht, Z. E., Gentry, L.,
     Rao, R., ... & Nevison, C. D. (2017). The role of oxidative stress,
     inflammation and acetaminophen exposure from birth to early
     childhood in the induction of autism. *Journal of International
     Medical Research, 45*(2), 407–438.

Chapter 1. Threats to Brain Health

8   Treffert, D. A. (1970). Epidemiology of infantile autism. *Archives
     of General Psychiatry, 22*(5), 431–438.
     Lotter, V. (1966). Epidemiology of autistic conditions in young
     children. *Social Psychiatry, 1*(3), 124–135.

9   Xu, G., Strathearn, L., Liu, B., & Bao, W. (2018). Prevalence of autism spectrum disorder among US children and adolescents, 2014-2016. *Jama, 319*(1), 81–82.

10   Xu, G., Strathearn, L., Liu, B., & Bao, W. (2018). Prevalence of autism spectrum disorder among US children and adolescents, 2014-2016. *Jama, 319*(1), 81–82.

11   Boyle, C. A., Boulet, S., Schieve, L. A., Cohen, R. A., Blumberg, S. J., Yeargin-Allsopp, M., ... & Kogan, M. D. (2011). Trends in the prevalence of developmental disabilities in US children, 1997–2008. *Pediatrics*, peds-2010.

12   Danielson, M. L., Bitsko, R. H., Ghandour, R. M., Holbrook, J. R., Kogan, M. D., & Blumberg, S. J. (2018). Prevalence of parent-reported ADHD diagnosis and associated treatment among US children and adolescents, 2016. *Journal of Clinical Child & Adolescent Psychology, 47*(2), 199–212.

13   U.S. Centers for Disease Control and Prevention. *Data & Statistics on Autism Spectrum Disorder.* https://www.cdc.gov/ncbddd/autism/data.html

14   Silberman, S. (2015). *Neurotribes: The Legacy of Autism and the Future of Neurodiversity.* Penguin.

15   Handley, J. B. (2018). *How to End the Autism Epidemic.* Chelsea Green Publishing.

16   American Psychiatric Association. (2013). Diagnostic and statistical manual of mental disorders (DSM-5®). *American Psychiatric Pub.*

17   Olmsted, D, Blaxill, M. *Denial: How Refusing to Face the Facts about Our Autism Epidemic Hurts Children, Families, and Our Future.* Skyhorse Publishing, 2017.

18   Buescher, A. V., Cidav, Z., Knapp, M., & Mandell, D. S. (2014). Costs of autism spectrum disorders in the United Kingdom and the United States. *JAMA Pediatrics, 168*(8), 721–728.

19   Mazurek, M. O., Kanne, S. M., & Wodka, E. L. (2013). Physical aggression in children and adolescents with autism spectrum disorders. *Research in Autism Spectrum Disorders, 7*(3), 455–465.

20   Hallmayer, J., Cleveland, S., Torres, A., Phillips, J., Cohen, B., Torigoe, T., ... & Lotspeich, L. (2011). Genetic heritability and shared environmental factors among twin pairs with autism. *Archives of General Psychiatry, 68*(11), 1095–1102.

Bourgeron, T. (2016). Current knowledge on the genetics of autism and propositions for future research. *Comptes rendus biologies, 339*(7-8), 300–307.

21   Nevison, C. D. (2014). A comparison of temporal trends in United States autism prevalence to trends in suspected environmental factors. *Environmental Health, 13*(1), 73.
Parker, W., Hornik, C. D., Bilbo, S., Holzknecht, Z. E., Gentry, L., Rao, R., ... & Nevison, C. D. (2017). The role of oxidative stress, inflammation and acetaminophen exposure from birth to early childhood in the induction of autism. *Journal of International Medical Research, 45*(2), 407–438

22   Handley, J. B. (2018). *How to End the Autism Epidemic.* Chelsea Green Publishing.

23   Xu, G., Strathearn, L., Liu, B., & Bao, W. (2018). Prevalence of autism spectrum disorder among US children and adolescents, 2014-2016. *Jama, 319*(1), 81–82.

24   Parker, W., Hornik, C. D., Bilbo, S., Holzknecht, Z. E., Gentry, L., Rao, R., ... & Nevison, C. D. (2017). The role of oxidative stress, inflammation and acetaminophen exposure from birth to early childhood in the induction of autism. *Journal of International Medical Research, 45*(2), 407–438.
Copyright © 2017 by William Parker.
Reprinted by Permission of SAGE Publications, Ltd.
Data compiled by Nevison, C. D. (2014). A comparison of temporal trends in United States autism prevalence to trends in suspected environmental factors. *Environmental Health, 13*(1), 73.

25   Treffert, D. A. (1970). Epidemiology of infantile autism. *Archives of General Psychiatry, 22*(5), 431–438.
Burd, L., Fisher, W., & Kerbeshian, J. (1987). A prevalence study of pervasive developmental disorders in North Dakota. *Journal of the American Academy of Child & Adolescent Psychiatry, 26*(5), 700–703.
Wing, L., Yeates, S. R., Brierley, L. M., & Gould, J. (1976). The prevalence of early childhood autism: comparison of administrative and epidemiological studies. *Psychological Medicine, 6*(1), 89–100.

26   Nevison, C. D. (2014). A comparison of temporal trends in United States autism prevalence to trends in suspected environmental factors. *Environmental Health, 13*(1), 73.

27   Saylor, K. E., & Amann, B. H. (2016). Impulsive aggression
     as a comorbidity of attention-deficit/hyperactivity disorder
     in children and adolescents. *Journal of Child and Adolescent
     Psychopharmacology, 26*(1), 19–25.

28   Saylor, K. E., & Amann, B. H. (2016). Impulsive aggression
     as a comorbidity of attention-deficit/hyperactivity disorder
     in children and adolescents. *Journal of Child and Adolescent
     Psychopharmacology, 26*(1), 19–25.

29   Wu, S., Ding, Y., Wu, F., Li, R., Xie, G., Hou, J., & Mao, P.
     (2015). Family history of autoimmune diseases is associated
     with an increased risk of autism in children: A systematic
     review and meta-analysis. *Neuroscience & Biobehavioral
     Reviews, 55,* 322–332.
     Chen, S. W., Zhong, X. S., Jiang, L. N., Zheng, X. Y., Xiong,
     Y. Q., Ma, S. J., … & Chen, Q. (2016). Maternal autoimmune
     diseases and the risk of autism spectrum disorders in offspring:
     a systematic review and meta-analysis. *Behavioural Brain
     Research, 296,* 61–69
     Croen, L. A., Qian, Y., Ashwood, P., Daniels, J. L., Fallin, D.,
     Schendel, D., … & Zerbo, O. (2018). Family history of immune
     conditions and autism spectrum and developmental disorders:
     Findings from the study to explore early development. *Autism
     Research.*

30   Instanes, J. T., Halmøy, A., Engeland, A., Haavik, J., Furu, K., &
     Klungsøyr, K. (2017). Attention-deficit/hyperactivity disorder
     in offspring of mothers with inflammatory and immune system
     diseases. *Biological Psychiatry, 81*(5), 452–459.

31   Köhler-Forsberg, O., Petersen, L., Gasse, C., Mortensen, P.
     B., Dalsgaard, S., Yolken, R. H., … & Benros, M. E. (2019). A
     nationwide study in Denmark of the association between treated
     infections and the subsequent risk of treated mental disorders in
     children and adolescents. *JAMA Psychiatry, 76*(3), 271–279.

32   Nevison, C. D. (2014). A comparison of temporal trends
     in United States autism prevalence to trends in suspected
     environmental factors. *Environmental Health, 13*(1), 73.

Chapter 2. Folate & Choline for Brain Development

33   Johns Hopkins University. (May 11, 2016). *Too Much Folate in
     Pregnant Women Increases Risk for Autism, Study Suggests.*

[Press release]. Retrieved from https://www.jhsph.edu/news/news-releases/2016/too-much-folate-in-pregnant-women-increases-risk-for-autism-study-suggests.html

34 Levine, S. Z., Kodesh, A., Viktorin, A., Smith, L., Uher, R., Reichenberg, A., & Sandin, S. (2018). Association of maternal use of folic acid and multivitamin supplements in the periods before and during pregnancy with the risk of autism spectrum disorder in offspring. *JAMA Psychiatry, 75*(2), 176–184.
   Schmidt, R. J., Hansen, R. L., Hartiala, J., Allayee, H., Schmidt, L. C., Tancredi, D. J., ... & Hertz-Picciotto, I. (2011). Prenatal vitamins, one-carbon metabolism gene variants, and risk for autism. *Epidemiology (Cambridge, Mass.), 22*(4), 476.
   Surén, P., Roth, C., Bresnahan, M., Haugen, M., Hornig, M., Hirtz, D., ... & Schjølberg, S. (2013). Association between maternal use of folic acid supplements and risk of autism spectrum disorders in children. *Jama, 309*(6), 570–577.

35 NIH Factsheet for Health Professionals, Folate (2018). https://ods.od.nih.gov/factsheets/folate-healthprofessional/

36 Schmidt, R. J., Kogan, V., Shelton, J. F., Delwiche, L., Hansen, R. L., Ozonoff, S., ... & Tancredi, D. J. (2017). Combined prenatal pesticide exposure and folic acid intake in relation to autism spectrum disorder. *Environmental Health Perspectives, 125*(9).

37 Raghavan, R., Riley, A. W., Volk, H., Caruso, D., Hironaka, L., Sices, L., ... & Wahl, A. (2018). Maternal multivitamin intake, plasma folate and vitamin B12 levels and autism spectrum disorder risk in offspring. *Paediatric and Perinatal Epidemiology, 32*(1), 100–111.

38 Wiens, D., & DeSoto, M. (2017). Is high folic acid intake a risk factor for autism?—a review. *Brain sciences, 7*(11), 149.

39 NIH Factsheet for Health Professionals, Folate (2018). https://ods.od.nih.gov/factsheets/folate-healthprofessional/

40 Valera-Gran, D., Navarrete-Muñoz, E. M., Garcia de la Hera, M., Fernández-Somoano, A., Tardón, A., Ibarluzea, J., ... & Julvez, J. (2017). Effect of maternal high dosages of folic acid supplements on neurocognitive development in children at 4–5 y of age: the prospective birth cohort Infancia y Medio Ambiente (INMA) study. *The American Journal of Clinical Nutrition, 106*(3), 878–887.

41 Harvard School of Public Health, *Keep the Multi, Skip the Heavily Fortified Foods*, https://www.hsph.harvard.edu/nutritionsource/folic-acid/,

42   Pu, D., Shen, Y., & Wu, J. (2013). Association between MTHFR Gene Polymorphisms and the Risk of Autism Spectrum Disorders: A Meta-Analysis. *Autism Research, 6*(5), 384–392.

43   NIH Factsheet for Health Professionals, Folate (2018). https://ods. od.nih.gov/factsheets/folate-healthprofessional/

44   Valera-Gran, D., Navarrete-Muñoz, E. M., Garcia de la Hera, M., Fernández-Somoano, A., Tardón, A., Ibarluzea, J., ... & Julvez, J. (2017). Effect of maternal high dosages of folic acid supplements on neurocognitive development in children at 4–5 y of age: the prospective birth cohort Infancia y Medio Ambiente (INMA) study. *The American Journal of Clinical Nutrition, 106*(3), 878–887.

45   Bentley, S., Hermes, A., Phillips, D., Daoud, Y. A., & Hanna, S. (2011). Comparative effectiveness of a prenatal medical food to prenatal vitamins on hemoglobin levels and adverse outcomes: a retrospective analysis. *Clinical Therapeutics, 33*(2), 204–210.

46   McMahon, K. E., & Farrell, P. M. (1985). Measurement of free choline concentrations in maternal and neonatal blood by micropyrolysis gas chromatography. *Clinica Chimica Acta, 149*(1), 1–12.

47   Zeisel, S. H. (2006). Choline: critical role during fetal development and dietary requirements in adults. *Annu. Rev. Nutr., 26*, 229–250.

48   Shaw, G. M., Carmichael, S. L., Yang, W., Selvin, S., & Schaffer, D. M. (2004). Periconceptional dietary intake of choline and betaine and neural tube defects in offspring. *American Journal of Epidemiology, 160*(2), 102-109.

49   Brunst, K. J., Wright, R. O., DiGioia, K., Enlow, M. B., Fernandez, H., Wright, R. J., & Kannan, S. (2014). Racial/ethnic and sociodemographic factors associated with micronutrient intakes and inadequacies among pregnant women in an urban US population. *Public Health Nutrition, 17*(9), 1960–1970. Wallace, T. C., & Fulgoni, V. L. (2017). Usual choline intakes are associated with egg and protein food consumption in the United States. *Nutrients, 9*(8), 839.

50   Wallace, T. (2017). *AMA Recommends Choline for Pregnant and Lactating Women.* https://drtaylorwallace.com/ama-choline/

51   Bell, C. C. (2017). AMA's stance on choline, prenatal vitamins could bring 'staggering'results. *Clinical Psychiatry News, 45*(10), 8.

52   Zeisel, S. H. (2006). Choline: critical role during fetal development and dietary requirements in adults. *Annu. Rev. Nutr., 26*, 229–250.

53   Moreno, H. C., de Brugada, I., Carias, D., & Gallo, M. (2013). Long-lasting effects of prenatal dietary choline availability on object recognition memory ability in adult rats. *Nutritional Neuroscience, 16*(6), 269–274.

       Meck, W. H., & Williams, C. L. (1997). Characterization of the facilitative effects of perinatal choline supplementation on timing and temporal memory. *Neuroreport, 8*(13), 2831–2835.

       Meck, W. H., & Williams, C. L. (1997). Perinatal choline supplementation increases the threshold for chunking in spatial memory. *Neuroreport, 8*(14), 3053–3059.

       Meck, W. H., & Williams, C. L. (1997). Simultaneous temporal processing is sensitive to prenatal choline availability in mature and aged rats. *Neuroreport, 8*(14), 3045–3051.

       Meck, W. H., Smith, R. A., & Williams, C. L. (1988). Pre- and postnatal choline supplementation produces long-term facilitation of spatial memory. Developmental Psychobiology: *The Journal of the International Society for Developmental Psychobiology, 21*(4), 339–353.

       Zeisel, S. H. (2006). Choline: critical role during fetal development and dietary requirements in adults. *Annu. Rev. Nutr., 26*, 229–250.

       Williams, C. L., Meck, W. H., Heyer, D. D., & Loy, R. (1998). Hypertrophy of basal forebrain neurons and enhanced visuospatial memory in perinatally choline-supplemented rats. *Brain Research, 794*(2), 225–238.

54   Wu, B. T., Dyer, R. A., King, D. J., Richardson, K. J., & Innis, S. M. (2012). Early second trimester maternal plasma choline and betaine are related to measures of early cognitive development in term infants. *PloS One, 7*(8), e43448.

55   Boeke, C. E., Gillman, M. W., Hughes, M. D., Rifas-Shiman, S. L., Villamor, E., & Oken, E. (2012). Choline intake during pregnancy and child cognition at age 7 years. *American Journal of Epidemiology, 177*(12), 1338–1347.

56   Nichols, L. (2018). *Real Food for Pregnancy*. p. 97.

Chapter 3. The Surprising New Science on Vitamin D & Preterm Birth

57   Behrman, R. E., & Butler, A. S. (2007). *Preterm Birth: Causes, Consequences and Prevention.* Chapter 11: Neurodevelopmental, Health, and Family Outcomes for Infants Born Preterm.

58   Agrawal, S., Rao, S. C., Bulsara, M. K., & Patole, S. K. (2018). Prevalence of autism spectrum disorder in preterm infants: a meta-analysis. *Pediatrics, 142*(3), e20180134.
     Johnson, S., Hollis, C., Kochhar, P., Hennessy, E., Wolke, D., & Marlow, N. (2010). Autism spectrum disorders in extremely preterm children. *The Journal of Pediatrics, 156*(4), 525–531.
     Buchmayer, S., Johansson, S., Johansson, A., Hultman, C. M., Sparén, P., & Cnattingius, S. (2009). Can association between preterm birth and autism be explained by maternal or neonatal morbidity? *Pediatrics, 124*(5), e817–e825.
     Limperopoulos, C., Bassan, H., Sullivan, N. R., Soul, J. S., Robertson Jr, R. L., Moore, M., … & du Plessis, A. J. (2008). Positive screening for autism in ex-preterm infants: prevalence and risk factors. *Pediatrics, 121*(4), 758.
     Glasson EJ, Bower C, Petterson B, de Klerk N, Chaney G, Hallmayer JF. Perinatal factors and the development of autism: a population study. *Arch Gen Psychiatry. 2004;61*(6):618–627

59   Padilla, N., Eklöf, E., Mårtensson, G. E., Bölte, S., Lagercrantz, H., & Ådén, U. (2015). Poor brain growth in extremely preterm neonates long before the onset of autism spectrum disorder symptoms. *Cerebral Cortex*, bhv300.

60   Caravale, B., Tozzi, C., Albino, G., & Vicari, S. (2005). Cognitive development in low risk preterm infants at 3–4 years of life. *Archives of Disease in Childhood-Fetal and Neonatal Edition, 90*(6), F474–F479.

61   Huddy, C. L. J., Johnson, A., & Hope, P. L. (2001). Educational and behavioural problems in babies of 32–35 weeks gestation. *Archives of Disease in Childhood-Fetal and Neonatal Edition, 85*(1), F23–F28

62   Bodnar, L. M., Simhan, H. N., Powers, R. W., Frank, M. P., Cooperstein, E., & Roberts, J. M. (2007). High prevalence of vitamin D insufficiency in black and white pregnant women residing in the northern United States and their neonates. *The Journal of Nutrition, 137*(2), 447–452.

63   McDonnell, S. L., Baggerly, K. A., Baggerly, C. A., Aliano, J. L., French, C. B., Baggerly, L. L., ... & Wineland, R. J. (2017). Maternal 25 (OH) D concentrations≥ 40 ng/mL associated with 60% lower preterm birth risk among general obstetrical patients at an urban medical center. *PloS One, 12*(7), e0180483.

64   McDonnell, S. L., Baggerly, K. A., Baggerly, C. A., Aliano, J. L., French, C. B., Baggerly, L. L., ... & Wineland, R. J. (2017). Maternal 25 (OH) D concentrations≥ 40 ng/mL associated with 60% lower preterm birth risk among general obstetrical patients at an urban medical center. *PloS One, 12*(7), e0180483.

65   Bodnar, L. M., Platt, R. W., & Simhan, H. N. (2015). Early-pregnancy vitamin D deficiency and risk of preterm birth subtypes. *Obstetrics and Gynecology, 125*(2), 439.
      Qin, L. L., Lu, F. G., Yang, S. H., Xu, H. L., & Luo, B. A. (2016). Does maternal vitamin D deficiency increase the risk of preterm birth: a meta-analysis of observational studies. *Nutrients, 8*(5), 301.

66   De-Regil, L. M., Palacios, C., Lombardo, L. K., & Peña-Rosas, J. P. (2016). Vitamin D supplementation for women during pregnancy. *Sao Paulo Medical Journal, 134*(3), 274-275.

67   Sorokin, Y., Romero, R., Mele, L., Wapner, R. J., Iams, J. D., Dudley, D. J., ... & Caritis, S. N. (2010). Maternal serum interleukin-6, C-reactive protein, and matrix metalloproteinase-9 concentrations as risk factors for preterm birth< 32 weeks and adverse neonatal outcomes. *American Journal of Perinatology, 27*(08), 631–640.

68   Li, N., Wu, H. M., Hang, F., Zhang, Y. S., & Li, M. J. (2017). Women with recurrent spontaneous abortion have decreased 25 (OH) vitamin D and VDR at the fetal-maternal interface. *Brazilian Journal of Medical and Biological Research, 50*(11).
      Chen, X., Yin, B., Lian, R. C., Zhang, T., Zhang, H. Z., Diao, L. H., ... & Zeng, Y. (2016). Modulatory effects of vitamin D on peripheral cellular immunity in patients with recurrent miscarriage. *American Journal of Reproductive Immunology, 76*(6), 432–438.

69   Ota, K., Dambaeva, S., Han, A. R., Beaman, K., Gilman-Sachs, A., & Kwak-Kim, J. (2013). Vitamin D deficiency may be a risk factor for recurrent pregnancy losses by increasing cellular immunity and autoimmunity. *Human Reproduction, 29*(2), 208–219.

70   Vinkhuyzen, A. A., Eyles, D. W., Burne, T. H., Blanken, L.
      M., Kruithof, C. J., Verhulst, F., ... & McGrath, J. J. (2018).
      Gestational vitamin D deficiency and autism-related traits: the
      Generation R Study. *Molecular Psychiatry, 23*(2), 240.
      Vinkhuyzen AAE, Eyles DW, Burne THJ, Blanken LME,
      Kruithof CJ, Verhulst F, White T, Jaddoe VW, Tiemeier H,
      McGrath JJ. (2017) Gestational vitamin D deficiency and autism
      spectrum disorder. *BJPsych Open, 3*: 85–90.

71   Chen, J., Xin, K., Wei, J., Zhang, K., & Xiao, H. (2016). Lower
      maternal serum 25 (OH) D in first trimester associated
      with higher autism risk in Chinese offspring. *Journal of
      Psychosomatic Research, 89*, 98–101.
      Magnusson, C., Kosidou, K., Dalman, C., Lundberg, M., Lee, B.
      K., Rai, D., ... & Arver, S. (2016). Maternal vitamin D deficiency
      and the risk of autism spectrum disorders: population-based
      study. *BJPsych Open, 2*(2), 170–172.

72   Vinkhuyzen, A. A., Eyles, D. W., Burne, T. H., Blanken, L.
      M., Kruithof, C. J., Verhulst, F., ... & McGrath, J. J. (2018).
      Gestational vitamin D deficiency and autism-related traits: the
      Generation R Study. *Molecular Psychiatry, 23*(2), 240.

73   Nichols, L. (2018). *Real Food For Pregnancy.*

74   Holick, M. F., Binkley, N. C., Bischoff-Ferrari, H. A., Gordon,
      C. M., Hanley, D. A., Heaney, R. P., ... & Weaver, C. M. (2011).
      Evaluation, treatment, and prevention of vitamin D deficiency:
      an Endocrine Society clinical practice guideline. *The Journal of
      Clinical Endocrinology & Metabolism, 96*(7), 1911–1930.

75   Larqué, E., Morales, E., Leis, R., & Blanco-Carnero, J. E. (2018).
      Maternal and foetal health implications of vitamin D status
      during pregnancy. *Annals of Nutrition and Metabolism, 72*(3),
      179–192.

76   Björkhem-Bergman, L., Nylén, H., Norlin, A. C., Lindh, J. D.,
      Ekström, L., Eliasson, E., ... & Diczfalusy, U. (2013). Serum
      levels of 25-hydroxyvitamin D and the CYP3A biomarker
      4β-hydroxycholesterol in a high-dose vitamin D supplementation
      study. *Drug Metabolism and Disposition, 41*(4), 704–708.
      Yin, K., & Agrawal, D. K. (2014). Vitamin D and inflammatory
      diseases. *Journal of Inflammation Research, 7*, 69.
      Olliver, M., Spelmink, L., Hiew, J., Meyer-Hoffert, U., Henriques-
      Normark, B., & Bergman, P. (2013). Immunomodulatory effects
      of vitamin D on innate and adaptive immune responses to

Streptococcus pneumoniae. *The Journal of Infectious Diseases, 208*(9), 1474–1481.

McDonnell, S. L., Baggerly, C. A., French, C. B., Baggerly, L. L., Garland, C. F., Gorham, E. D., ... & Lappe, J. M. (2018). Breast cancer risk markedly lower with serum 25-hydroxyvitamin D concentrations≥ 60 vs< 20 ng/mL (150 vs 50 nmol/L): pooled analysis of two randomized trials and a prospective cohort. *PloS One, 13*(6), e0199265

77   Holick, M. F., Binkley, N. C., Bischoff-Ferrari, H. A., Gordon, C. M., Hanley, D. A., Heaney, R. P., ... & Weaver, C. M. (2011). Evaluation, treatment, and prevention of vitamin D deficiency: an Endocrine Society clinical practice guideline. *The Journal of Clinical Endocrinology & Metabolism, 96*(7), 1911–1930.

78   Garland, C. F., French, C. B., Baggerly, L. L., & Heaney, R. P. (2011). Vitamin D supplement doses and serum 25-hydroxyvitamin D in the range associated with cancer prevention. *Anticancer Research, 31*(2), 607–611.

79   Stubbs, G., Henley, K., & Green, J. (2016). Autism: will vitamin D supplementation during pregnancy and early childhood reduce the recurrence rate of autism in newborn siblings? *Medical Hypotheses, 88*, 74–78.

80   Tripkovic, L., Lambert, H., Hart, K., Smith, C. P., Bucca, G., Penson, S., ... & Lanham-New, S. (2012). Comparison of vitamin D2 and vitamin D3 supplementation in raising serum 25-hydroxyvitamin D status: a systematic review and meta-analysis. *The American Journal of Clinical Nutrition, 95*(6), 1357–1364.

Chapter 4. Baby Brain Food: Fish & Omega-3 Fats

81   Olsen, S., So/rensen, T. A., Secher, N., Hansen, H., Jensen, B., Sommer, S., & Knudsen, L. (1986). Intake of marine fat, rich in (n-3)-polyunsaturated fatty acids, may increase birthweight by prolonging gestation. *The Lancet, 328*(8503), 367–369.

82   Middleton, P. Gomersall JC, Gould JF, Shepherd E, Olsen SF, Makrides M. (2018) Omega-3 fatty acid addition during pregnancy. *Cochrane Database Syst Rev. 2018* Nov 15.

83   Olsen, S. F., Halldorsson, T. I., Thorne-Lyman, A. L., Strøm, M., Gørtz, S., Granstrøm, C., ... & Cohen, A. S. (2018). Plasma Concentrations of Long Chain N-3 Fatty Acids in Early and

Mid-Pregnancy and Risk of Early Preterm Birth. *EBioMedicine,* *35,* 325–333.

84 https://www.cochrane.org/news/new-research-finds-omega-3-fatty-acids-reduce-risk-premature-birth

85 Lauterbach, R. (2018). EPA+ DHA in Prevention of Early Preterm Birth–Do We Know How to Apply it? *EBioMedicine, 35,* 16–17.

86 Judge, M. P., Harel, O., & Lammi-Keefe, C. J. (2007). Maternal consumption of a docosahexaenoic acid–containing functional food during pregnancy: benefit for infant performance on problem-solving but not on recognition memory tasks at age 9 mo. *The American Journal of Clinical Nutrition, 85*(6), 1572–1577.
Hibbeln, J. R., Davis, J. M., Steer, C., Emmett, P., Rogers, I., Williams, C., & Golding, J. (2007). Maternal seafood consumption in pregnancy and neurodevelopmental outcomes in childhood (ALSPAC study): an observational cohort study. *The Lancet, 369*(9561), 578–585.
Dunstan, J. A., Simmer, K., Dixon, G., & Prescott, S. L. (2008). Cognitive assessment of children at age 2½ years after maternal fish oil supplementation in pregnancy: a randomised controlled trial. *Archives of Disease in Childhood-Fetal and Neonatal Edition, 93*(1), F45–F50.

87 Helland, I. B., Smith, L., Saarem, K., Saugstad, O. D., & Drevon, C. A. (2003). Maternal supplementation with very-long-chain n-3 fatty acids during pregnancy and lactation augments children's IQ at 4 years of age. *PEDIATRICS-SPRINGFIELD-, 111*(1), 189–189.

88 Carlson, S. E., Colombo, J., Gajewski, B. J., Gustafson, K. M., Mundy, D., Yeast, J., ... & Shaddy, D. J. (2013). DHA supplementation and pregnancy outcomes. *The American Journal of Clinical Nutrition, 97*(4), 808–815.

89 Middleton, P., Gomersall, J. C., Gould, J. F., Shepherd, E., Olsen, S. F., & Makrides, M. (2018). Omega-3 fatty acid addition during pregnancy. *Cochrane Database of Systematic Reviews,* (11).

90 De Groot, R. H., Hornstra, G., van Houwelingen, A. C., & Roumen, F. (2004). Effect of α-linolenic acid supplementation during pregnancy on maternal and neonatal polyunsaturated fatty acid status and pregnancy outcome. *The American Journal of Clinical Nutrition, 79*(2), 251–260.

91 Bays, H. E. (2007). Safety considerations with omega-3 fatty acid therapy. *The American Journal of Cardiology, 99*(6), S35–S43.

92   Olsen, S. F., Secher, N. J., Tabor, A., Weber, T., Walker, J. J., & Gluud, C. (2000). Randomised clinical trials of fish oil supplementation in high risk pregnancies. *BJOG: An International Journal of Obstetrics & Gynaecology, 107*(3), 382–395.

93   https://www.epa.gov/international-cooperation/mercury-emissions-global-context

94   Hibbeln, J. R., Davis, J. M., Steer, C., Emmett, P., Rogers, I., Williams, C., & Golding, J. (2007). Maternal seafood consumption in pregnancy and neurodevelopmental outcomes in childhood (ALSPAC study): an observational cohort study. *The Lancet, 369*(9561), 578–585.

95   FDA (2014). *New Advice: Pregnant Women and Young Children Should Eat More Fish.* https://www.fda.gov/consumers/consumer-updates/new-advice-pregnant-women-and-young-children-should-eat-more-fish

96   Centers for Disease Control (2019). *Outbreak of Listeria Infections Linked to Deli-Sliced Meats and Cheeses.* https://www.cdc.gov/listeria/outbreaks/deliproducts-04-19/index.html

Chapter 5. Iodine, Thyroid Hormones, & Your Baby

97   Nazarpour, S., Tehrani, F. R., Simbar, M., Tohidi, M., Majd, H. A., & Azizi, F. (2017). Effects of levothyroxine treatment on pregnancy outcomes in pregnant women with autoimmune thyroid disease. *European Journal of Endocrinology, 176*(2), 253–265.

Johns, L. E., Ferguson, K. K., McElrath, T. F., Mukherjee, B., Seely, E. W., & Meeker, J. D. (2017). Longitudinal profiles of thyroid hormone parameters in pregnancy and associations with preterm birth. *PloS One, 12*(1), e0169542.

Alexander, E. K., Pearce, E. N., Brent, G. A., Brown, R. S., Chen, H., Dosiou, C., ... & Peeters, R. P. (2017). 2017 Guidelines of the American Thyroid Association for the diagnosis and management of thyroid disease during pregnancy and the postpartum. *Thyroid, 27*(3), 315–389.

He, X., Wang, P., Wang, Z., He, X., Xu, D., & Wang, B. (2012). Thyroid antibodies and risk of preterm delivery: a meta-analysis of prospective cohort studies. *European Journal of Endocrinology*, EJE–12.

98   Andersen, S. L., Andersen, S., Vestergaard, P., & Olsen, J.
      (2018). Maternal thyroid function in early pregnancy and child
      neurodevelopmental disorders: a Danish nationwide case-cohort
      study. *Thyroid, 28*(4), 537–546.
      Getahun, D., Jacobsen, S. J., Fassett, M. J., Wing, D. A., Xiang,
      A. H., Chiu, V. Y., & Peltier, M. R. (2018). Association between
      maternal hypothyroidism and autism spectrum disorders in
      children. *Pediatric Research, 83*(3), 580.

99   Getahun, D., Jacobsen, S. J., Fassett, M. J., Wing, D. A., Xiang,
      A. H., Chiu, V. Y., & Peltier, M. R. (2018). Association between
      maternal hypothyroidism and autism spectrum disorders in
      children. *Pediatric Research, 83*(3), 580.

100   Nazarpour, S., Tehrani, F. R., Simbar, M., Tohidi, M., Majd,
      H. A., & Azizi, F. (2017). Effects of levothyroxine treatment on
      pregnancy outcomes in pregnant women with autoimmune
      thyroid disease. *European Journal of Endocrinology, 176*(2), 253–
      265.
      Blumenthal, N. J., & Eastman, C. J. (2017). Beneficial effects
      on pregnancy outcomes of thyroid hormone replacement for
      subclinical hypothyroidism. *Journal of Thyroid Research*, 2017.

101   Alexander, E. K., Pearce, E. N., Brent, G. A., Brown, R. S.,
      Chen, H., Dosiou, C., ... & Peeters, R. P. (2017). 2017 Guidelines
      of the American Thyroid Association for the diagnosis and
      management of thyroid disease during pregnancy and the
      postpartum. *Thyroid, 27*(3), 315–389.

102   de Benoist, B., Andersson, M., Takkouche, B., & Egli, I.
      (2003). Prevalence of iodine deficiency worldwide. *The Lancet,
      362*(9398), 1859–1860.

103   Nazarpour, S., Tehrani, F. R., Simbar, M., Tohidi, M., Majd, H. A.,
      & Azizi, F. (2017). Effects of levothyroxine treatment on pregnancy
      outcomes in pregnant women with autoimmune thyroid disease.
      European Journal of Endocrinology, 176(2), 253–265.

104   Rogan, W. J., Paulson, J. A., Baum, C., Brock-Utne, A. C.,
      Brumberg, H. L., Campbell, C. C., ... & Spanier, A. (2014). Iodine
      deficiency, pollutant chemicals, and the thyroid: new information
      on an old problem. *Pediatrics, 133*(6), 1163–1166.

105   Bath, S. C., Steer, C. D., Golding, J., Emmett, P., & Rayman,
      M. P. (2013). Effect of inadequate iodine status in UK pregnant
      women on cognitive outcomes in their children: results from the

Avon Longitudinal Study of Parents and Children (ALSPAC). *The Lancet, 382*(9889), 331–337.

106   Hollowell, J. G., & Haddow, J. E. (2007). The prevalence of iodine deficiency in women of reproductive age in the United States of America. *Public Health Nutrition, 10*(12A), 1532–1539.
Lumen, A., & George, N. I. (2017). Estimation of iodine nutrition and thyroid function status in late-gestation pregnant women in the United States: Development and application of a population-based pregnancy model. *Toxicology and Applied Pharmacology, 314*, 24–38.

107   Lee, S. Y., Stagnaro-Green, A., MacKay, D., Wong, A. W., & Pearce, E. N. (2017). Iodine Contents in Prenatal Vitamins in the United States. *Thyroid, 27*(8), 1101–1102.

108   Leung, A. M., & Braverman, L. E. (2014). Consequences of excess iodine. *Nature Reviews Endocrinology, 10*(3), 136.

109   Food Standards Australia and New Zealand (2011). *Advice on brown seaweed for pregnant women; breastfeeding women and children* (27 June 2011). http://www.foodstandards.gov.au/consumer/safety/brownseaweed/Pages/default.aspx

110   Rink, T., Schroth, H. J., Holle, L. H., & Garth, H. (1999). Effect of iodine and thyroid hormones in the induction and therapy of Hashimoto's thyroiditis. *Nuklearmedizin. Nuclear medicine, 38*(5), 144-149.

Chapter 6. Iron, Anemia & When to Cut the Cord

111   Hytten, F. (1985). Blood volume changes in normal pregnancy. *Clinics in Haematology, 14*(3), 601–612.

112   Peña-Rosas, J. P., De-Regil, L. M., Dowswell, T., & Viteri, F. E. (2012). Daily oral iron supplementation during pregnancy. *The Cochrane Database of Systematic Reviews, 12*, CD004736.

113   Peña-Rosas, J. P., De-Regil, L. M., Dowswell, T., & Viteri, F. E. (2012). Daily oral iron supplementation during pregnancy. *The Cochrane Database of Systematic Reviews, 12*, CD004736.
Thomas, D. G., Kennedy, T. S., Colaizzi, J., Aubuchon-Endsley, N., Grant, S., Stoecker, B., & Duell, E. (2017). Multiple Biomarkers of Maternal Iron Predict Infant Cognitive Outcomes. *Developmental Neuropsychology, 42*(3), 146–159.
Tran, T. D., Biggs, B. A., Tran, T., Simpson, J. A., Hanieh, S., Dwyer, T., & Fisher, J. (2013). Impact on infants' cognitive

development of antenatal exposure to iron deficiency disorder and common mental disorders. *Plos One, 8*(9), e74876.

Cusick, S. E., Georgieff, M. K., & Rao, R. (2018). Approaches for reducing the risk of early-life iron deficiency-induced brain dysfunction in children. *Nutrients, 10*(2), 227.

Levy, A., Fraser, D., Katz, M., Mazor, M., & Sheiner, E. (2005). Maternal anemia during pregnancy is an independent risk factor for low birthweight and preterm delivery. *European Journal of Obstetrics & Gynecology and Reproductive Biology, 122*(2), 182–186.

Thomas, D. G., Kennedy, T. S., Colaizzi, J., Aubuchon-Endsley, N., Grant, S., Stoecker, B., & Duell, E. (2017). Multiple Biomarkers of Maternal Iron Predict Infant Cognitive Outcomes. *Developmental Neuropsychology, 42*(3), 146–159.

114 Cusick, S., Georgieff, M., & Rao, R. (2018). Approaches for reducing the risk of early-life iron deficiency-induced brain dysfunction in children. *Nutrients, 10*(2), 227.

115 Milman, N., Jønsson, L., Dyre, P., Pedersen, P. L., & Larsen, L. G. (2014). Ferrous bisglycinate 25 milligrams iron is as effective as ferrous sulfate 50 milligrams iron in the prophylaxis of iron deficiency and anemia during pregnancy in a randomized trial. *Journal of Perinatal Medicine, 42*(2), 197–206.

116 Milman, N., Jønsson, L., Dyre, P., Pedersen, P. L., & Larsen, L. G. (2014). Ferrous bisglycinate 25 milligrams iron is as effective as ferrous sulfate 50 milligrams iron in the prophylaxis of iron deficiency and anemia during pregnancy in a randomized trial. *Journal of Perinatal Medicine, 42*(2), 197–206.

117 Paesano, R., Berlutti, F., Pietropaoli, M., Pantanella, F., Pacifici, E., Goolsbee, W., & Valenti, P. (2010). Lactoferrin efficacy versus ferrous sulfate in curing iron deficiency and iron deficiency anemia in pregnant women. *Biometals, 23*(3), 411–417.

Hashim, H. A., Foda, O., & Ghayaty, E. (2017). Lactoferrin or ferrous salts for iron deficiency anemia in pregnancy: A meta-analysis of randomized trials. *European Journal of Obstetrics & Gynecology and Reproductive Biology.*

118 McDonald, S. J., & Middleton, P. (2008). Effect of timing of umbilical cord clamping of term infants on maternal and neonatal outcomes. *Cochrane Database Syst Rev, 2*(2), CD004074.

119 Ashish, K. C., Rana, N., Målqvist, M., Ranneberg, L. J., Subedi, K., & Andersson, O. (2017). Effects of delayed umbilical cord clamping vs early clamping on anemia in infants at 8 and 12 months: a randomized clinical trial. *JAMA Pediatrics, 171*(3), 264–270.

120 Ashish, K. C., Rana, N., Målqvist, M., Ranneberg, L. J., Subedi, K., & Andersson, O. (2017). Effects of delayed umbilical cord clamping vs early clamping on anemia in infants at 8 and 12 months: a randomized clinical trial. *JAMA Pediatrics, 171*(3), 264–270.
     Andersson, O., Hellström-Westas, L., Andersson, D., & Domellöf, M. (2011). Effect of delayed versus early umbilical cord clamping on neonatal outcomes and iron status at 4 months: a randomised controlled trial. *BMJ, 343*, d7157.

121 Rana, N., Ashish, K. C., Målqvist, M., Subedi, K., & Andersson, O. (2019). Effect of Delayed Cord Clamping of Term Babies on Neurodevelopment at 12 Months: A Randomized Controlled Trial. *Neonatology, 115*(1), 36–42.

122 Andersson, O., Hellström-Westas, L., Andersson, D., & Domellöf, M. (2011). Effect of delayed versus early umbilical cord clamping on neonatal outcomes and iron status at 4 months: a randomised controlled trial. *BMJ, 343*, d7157.

123 Mercer, J. S., Erickson-Owens, D. A., Deoni, S. C., Dean III, D. C., Collins, J., Parker, A. B., … & Padbury, J. F. (2018). Effects of Delayed Cord Clamping on 4-Month Ferritin Levels, Brain Myelin Content, and Neurodevelopment: A Randomized Controlled Trial. *The Journal of Pediatrics, 203*, 266–272.

124 American College of Obstetricians and Gynecologists (2017), Committee Opinion Number 684. Delayed Umbilical Cord Clamping After Birth.

125 CBR (2019). *Your Guide to Delayed Cord Clamping.* https://www.cordblood.com/how-banking-works/delayed-cord-clamping

126 American College of Obstetricians and Gynecologists (2017), Committee Opinion Number 684. Delayed Umbilical Cord Clamping After Birth

127 World Health Organization. *Optimal timing of cord clamping for the prevention of iron deficiency anaemia in infants.* https://www.who.int/elena/titles/full_recommendations/cord_clamping/en

Chapter 7. Antidepressants & Acetaminophen During Pregnancy

128 Mallet, C., Barrière, D. A., Ermund, A., Jönsson, B. A., Eschalier, A., Zygmunt, P. M., & Högestätt, E. D. (2010). TRPV1 in brain is involved in acetaminophen-induced antinociception. *PLoS One, 5*(9), e12748.
Mallet, C., Daulhac, L., Bonnefont, J., Ledent, C., Etienne, M., Chapuy, E., ... & Eschalier, A. (2008). Endocannabinoid and serotonergic systems are needed for acetaminophen-induced analgesia. *Pain, 139*(1), 190–200.
129 U.S. Food & Drug Administration (2015). *FDA Drug Safety Communication*: FDA has reviewed possible risks of pain medicine use during pregnancy. January 9, 2015.
130 Ji, Y., Riley, A., Lee, L. C., Hong, X., Wang, G., Tsai, H. J., ... & Ji, H. (2018). Maternal biomarkers of acetaminophen use and offspring attention deficit hyperactivity disorder. *Brain Sciences, 8*(7), 127.
Liew, Z., Ritz, B., Rebordosa, C., Lee, P. C., & Olsen, J. (2014). Acetaminophen use during pregnancy, behavioral problems, and hyperkinetic disorders. *JAMA Pediatrics, 168*(4), 313–320.
Thompson, J. M., Waldie, K. E., Wall, C. R., Murphy, R., Mitchell, E. A., & ABC Study Group. (2014). Associations between acetaminophen use during pregnancy and ADHD symptoms measured at ages 7 and 11 years. *PloS One, 9*(9), e108210.
Ystrom, E., Gustavson, K., Brandlistuen, R. E., Knudsen, G. P., Magnus, P., Susser, E., ... & Hornig, M. (2017). Prenatal exposure to acetaminophen and risk of ADHD. *Pediatrics*, e20163840.
131 Liew, Z., Ritz, B., Virk, J., & Olsen, J. (2016). Maternal use of acetaminophen during pregnancy and risk of autism spectrum disorders in childhood: AD anish national birth cohort study. *Autism Research, 9*(9), 951–958.
Masarwa, R., Levine, H., Gorelik, E., Reif, S., Perlman, A., & Matok, I. (2018). Prenatal exposure to acetaminophen and risk for attention deficit hyperactivity disorder and autistic Spectrum disorder: a systematic review, meta-analysis, and meta-regression analysis of cohort studies. *American Journal of Epidemiology, 187*(8), 1817–1827.
132 Masarwa, R., Levine, H., Gorelik, E., Reif, S., Perlman, A., & Matok, I. (2018). Prenatal exposure to acetaminophen and risk for attention deficit hyperactivity disorder and autistic Spectrum

disorder: a systematic review, meta-analysis, and meta-regression analysis of cohort studies. *American Journal of Epidemiology, 187*(8), 1817–1827.

133 Ystrom, E., Gustavson, K., Brandlistuen, R. E., Knudsen, G. P., Magnus, P., Susser, E., ... & Hornig, M. (2017). Prenatal exposure to acetaminophen and risk of ADHD. *Pediatrics*, e20163840.

134 Bornehag, C. G., Reichenberg, A., Hallerback, M. U., Wikstrom, S., Koch, H. M., Jonsson, B. A., & Swan, S. H. (2018). Prenatal exposure to acetaminophen and children's language development at 30 months. *European Psychiatry, 51*, 98–103.
Liew, Z., Ritz, B., Virk, J., & Olsen, J. (2016). Maternal use of acetaminophen during pregnancy and risk of autism spectrum disorders in childhood: AD anish national birth cohort study. *Autism Research, 9*(9), 951–958.

135 Stergiakouli, E., Thapar, A., & Smith, G. D. (2016). Association of acetaminophen use during pregnancy with behavioral problems in childhood: evidence against confounding. JAMA pediatrics, 170(10), 964-970.

136 Brandlistuen, R. E., Ystrom, E., Nulman, I., Koren, G., & Nordeng, H. (2013). Prenatal paracetamol exposure and child neurodevelopment: a sibling-controlled cohort study. *International Journal of Epidemiology, 42*(6), 1702–1713.

137 Stergiakouli, E., Thapar, A., & Smith, G. D. (2016). Association of acetaminophen use during pregnancy with behavioral problems in childhood: evidence against confounding. *JAMA Pediatrics, 170*(10), 964–970.
Brandlistuen, R. E., Ystrom, E., Nulman, I., Koren, G., & Nordeng, H. (2013). Prenatal paracetamol exposure and child neurodevelopment: a sibling-controlled cohort study. *International Journal of Epidemiology, 42*(6), 1702–1713.

138 Society for Maternal Fetal Medicine (2017). *SMFM Statement: Prenatal acetaminophen and outcomes in children* https://www.smfm.org/publications/234-smfm-statement-prenatal-acetaminophen-and-outcomes-in-children

139 Interrante, J. D., Ailes, E. C., Lind, J. N., Anderka, M., Feldkamp, M. L., Werler, M. M., ... & Study, T. N. B. D. P. (2017). Risk comparison for prenatal use of analgesics and selected birth defects, National Birth Defects Prevention Study 1997–2011. *Annals of Epidemiology, 27*(10), 645–653.

140 Franklin, M. E., & Conner-Kerr, T. (2018). Pregnancy and Low Back Pain: Physical Therapy Can Reduce Back and Pelvic Pain During and After Pregnancy. *Journal of Orthopaedic & Sports Physical Therapy, 44*(7).

141 Turner, L, (2018). Should Pregnant Women Take Anti-Anxiety Medication? Some Have No Choice. *Slate.* November 12, 2018.

142 Boukhris, T., Sheehy, O., Mottron, L., & Bérard, A. (2016). Antidepressant use during pregnancy and the risk of autism spectrum disorder in children. *JAMA Pediatrics, 170*(2), 117–124.

143 Underood, E. (2015). Reality check: Taking antidepressants while pregnant unlikely to double autism risk in kids. *Science.* Dec. 14, 2015.

144 Underood, E. (2015). Reality check: Taking antidepressants while pregnant unlikely to double autism risk in kids. *Science.* Dec. 14, 2015.

145 Brown, H. K., Ray, J. G., Wilton, A. S., Lunsky, Y., Gomes, T., & Vigod, S. N. (2017). Association between serotonergic antidepressant use during pregnancy and autism spectrum disorder in children. *Jama, 317*(15), 1544–1552.
Sujan, A. C., Rickert, M. E., Öberg, A. S., Quinn, P. D., Hernández-Díaz, S., Almqvist, C., … & D'Onofrio, B. M. (2017). Associations of maternal antidepressant use during the first trimester of pregnancy with preterm birth, small for gestational age, autism spectrum disorder, and attention-deficit/ hyperactivity disorder in offspring. *Jama, 317*(15), 1553–1562.
Janecka, M., Kodesh, A., Levine, S. Z., Lusskin, S. I., Viktorin, A., Rahman, R., … & Reichenberg, A. (2018). Association of autism spectrum disorder with prenatal exposure to medication affecting neurotransmitter systems. *JAMA Psychiatry, 75*(12), 1217–1224.

146 Yu, W., Yen, Y. C., Lee, Y. H., Tan, S., Xiao, Y., Lokman, H., … & Je, H. S. (2019). Prenatal selective serotonin reuptake inhibitor (SSRI) exposure induces working memory and social recognition deficits by disrupting inhibitory synaptic networks in male mice. *Molecular Brain, 12*(1), 29.

147 Maes, M. (2011). Depression is an inflammatory disease, but cell-mediated immune activation is the key component of depression. *Progress in Neuro-Psychopharmacology and Biological Psychiatry, 35*(3), 664–675.

Miller, A. H., Maletic, V., & Raison, C. L. (2009). Inflammation and its discontents: the role of cytokines in the pathophysiology of major depression. *Biological Psychiatry, 65*(9), 732–741.

Raison, C. L., Capuron, L., & Miller, A. H. (2006). Cytokines sing the blues: inflammation and the pathogenesis of depression. *Trends in Immunology, 27*(1), 24–31.

148 Osborne, S., Biaggi, A., Chua, T. E., Du Preez, A., Hazelgrove, K., Nikkheslat, N., … & Pariante, C. M. (2018). Antenatal depression programs cortisol stress reactivity in offspring through increased maternal inflammation and cortisol in pregnancy: The Psychiatry Research and Motherhood–Depression (PRAM-D) Study. *Psychoneuroendocrinology, 98*, 211–221.

149 Raison, C. L., Capuron, L., & Miller, A. H. (2006). Cytokines sing the blues: inflammation and the pathogenesis of depression. *Trends in Immunology, 27*(1), 24–31.

Chapter 8. Vaccine Decisions During Pregnancy

150 Zerbo, O., Qian, Y., Yoshida, C., Fireman, B. H., Klein, N. P., & Croen, L. A. (2017). Association between influenza infection and vaccination during pregnancy and risk of autism spectrum disorder. *JAMA Pediatrics, 171*(1), e163609–e163609.

151 Hooker, B. S. (2017). Influenza Vaccination in the First Trimester of Pregnancy and Risk of Autism Spectrum Disorder. *JAMA Pediatrics, 171*(6), 600–600.

152 Christian, L. M., Porter, K., Karlsson, E., Schultz-Cherry, S., & Iams, J. D. (2013). Serum proinflammatory cytokine responses to influenza virus vaccine among women during pregnancy versus non-pregnancy. *American Journal of Reproductive Immunology, 70*(1), 45–53.

153 Jiang, H. Y., Xu, L. L., Shao, L., Xia, R. M., Yu, Z. H., Ling, Z. X., … & Ruan, B. (2016). Maternal infection during pregnancy and risk of autism spectrum disorders: a systematic review and meta-analysis. *Brain, Behavior, and Immunity, 58*, 165–172.

154 Donahue, J. G., Kieke, B. A., King, J. P., DeStefano, F., Mascola, M. A., Irving, S. A., … & Naleway, A. L. (2017). Association of spontaneous abortion with receipt of inactivated influenza vaccine containing H1N1pdm09 in 2010–11 and 2011–12. *Vaccine, 35*(40), 5314–5322.

155 Håberg, S. E., Trogstad, L., Gunnes, N., Wilcox, A. J., Gjessing, H. K., Samuelsen, S. O., ... & Madsen, S. (2013). Risk of fetal death after pandemic influenza virus infection or vaccination. *New England Journal of Medicine, 368*(4), 333–340.
Moro, P. L., Broder, K., Zheteyeva, Y., Walton, K., Rohan, P., Sutherland, A., ... & Vellozzi, C. (2011). Adverse events in pregnant women following administration of trivalent inactivated influenza vaccine and live attenuated influenza vaccine in the Vaccine Adverse Event Reporting System, 1990-2009. *American Journal of Obstetrics and Gynecology, 204*(2), 146–e1.

156 Håberg, S. E., Trogstad, L., Gunnes, N., Wilcox, A. J., Gjessing, H. K., Samuelsen, S. O., ... & Madsen, S. (2013). Risk of fetal death after pandemic influenza virus infection or vaccination. *New England Journal of Medicine, 368*(4), 333–340.

157 https://www.aafp.org/news/health-of-the-public/20170920flumiscarry.html

158 Black, S. B., Shinefield, H. R., France, E. K., Fireman, B. H., Platt, S. T., & Shay, D. (2004). Effectiveness of influenza vaccine during pregnancy in preventing hospitalizations and outpatient visits for respiratory illness in pregnant women and their infants. *American Journal of Perinatology, 21*(06), 333–339.

159 Thompson, M. G., Kwong, J. C., Regan, A. K., Katz, M. A., Drews, S. J., Azziz-Baumgartner, E., ... & Simmonds, K. (2018). Influenza Vaccine Effectiveness in Preventing Influenza-associated Hospitalizations During Pregnancy: A Multi-country Retrospective Test Negative Design Study, 2010–2016. *Clinical Infectious Diseases.*

160 Centers for Disease Control (2016), *Create a Circle of Protection Around Babies*, https://www.cdc.gov/vaccines/pregnancy/family-caregivers/index.html

161 Eick, A. A., Uyeki, T. M., Klimov, A., Hall, H., Reid, R., Santosham, M., & O'brien, K. L. (2011). Maternal influenza vaccination and effect on influenza virus infection in young infants. *Archives of Pediatrics & Adolescent Medicine, 165*(2), 104–111.

162 Shakib, J. H., Korgenski, K., Presson, A. P., Sheng, X., Varner, M. W., Pavia, A. T., & Byington, C. L. (2016). Influenza in infants born to women vaccinated during pregnancy. *Pediatrics*, e20152360.

163 Blanchard-Rohner, G., Meier, S., Bel, M., Combescure, C., Othenin-Girard, V., Swali, R. A., ... & Siegrist, C. A. (2013). Influenza vaccination given at least 2 weeks before delivery to pregnant women facilitates transmission of seroprotective influenza-specific antibodies to the newborn. *The Pediatric Infectious Disease Journal, 32*(12), 1374–1380.

164 Blanchard-Rohner, G., Meier, S., Bel, M., Combescure, C., Othenin-Girard, V., Swali, R. A., ... & Siegrist, C. A. (2013). Influenza vaccination given at least 2 weeks before delivery to pregnant women facilitates transmission of seroprotective influenza-specific antibodies to the newborn. *The Pediatric Infectious Disease Journal, 32*(12), 1374–1380.

165 Salahi, L. (2010). 38-Day-Old Baby Dies After Persisting Cough. ABC News. April 28, 2010.

166 Baxter, R., Bartlett, J., Fireman, B., Lewis, E., & Klein, N. P. (2017). Effectiveness of vaccination during pregnancy to prevent infant pertussis. *Pediatrics*, e20164091.

167 Becerra-Culqui, T. A., Getahun, D., Chiu, V., Sy, L. S., & Tseng, H. F. (2018). Prenatal Tetanus, Diphtheria, Acellular Pertussis Vaccination and Autism Spectrum Disorder. *Pediatrics, 142*(3), e20180120.

Chapter 9. The Risks & Benefits of Ultrasounds

168 Rosman, N. P., Vassar, R., Doros, G., DeRosa, J., Froman, A., DiMauro, A., ... & Abbott, J. (2018). Association of prenatal ultrasonography and autism spectrum disorder. *JAMA Pediatrics, 172*(4), 336–344.

169 Abramowicz, J. S. (2012). Ultrasound and autism: association, link, or coincidence?. *Journal of Ultrasound in Medicine, 31*(8), 1261–1269.
Grether, J. K., Li, S. X., Yoshida, C. K., & Croen, L. A. (2010). Antenatal ultrasound and risk of autism spectrum disorders. *Journal of Autism and Developmental Disorders, 40*(2), 238–245.
Stoch, Y. K., Williams, C. J., Granich, J., Hunt, A. M., Landau, L. I., Newnham, J. P., & Whitehouse, A. J. (2012). Are prenatal ultrasound scans associated with the autism phenotype? Follow-up of a randomised controlled trial. *Journal of Autism and Developmental Disorders, 42*(12), 2693–2701.

Carlsson, L. H., Saltvedt, S., Anderlid, B. M., Westerlund, J., Gillberg, C., Westgren, M., & Fernell, E. (2016). Prenatal ultrasound and childhood autism: long-term follow-up after a randomized controlled trial of first- vs second-trimester ultrasound. *Ultrasound in Obstetrics & Gynecology, 48*(3), 285–288.

170 Webb, S. J., & Mourad, P. D. (2018). Prenatal ultrasonography and the incidence of autism spectrum disorder. *JAMA Pediatrics, 172*(4), 319–320.

171 Webb, S. J., Garrison, M. M., Bernier, R., McClintic, A. M., King, B. H., & Mourad, P. D. (2017). Severity of ASD symptoms and their correlation with the presence of copy number variations and exposure to first trimester ultrasound. *Autism Research, 10*(3), 472–484.

172 ACOG Committee Opinion (2017). Guidelines for Diagnostic Imaging During Pregnancy and Lactation. Number 723, October 2017.

173 Bricker, L., Medley, N., & Pratt, J. J. (2015). Routine ultrasound in late pregnancy (after 24 weeks' gestation). *Cochrane Database of Systematic Reviews*, (6).

174 Bricker, L., Medley, N., & Pratt, J. J. (2015). Routine ultrasound in late pregnancy (after 24 weeks' gestation). *Cochrane Database of Systematic Reviews*, (6).

175 Whitworth, M., Bricker, L., & Mullan, C. (2015). Ultrasound for fetal assessment in early pregnancy. *Cochrane Database of Systematic Reviews*, (7).

176 Sovio, U., White, I. R., Dacey, A., Pasupathy, D., & Smith, G. C. (2015). Screening for fetal growth restriction with universal third trimester ultrasonography in nulliparous women in the Pregnancy Outcome Prediction (POP) study: a prospective cohort study. *The Lancet, 386*(10008), 2089–2097.
Imdad, A., Yakoob, M. Y., Siddiqui, S., & Bhutta, Z. A. (2011). Screening and triage of intrauterine growth restriction (IUGR) in general population and high risk pregnancies: a systematic review with a focus on reduction of IUGR related stillbirths. *BMC Public Health, 11*(3), S1.
Breeze, A. C., & Lees, C. C. (2007, October). Prediction and perinatal outcomes of fetal growth restriction. *In Seminars in Fetal and Neonatal Medicine* (Vol. 12, No. 5, pp. 383–397). WB Saunders.

177 American College of Obstetricians and Gynecologists (2017). *Ultrasound Exams.* https://www.acog.org/Patients/FAQs/Ultrasound-Exams

178 U.S. Food and Drug Administration. (2018). *Ultrasound Imaging.* https://www.fda.gov/radiation-emitting-products/medical-imaging/ultrasound-imaging

179 U.S. Food and Drug Administration. (2018). Ultrasound Imaging. https://www.fda.gov/radiation-emitting-products/medical-imaging/ultrasound-imaging

180 U.S. Food and Drug Administration. (2014). *Avoid Fetal "Keepsake" Images, Heartbeat Monitors.* https://www.fda.gov/consumers/consumer-updates/avoid-fetal-keepsake-images-heartbeat-monitors

181 Parker-Pope, Tara. The Risk of Home Fetal Heart Monitor. *The New York Times*, November 6, 2009.

182 Parker-Pope, Tara. The Risk of Home Fetal Heart Monitor. *The New York Times*, November 6, 2009.

Chapter 10. Baby Steps to a Cleaner, Greener Home

183 Houlihan, J., Kropp, T., Wiles, R., Gray, S., & Campbell, C. (2005). Body burden. the pollution in newborns: a benchmark investigation of industrial chemicals, pollutants, and pesticides in human umbilical cord blood. *Environmental Working Group.*

184 Woodruff, T. J., Zota, A. R., & Schwartz, J. M. (2011). Environmental chemicals in pregnant women in the United States: NHANES 2003–2004. *Environmental health perspectives, 119*(6), 878.

185 American Academy of Pediatrics. (2018). *American Academy of Pediatrics Says Some Common Food Additives May Pose Health Risks to Children.* https://www.aap.org/en-us/about-the-aap/aap-press-room/Pages/AAP-Says-Some-Common-Food-Additives-May-Pose-Health-Risks-to-Children.aspx

186 Greene, A. (2007). *Raising Baby Green: The Earth-Friendly Guide to Pregnancy, Childbirth, and Baby Care.* Jossey-Bass

187 Kalkbrenner, A. E., Schmidt, R. J., & Penlesky, A. C. (2014). Environmental chemical exposures and autism spectrum disorders: a review of the epidemiological evidence. *Current Problems in Pediatric and Adolescent Health Care, 44*(10), 277–318.

188 Mostafalou, S., & Abdollahi, M. (2017). Pesticides: an update of human exposure and toxicity. *Archives of Toxicology, 91*(2), 549–599.

189 El-Salam, M. A., Hegazy, A. A., Elhady, M., Ibrahim, G. E., & Hussein, R. (2017). Biomarkers of Organophosphate Pesticides and Attention-Deficit/Hyperactivity Disorder in Children: A Case-Control Study. *J Environ Anal Toxicol, 7*(460), 2161–0525. Roberts, J. R., Dawley, E. H., & Reigart, J. R. (2018). Children's low-level pesticide exposure and associations with autism and ADHD: a review. *Pediatric Research, 1.* Schmidt, R. J., Kogan, V., Shelton, J. F., Delwiche, L., Hansen, R. L., Ozonoff, S., ... & Tancredi, D. (2018, February). *Combined Exposures to Prenatal Pesticides and Folic Acid Intake in Relation to Autism Spectrum Disorder.* In ISEE Conference Abstracts.

190 Roberts, J. R., & Karr, C. J. (2012). Pesticide exposure in children. *Pediatrics, peds-2012.*

191 Roberts, J. R., & Karr, C. J. (2012). Pesticide exposure in children. *Pediatrics, peds-2012.*

192 Hertz-Picciotto, I., Sass, J. B., Engel, S., Bennett, D. H., Bradman, A., Eskenazi, B., ... & Whyatt, R. (2018). Organophosphate exposures during pregnancy and child neurodevelopment: Recommendations for essential policy reforms. *PLoS Medicine, 15*(10), e1002671.

193 von Ehrenstein, O. S., Ling, C., Cui, X., Cockburn, M., Park, A. S., Yu, F., ... & Ritz, B. (2019). Prenatal and infant exposure to ambient pesticides and autism spectrum disorder in children: population based case-control study. *BMJ, 364,* l962. Shelton, J. F., Geraghty, E. M., Tancredi, D. J., Delwiche, L. D., Schmidt, R. J., Ritz, B., ... & Hertz-Picciotto, I. (2014). Neurodevelopmental disorders and prenatal residential proximity to agricultural pesticides: the CHARGE study. *Environmental Health Perspectives, 122*(10), 1103.

194 Shelton, J. F., Geraghty, E. M., Tancredi, D. J., Delwiche, L. D., Schmidt, R. J., Ritz, B., ... & Hertz-Picciotto, I. (2014). Neurodevelopmental disorders and prenatal residential proximity to agricultural pesticides: the CHARGE study. *Environmental Health Perspectives, 122*(10), 1103.

195 Furlong, M. A., Barr, D. B., Wolff, M. S., & Engel, S. M. (2017). Prenatal exposure to pyrethroid pesticides and childhood behavior and executive functioning. *Neurotoxicology, 62*, 231–238.

196 Yang, T., Doherty, J., Zhao, B., Kinchla, A. J., Clark, J. M., & He, L. (2017). Effectiveness of commercial and homemade washing agents in removing pesticide residues on and in apples. *Journal of Agricultural and Food Chemistry, 65*(44), 9744–9752.

197 Aspelin, A. L., & Grube, A. H. (1999). *Pesticides industry sales and usage: 1996 and 1997 market estimates.* Biological and Economic Analysis Division, Office of Pesticide Programs, Office of Prevention, Pesticides and Toxic Substances, US Environmental Protection Agency.

198 Benbrook, C. M. (2016). Trends in glyphosate herbicide use in the United States and globally. *Environmental Sciences Europe, 28*(1), 3.

199 Myers, J. P., Antoniou, M. N., Blumberg, B., Carroll, L., Colborn, T., Everett, L. G., ... & Vandenberg, L. N. (2016). Concerns over use of glyphosate-based herbicides and risks associated with exposures: a consensus statement. *Environmental Health, 15*(1), 19.

200 Beecham, J. E., & Seneff, S. (2016). Is there a link between autism and glyphosate-formulated herbicides? *Journal of Autism, 3*(1), 1.

201 Gallegos, C. E., Bartos, M., Bras, C., Gumilar, F., Antonelli, M. C., & Minetti, A. (2016). Exposure to a glyphosate-based herbicide during pregnancy and lactation induces neurobehavioral alterations in rat offspring. *Neurotoxicology, 53*, 20–28.
      Roy, N. M., Carneiro, B., & Ochs, J. (2016). Glyphosate induces neurotoxicity in zebrafish. *Environmental Toxicology and Pharmacology, 42*, 45–54.
      Coullery, R. P., Ferrari, M. E., & Rosso, S. B. (2016). Neuronal development and axon growth are altered by glyphosate through a WNT non-canonical signaling pathway. *Neurotoxicology, 52*, 150–161.
      Cattani, D., Cavalli, V. L. D. L. O., Rieg, C. E. H., Domingues, J. T., Dal-Cim, T., Tasca, C. I., ... & Zamoner, A. (2014). Mechanisms underlying the neurotoxicity induced by glyphosate-based herbicide in immature rat hippocampus: involvement of glutamate excitotoxicity. *Toxicology, 320*, 34–45.
      Martínez, M. A., Ares, I., Rodríguez, J. L., Martínez, M., Martínez-Larrañaga, M. R., & Anadón, A. (2018).

Neurotransmitter changes in rat brain regions following glyphosate exposure. *Environmental Research, 161,* 212–219.

202 Vandenberg, L. N., Blumberg, B., Antoniou, M. N., Benbrook, C. M., Carroll, L., Colborn, T., ... & Mesnage, R. (2017). Is it time to reassess current safety standards for glyphosate-based herbicides? *J Epidemiol Community Health, 71*(6), 613–618.

Myers, J. P., Antoniou, M. N., Blumberg, B., Carroll, L., Colborn, T., Everett, L. G., ... & Vandenberg, L. N. (2016). Concerns over use of glyphosate-based herbicides and risks associated with exposures: a consensus statement. *Environmental Health, 15*(1), 19.

203 World Health Organization. (2017). *IARC Monographs on the Evaluation of Carcinogenic Risks to Humans. Some Organophosphate Insecticides and Herbicides. Volume 112* (2017)

204 Myers, J. P., Antoniou, M. N., Blumberg, B., Carroll, L., Colborn, T., Everett, L. G., ... & Vandenberg, L. N. (2016). Concerns over use of glyphosate-based herbicides and risks associated with exposures: a consensus statement. *Environmental Health, 15*(1), 19.

205 Temkin, A. (2018) *Breakfast With a Dose of Roundup. Environmental Working Group.* https://www.ewg.org/childrenshealth/glyphosateincereal/

206 Abrams, L. (2014). Study reinforces link between autism and pesticides. *Salon,* June 23, 2014.

207 Brown University. *News from Brown - Joseph Braun.* https://news.brown.edu/new-faculty/life-sciences/joseph-braun

208 Braun, J. M., Kalkbrenner, A. E., Just, A. C., Yolton, K., Calafat, A. M., Sjödin, A., ... & Lanphear, B. P. (2014). Gestational exposure to endocrine-disrupting chemicals and reciprocal social, repetitive, and stereotypic behaviors in 4-and 5-year-old children: the HOME study. *Environmental Health Perspectives, 122*(5), 513.

Braun, J. M., Yolton, K., Dietrich, K. N., Hornung, R., Ye, X., Calafat, A. M., & Lanphear, B. P. (2009). Prenatal bisphenol A exposure and early childhood behavior. *Environmental Health Perspectives, 117*(12), 1945.

Evans, S. F., Kobrosly, R. W., Barrett, E. S., Thurston, S. W., Calafat, A. M., Weiss, B., ... & Swan, S. H. (2014). Prenatal bisphenol A exposure and maternally reported behavior in boys and girls. *Neurotoxicology, 45,* 91–99.

Harley, K. G., Gunier, R. B., Kogut, K., Johnson, C., Bradman, A., Calafat, A. M., & Eskenazi, B. (2013). Prenatal and early childhood bisphenol A concentrations and behavior in school-aged children. *Environmental Research, 126*, 43–50.

Hong, S. B., Hong, Y. C., Kim, J. W., Park, E. J., Shin, M. S., Kim, B. N., ... & Cho, S. C. (2013). Bisphenol A in relation to behavior and learning of school-age children. *Journal of Child Psychology and Psychiatry, 54*(8), 890–899.

Miodovnik, A., Engel, S. M., Zhu, C., Ye, X., Soorya, L. V., Silva, M. J., ... & Wolff, M. S. (2011). Endocrine disruptors and childhood social impairment. *Neurotoxicology, 32*(2), 261–267.

Perera, F., Vishnevetsky, J., Herbstman, J. B., Calafat, A. M., Xiong, W., Rauh, V., & Wang, S. (2012). Prenatal bisphenol a exposure and child behavior in an inner-city cohort. *Environmental Health Perspectives, 120*(8), 1190.

Roen, E. L., Wang, Y., Calafat, A. M., Wang, S., Margolis, A., Herbstman, J., ... & Perera, F. P. (2015). Bisphenol A exposure and behavioral problems among inner city children at 7–9 years of age. *Environmental Research, 142*, 739–745.

209 Tewar, S., Auinger, P., Braun, J. M., Lanphear, B., Yolton, K., Epstein, J. N., ... & Froehlich, T. E. (2016). Association of bisphenol A exposure and attention-deficit/hyperactivity disorder in a national sample of US children. *Environmental Research, 150*, 112–118.

Hong, S. B., Hong, Y. C., Kim, J. W., Park, E. J., Shin, M. S., Kim, B. N., ... & Cho, S. C. (2013). Bisphenol A in relation to behavior and learning of school-age children. *Journal of Child Psychology and Psychiatry, 54*(8), 890–899.

Harley, K. G., Gunier, R. B., Kogut, K., Johnson, C., Bradman, A., Calafat, A. M., & Eskenazi, B. (2013). Prenatal and early childhood bisphenol A concentrations and behavior in school-aged children. *Environmental Research, 126*, 43–50

Perera, F., Vishnevetsky, J., Herbstman, J. B., Calafat, A. M., Xiong, W., Rauh, V., & Wang, S. (2012). Prenatal bisphenol a exposure and child behavior in an inner-city cohort. *Environmental Health Perspectives, 120*(8), 1190.

Roen, E. L., Wang, Y., Calafat, A. M., Wang, S., Margolis, A., Herbstman, J., ... & Perera, F. P. (2015). Bisphenol A exposure and behavioral problems among inner city children at 7–9 years of age. *Environmental Research, 142*, 739–745.

210 Braun, J. M., Kalkbrenner, A. E., Calafat, A. M., Bernert, J. T., Ye, X., Silva, M. J., ... & Lanphear, B. P. (2010). Variability and predictors of urinary bisphenol A concentrations during pregnancy. *Environmental Health Perspectives, 119*(1), 131–137.

211 Von Goetz, N., Wormuth, M., Scheringer, M., & Hungerbühler, K. (2010). Bisphenol A: how the most relevant exposure sources contribute to total consumer exposure. *Risk Analysis: An International Journal, 30*(3), 473–487.
Hartle, J. C., Navas-Acien, A., & Lawrence, R. S. (2016). The consumption of canned food and beverages and urinary Bisphenol A concentrations in NHANES 2003–2008. *Environmental Research, 150*, 375-382.

212 Liu, J., Wattar, N., Field, C. J., Dinu, I., Dewey, D., Martin, J. W., & APrON study team. (2018). Exposure and dietary sources of bisphenol A (BPA) and BPA-alternatives among mothers in the APrON cohort study. *Environment International, 119*, 319–326.

213 Bae B, Jeong JH, Lee SJ. The quantification and characterization of endocrine disruptor bisphenol-A leaching from epoxy resin. *Water Sci Technol. 2002;46*(11-12):381–7.

214 Chen, L. W., Wu, Y., Neelakantan, N., Chong, M. F. F., Pan, A., & van Dam, R. M. (2016). Maternal caffeine intake during pregnancy and risk of pregnancy loss: a categorical and dose-response meta-analysis of prospective studies. *Public Health Nutrition, 19*(7), 1233–1244.

215 Zhang, Z., Hu, Y., Guo, J., Yu, T., Sun, L., Xiao, X., ... & Fan, X. (2017). Fluorene-9-bisphenol is anti-oestrogenic and may cause adverse pregnancy outcomes in mice. *Nature Communications, 8*, 14585.

216 Meuwly, R., Brunner, K., Fragnière, C., Sager, F., & Dudler, V. (2005). Heat stability and migration from silicone baking moulds. *Mitteilungen aus Lebensmitteluntersuchung und Hygiene, 96*(5), 281.

217 Meng, Q., Inoue, K., Ritz, B., Olsen, J., & Liew, Z. (2018). Prenatal Exposure to Perfluoroalkyl Substances and Birth Outcomes; An Updated Analysis from the Danish National Birth Cohort. *International Journal of Environmental Research and Public Health, 15*(9), 1832.
Manzano-Salgado, C. B., Casas, M., Lopez-Espinosa, M. J., Ballester, F., Iñiguez, C., Martinez, D., ... & Sunyer, J. (2017). Prenatal exposure to perfluoroalkyl substances and birth

outcomes in a Spanish birth cohort. *Environment International, 108*, 278–284.

Woods, M. M., Lanphear, B. P., Braun, J. M., & McCandless, L. C. (2017). Gestational exposure to endocrine disrupting chemicals in relation to infant birth weight: a Bayesian analysis of the HOME Study. *Environmental Health, 16*(1), 115.

218 Ghassabian, A., Bell, E. M., Ma, W. L., Sundaram, R., Kannan, K., Louis, G. M. B., & Yeung, E. (2018). Concentrations of perfluoroalkyl substances and bisphenol A in newborn dried blood spots and the association with child behavior. *Environmental Pollution.*

219 Bondy, S. C. (2014). Prolonged exposure to low levels of aluminum leads to changes associated with brain aging and neurodegeneration. *Toxicology, 315*, 1–7.

220 Soni, M. G., White, S. M., Flamm, W. G., & Burdock, G. A. (2001). Safety evaluation of dietary aluminum. *Regulatory Toxicology and Pharmacology, 33*(1), 66–79.

221 Swan SH, Main KM, Liu F, Stewart SL, Kruse RL, Calafat AM, Mao CS, Redmon JB, Ternand CL, Sullivan S, Teague JL; Study for Future Families Research Team. Decrease in anogenital distance among male infants with prenatal phthalateexposure. *Environ Health Perspect. 2005 Aug;113*(8), 1056–61. Erratum in: *Environ Health Perspect. 2005 Sep;113*(9), A583. ("Swan 2005"). Swan SH. Environmental phthalate exposure in relation to reproductive outcomes and other health endpoints in humans. *Environ Res. 2008 Oct; 108*(2), 177–84.

222 Foster, P. M. (2006). Disruption of reproductive development in male rat offspring following in utero exposure to phthalate esters. *International Journal of Andrology, 29*(1), 140–147.

Howdeshell KL, Wilson VS, Furr J, Lambright CR, Rider CV, Blystone CR, Hotchkiss AK, Gray LE Jr. A mixture of five phthalate esters inhibits fetal testicular testosterone production in the sprague-dawley rat in a cumulative, dose-additive manner. *Toxicol Sci. 2008 Sep;105*(1), 153–65.

Akingbemi BT, Ge R, Klinefelter GR, Zirkin BR, Hardy MP. Phthalate-induced Leydig cell hyperplasia is associated with multiple endocrine disturbances. *Proc Natl Acad Sci U S A. 2004 Jan 20;101*(3), 775–80

Borch J, Ladefoged O, Hass U, Vinggaard AM. Steroidogenesis in fetal male rats is reduced by DEHP and DINP, but endocrine effects of DEHP are not modulated by DEHA in fetal, prepubertal and adult male rats. *Reprod Toxicol. 2004 Jan-Feb;18*(1), 53–61;

Klinefelter GR, Laskey JW, Winnik WM, Suarez JD, Roberts NL, Strader LF, Riffle BW, Veeramachaneni DN. Novel molecular targets associated with testicular dysgenesis induced by gestational exposure to diethylhexyl phthalate in the rat: a role for estradiol. *Reproduction. 2012 Dec; 144*(6), 747–61

223 Latini G, et al. In utero exposure to di-(2-ethylhexyl)phthalate and duration of human pregnancy. *Environmental Health Perspectives. 2003;111*, 1783–1785.

Meeker JD, Hu H, Cantonwine DE, Lamadrid-Figueroa H, Calafat AM, Ettinger AS, Hernandez-Avila M, Loch-Caruso R, Téllez-Rojo MM. Urinary phthalate metabolites in relation to preterm birth in Mexico city. *Environ. Health Perspect. 2009;117*(10), 1587–1592.

Whyatt RM, Adibi JJ, Calafat AM, Camann DE, Rauh V, Bhat HK, Perera FP, Andrews H, Just AC, Hoepner L, Tang D, Hauser R. Prenatal di(2-ethylhexyl) phthalate exposure and length of gestation among an inner-city cohort. *Pediatrics. 2009;124*(6), e1213–e1220.

Meeker JD, Hu H, Cantonwine DE, Lamadrid-Figueroa H, Calafat AM, Ettinger AS, Hernandez-Avila M, Loch-Caruso R, Téllez-Rojo MM. Urinary phthalate metabolites in relation to preterm birth in Mexico city. *Environ. Health Perspect. 2009;117*(10), 1587–1592.

224 Latini G, Del Vecchio A, Massaro M, Verrotti A, De Felice C. In utero exposure to phthalates and fetal development. *Curr Med Chem. 2006;13*, 2527–2534.

Ferguson, K. K., Chen, Y. H., VanderWeele, T. J., McElrath, T. F., Meeker, J. D., & Mukherjee, B. (2016). Mediation of the relationship between maternal phthalate exposure and preterm birth by oxidative stress with repeated measurements across pregnancy. *Environmental Health Perspectives, 125*(3), 488–494.

225 Meeker JD, Hu H, Cantonwine DE, Lamadrid-Figueroa H, Calafat AM, Ettinger AS, Hernandez-Avila M, Loch-Caruso R, Téllez-Rojo MM. Urinary phthalate metabolites in relation to preterm birth in Mexico city. *Environ. Health Perspect. 2009;117*(10), 1587–1592.

226 Whyatt RM, Liu X, Rauh VA, Calafat AM, Just AC, Hoepner L, Diaz D, Quinn J, Adibi J, Perera FP, Factor-Litvak P. Maternal prenatal urinary phthalate metabolite concentrations and child mental, psychomotor, and behavioral development at 3 years of age. *Environ Health Perspect 2012;120, 290* ("Whyatt 2012").

227 Yolton K, Xu Y, Strauss D, Altaye M, Calafat AM, Khoury J. Prenatal exposure to bisphenol A and phthalates and infant neurobehavior. *Neurotoxicol Teratol 2011;33*, 558–66; Engel SM, Zhu C, Berkowitz GS, Calafat AM, Silva MJ, Miodovnik A, Wolff MS. Prenatal phthalate exposure and performance on the Neonatal Behavioral Assessment Scale in a multiethnic birth cohort. *Neurotoxicology 2009;30*, 522–8; Kim Y, Ha EH, Kim EJ, Park H, Ha M, Kim JH, Hong YC, Chang N, Kim BN. Prenatal exposure to phthalates and infant development at 6 months: prospective Mothers and Children's Environmental Health (MOCEH) study. *Environ Health Perspect 2011;119*, 1495–500; Engel SM, Miodovnik A, Canfield RL, Zhu C, Silva MJ, Calafat AM, Wolff MS. Prenatal phthalate exposure is associated with childhood behavior and executive functioning. *Environ Health Perspect 2010;118*, 565–71; Swan SH, Liu F, Hines M, Kruse RL, Wang C, Redmon JB, Sparks A, Weiss B. Prenatal phthalate exposure and reduced masculine play in boys. *Int J Androl 2010;33*, 259–69; Miodovnik A, Engel SM, Zhu C, Ye X, Soorya LV, Silva MJ, Calafat AM, Wolff MS. Endocrine disruptors and childhood social impairment. *Neurotoxicology 2011;32*, 261–7; Whyatt 2012.

228 Philippat, C., Nakiwala, D., Calafat, A. M., Botton, J., De Agostini, M., Heude, B., ... & EDEN Mother–Child Study Group. (2017). Prenatal exposure to nonpersistent endocrine disruptors and behavior in boys at 3 and 5 years. *Environmental Health Perspectives, 125*(9). Whyatt, R. M., Liu, X., Rauh, V. A., Calafat, A. M., Just, A. C., Hoepner, L., ... & Factor-Litvak, P. (2011). Maternal prenatal urinary phthalate metabolite concentrations and child mental, psychomotor, and behavioral development at 3 years of age. *Environmental Health Perspectives, 120*(2), 290–295. Factor-Litvak, P., Insel, B., Calafat, A. M., Liu, X., Perera, F., Rauh, V. A., & Whyatt, R. M. (2014). Persistent associations

between maternal prenatal exposure to phthalates on child IQ at age 7 years. *PloS one, 9*(12), e114003.

Braun, J. M. (2017). Early-life exposure to EDCs: role in childhood obesity and neurodevelopment. *Nature Reviews Endocrinology, 13*(3), 161.

229 Kobrosly, R. W., Evans, S., Miodovnik, A., Barrett, E. S., Thurston, S. W., Calafat, A. M., & Swan, S. H. (2014). Prenatal phthalate exposures and neurobehavioral development scores in boys and girls at 6–10 years of age. *Environmental Health Perspectives, 122*(5), 521.

230 Olesen, T. S., Bleses, D., Andersen, H. R., Grandjean, P., Frederiksen, H., Trecca, F., … & Andersson, A. M. (2018). Prenatal phthalate exposure and language development in toddlers from the Odense Child Cohort. *Neurotoxicology and Teratology, 65*, 34–41.

Bornehag, C. G., Lindh, C., Reichenberg, A., Wikström, S., Hallerback, M. U., Evans, S. F., … & Swan, S. H. (2018). Association of Prenatal Phthalate Exposure With Language Development in Early Childhood. *JAMA Pediatrics.*

231 Zota, A. R., Calafat, A. M., & Woodruff, T. J. (2014). Temporal trends in phthalate exposures: findings from the National Health and Nutrition Examination Survey, 2001–2010. *Environmental Health Perspectives, 122*(3), 235–241.

Göen, T., Dobler, L., Koschorreck, J., Müller, J., Wiesmüller, G. A., Drexler, H., & Kolossa-Gehring, M. (2011). Trends of the internal phthalate exposure of young adults in Germany— follow-up of a retrospective human biomonitoring study. *International Journal of Hygiene and Environmental Health, 215*(1), 36–45.

232 Koch, H. M., Lorber, M., Christensen, K. L., Pälmke, C., Koslitz, S., & Brüning, T. (2013). Identifying sources of phthalate exposure with human biomonitoring: results of a 48 h fasting study with urine collection and personal activity patterns. *International Journal of Hygiene and Environmental Health, 216*(6), 672–681.

233 Koch, H. M., Lorber, M., Christensen, K. L., Pälmke, C., Koslitz, S., & Brüning, T. (2013). Identifying sources of phthalate exposure with human biomonitoring: results of a 48 h fasting study with urine collection and personal activity patterns.

International Journal of Hygiene and Environmental Health,
216(6), 672–681.

234 Zota, A. R., Phillips, C. A., & Mitro, S. D. (2016). Recent fast food
consumption and bisphenol A and phthalates exposures among
the US population in NHANES, 2003–2010. *Environmental
Health Perspectives, 124*(10), 1521.

235 http://kleanupkraft.org/PhthalatesLabReport.pdf
Rabin, R. C. (2017). The Chemicals in Your Mac and Cheese.
New York Times.

236 Rabin, R. C. (2017). The Chemicals in Your Mac and Cheese.
New York Times.

237 Rudel RA, Gray JM, Engel CL, Rawsthorne TW, Dodson RE,
Ackerman JM, Rizzo J, Nudelman JL, Brody JG. Food packaging
and bisphenol A and bis(2-ethyhexyl) phthalate exposure:
findings from a dietary intervention. *Environ Health Perspect.*
2011 Jul;119(7), 914–20.

238 Cao, X. L., Zhao, W., Churchill, R., & Hilts, C. (2014).
Occurrence of di-(2-ethylhexyl) adipate and phthalate plasticizers
in samples of meat, fish, and cheese and their packaging films.
Journal of Food Protection, 77(4), 610–620

239 Van Holderbeke, M., Geerts, L., Vanermen, G., Servaes, K.,
Sioen, I., De Henauw, S., & Fierens, T. (2014). Determination of
contamination pathways of phthalates in food products sold on
the Belgian market. *Environmental Research, 134*, 345–352.

240 Lin, J., Chen, W., Zhu, H., & Wang, C. (2015). Determination
of free and total phthalates in commercial whole milk products
in different packaging materials by gas chromatography-mass
spectrometry. *Journal of Dairy Science, 98*(12), 8278–8284.

241 Montuori P, Jover E, Morgantini M, Bayona JM, Triassi M.
Assessing human exposure to phthalic acid and phthalate esters
from mineral water stored in polyethylene terephthalate and glass
bottles. *Food Add Contamin. 2008;25*(4), 511–518;
Sax L. Polyethylene terephthalate may yield endocrine disruptors.
Environ Health Perspect. 2010;118, 445–8;
Farhoodi M, Emam-Djomeh Z, Ehsani MR, Oromiehie A.
Effect of environmental conditions on the migration of di(2-
ethylhexyl)phthalate from PET bottles into yogurt drinks:
influence of time, temperature, and food simulant. *Arabian J Sci
Eng. 2008;33*(2), 279–287.

242   Wittassek M, Koch HM, Angerer J, Bruning T. Assessing
      exposure to phthalates – the human biomonitoring approach.
      Mol Nutr Food Res. 2011;55, 7–31

243   Koniecki D, Wang R, Moody RP, Zhu J. Phthalates in cosmetic
      and personal care products: concentrations and possible dermal
      exposure. *Environ Res. 2011*
      Apr;111(3), 329–36. ("Koniecki 2011").
      Janjua NR, Mortensen GK, Andersson AM, Kongshoj B,
      Skakkebaek NE, Wulf HC.Systemic uptake of diethyl phthalate,
      dibutyl phthalate, and butyl paraben following whole-body
      topical application and reproductive and thyroid hormone levels
      in humans. *Environ Sci Technol. 2007 Aug 1;41*(15):5564–70.

244   Jiang, Y., Zhao, H., Xia, W., Li, Y., Liu, H., Hao, K., ... & Peng,
      Y. (2019). Prenatal exposure to benzophenones, parabens
      and triclosan and neurocognitive development at 2 years.
      Environment International, 126, 413–421.
      Kawaguchi, M., Morohoshi, K., Imai, H., Morita, M., Kato, N., &
      Himi, T. (2010). Maternal exposure to isobutyl-paraben impairs
      social recognition in adult female rats. *Experimental Animals,
      59*(5), 631–635.
      Ali, E. H., & Elgoly, A. H. M. (2013). Combined prenatal and
      postnatal butyl paraben exposure produces autism-like symptoms
      in offspring: comparison with valproic acid autistic model.
      Pharmacology Biochemistry and Behavior, 111, 102–110.

245   Wang, X., Ouyang, F., Feng, L., Wang, X., Liu, Z., & Zhang, J.
      (2017). Maternal urinary triclosan concentration in relation to
      maternal and neonatal thyroid hormone levels: a prospective
      study. *Environmental Health Perspectives, 125*(6), 067017.

246   Ghazipura, M., McGowan, R., Arslan, A., & Hossain, T. (2017).
      Exposure to benzophenone-3 and reproductive toxicity: a
      systematic review of human and animal studies. *Reproductive
      Toxicology, 73*, 175–183.
      Environmental Working Group (2018). *The Trouble with
      Ingredients in Sunscreens*. https://www.ewg.org/sunscreen/
      report/the-trouble-with-sunscreen-chemicals/

247   Chien, A. L., Qi, J., Rainer, B., Sachs, D. L., & Helfrich, Y. R.
      (2016). Treatment of acne in pregnancy. *J Am Board Fam Med,
      29*(2), 254–262.

Chapter 11. The Natural Nursery

248 Huang, H. B., Chen, H. Y., Su, P. H., Huang, P. C., Sun, C. W., Wang, C. J., ... & Wang, S. L. (2015). Fetal and childhood exposure to phthalate diesters and cognitive function in children up to 12 years of age: Taiwanese maternal and infant cohort study. *PloS One, 10*(6), e0131910.
Ku, H. Y., Su, P. H., Wen, H. J., Sun, H. L., Wang, C. J., Chen, H. Y., ... & TMICS Group. (2015). Prenatal and postnatal exposure to phthalate esters and asthma: a 9-year follow-up study of a taiwanese birth cohort. *PloS One, 10*(4), e0123309.
Bertelsen, R. J., Carlsen, K. C. L., Calafat, A. M., Hoppin, J. A., Håland, G., Mowinckel, P., ... & Løvik, M. (2012). Urinary biomarkers for phthalates associated with asthma in Norwegian children. *Environmental Health Perspectives, 121*(2), 251–256.
249 Philippat, C., Bennett, D. H., Krakowiak, P., Rose, M., Hwang, H. M., & Hertz-Picciotto, I. (2015). Phthalate concentrations in house dust in relation to autism spectrum disorder and developmental delay in the CHildhood Autism Risks from Genetics and the Environment (CHARGE) study. *Environmental Health, 14*(1), 56.
250 *U.S. Consumer Product Safety Commission (2015)*. https://www.cpsc.gov/Recalls/2015/babys-dream-recalls-cribs-and-furniture
251 Ecology Center (2016). *Children's Car Seat Study*. https://www.ecocenter.org/healthy-stuff/pages/childrens-car-seat-2016-executive-summary
252 Nelson, G. L., Sorathia, U., Jayakodi, C. & Myers, D. Fire-Retardant Characteristics of Water-Blown Molded Flexible Polyurethane Foam Materials. *Journal of Fire Sciences 18*, 430–455 (2000).
253 The Ecology Center. (2016). *Children's Car Seat Study 2016*. https://www.ecocenter.org/healthy-stuff/reports/childrens-car-seats-2016
254 Costa, L. G., & Giordano, G. (2007). Developmental neurotoxicity of polybrominated diphenyl ether (PBDE) flame retardants. *Neurotoxicology, 28*(6), 1047–1067.
Noyes, P. D., Haggard, D. E., Gonnerman, G. D., & Tanguay, R. L. (2015). Advanced morphological—behavioral test platform reveals neurodevelopmental defects in embryonic zebrafish exposed to comprehensive suite of halogenated and

organophosphate flame retardants. *Toxicological Sciences, 145*(1), 177–195.

255 Eskenazi, B., Chevrier, J., Rauch, S. A., Kogut, K., Harley, K. G., Johnson, C., ... & Bradman, A. (2012). In utero and childhood polybrominated diphenyl ether (PBDE) exposures and neurodevelopment in the CHAMACOS study. *Environmental Health Perspectives, 121*(2), 257–262.

Chen, A., Yolton, K., Rauch, S. A., Webster, G. M., Hornung, R., Sjödin, A., ... & Lanphear, B. P. (2014). Prenatal polybrominated diphenyl ether exposures and neurodevelopment in US children through 5 years of age: the HOME study. *Environmental Health Perspectives, 122*(8), 856–862.

256 Chemical Watch (2018). *Flame retardant ban signed into California law.* https://chemicalwatch.com/70521/flame-retardant-ban-signed-into-california-law

257 U.S. Environmental Protection Agency. (2016). *EPA Fact Sheet: Reducing Your Child's Exposure to Flame Retardant Chemicals.* https://www.epa.gov/sites/production/files/2016-05/documents/flame_retardant_fact_sheet_3-22-16.pdf

258 U.S. Environmental Protection Agency. (2016). *EPA Fact Sheet: Reducing Your Child's Exposure to Flame Retardant Chemicals.* https://www.epa.gov/sites/production/files/2016-05/documents/flame_retardant_fact_sheet_3-22-16.pdf

259 Gibson, E. A., Stapleton, H. M., Calero, L., Holmes, D., Burke, K., Martinez, R., ... & Herbstman, J. B. (2018). Flame retardant exposure assessment: findings from a behavioral intervention study. *Journal of Exposure Science & Environmental Epidemiology, 1.*

260 Raz, R., Roberts, A. L., Lyall, K., Hart, J. E., Just, A. C., Laden, F., & Weisskopf, M. G. (2014). Autism spectrum disorder and particulate matter air pollution before, during, and after pregnancy: a nested case–control analysis within the Nurses' Health Study II cohort. *Environmental Health Perspectives, 123*(3), 264–270.

Sun, X., Luo, X., Zhao, C., Zhang, B., Tao, J., Yang, Z., ... & Liu, T. (2016). The associations between birth weight and exposure to fine particulate matter (PM2. 5) and its chemical constituents during pregnancy: A meta-analysis. *Environmental Pollution, 211*, 38–47.

Suades-González, E., Gascon, M., Guxens, M., & Sunyer, J. (2015). Air pollution and neuropsychological development: a review of the latest evidence. *Endocrinology, 156*(10), 3473–3482.

Kioumourtzoglou, M. A., Raz, R., Wilson, A., Fluss, R., Nirel, R., Broday, D. M., ... & Weisskopf, M. G. (2019). Traffic-related Air Pollution and Pregnancy Loss. *Epidemiology, 30*(1), 4–10.

Ha, S., Sundaram, R., Louis, G. M. B., Nobles, C., Seeni, I., Sherman, S., & Mendola, P. (2018). Ambient air pollution and the risk of pregnancy loss: a prospective cohort study. *Fertility and Sterility, 109*(1), 148–153.

Rich, D. Q., Liu, K., Zhang, J., Thurston, S. W., Stevens, T. P., Pan, Y., ... & Duan, X. *Supplemental Material Differences in Birth Weight Associated with the 2008 Beijing Olympic Air Pollution Reduction: Results from a Natural Experiment.*

261 Anderson, J. O., Thundiyil, J. G., & Stolbach, A. (2012). Clearing the air: a review of the effects of particulate matter air pollution on human health. *Journal of Medical Toxicology, 8*(2), 166–175.

262 Allen, R. W., Carlsten, C., Karlen, B., Leckie, S., Eeden, S. V., Vedal, S., ... & Brauer, M. (2011). An air filter intervention study of endothelial function among healthy adults in a woodsmoke-impacted community. *American Journal of Respiratory and Critical Care Medicine, 183*(9), 1222–1230.

Chuang, H. C., Ho, K. F., Lin, L. Y., Chang, T. Y., Hong, G. B., Ma, C. M., ... & Chuang, K. J. (2017). Long-term indoor air conditioner filtration and cardiovascular health: a randomized crossover intervention study. *Environment International, 106*, 91–96.

263 Debra Lynn Dadd (2015). *Nonorganic Cotton Vs. Polyester Clothing.* https://www.debralynndadd.com/q-a/nonorganic-cotton-vs-polyester-clothing/

264 Plungis, Jeff (2010). Homeowners Exposed to Chemicals in Floors, Group Says. *Bloomberg.* October 19, 2010.

Chapter 12: Clean and Green Baby Care

265 Environment Agency (UK). (2005) *Life Cycle Assessment of Disposable and Reusable Nappies in the UK.* http://www.ahpma.co.uk/docs/LCA.pdf

266 Kosemund, K., Schlatter, H., Ochsenhirt, J. L., Krause, E. L., Marsman, D. S., & Erasala, G. N. (2009). Safety evaluation

of superabsorbent baby diapers. *Regulatory Toxicology and Pharmacology, 53*(2), 81–89.

Dey, S., Helmes, C. T., White, J. C., & Zhou, S. (2014). Safety of disposable diaper materials: Extensive evaluations validate use. *Clinical Pediatrics, 53*(9_suppl), 17S–19S.

267 Moyer, M. W. (2013). Are Jessica Alba's Trendy Diapers Really the Poop? *Slate*, June 20, 2013.

268 Ishii, S., Katagiri, R., Minobe, Y., Kuribara, I., Wada, T., Wada, M., & Imai, S. (2015). Investigation of the amount of transdermal exposure of newborn babies to phthalates in paper diapers and certification of the safety of paper diapers. *Regulatory Toxicology and Pharmacology, 73*(1), 85–92.

Park, C. J., Barakat, R., Ulanov, A., Li, Z., Lin, P. C., Chiu, K., … & Ko, C. J. (2019). Sanitary pads and diapers contain higher phthalate contents than those in common commercial plastic products. *Reproductive Toxicology, 84*, 114–121.

269 Sathyanarayana, S., Karr, C. J., Lozano, P., Brown, E., Calafat, A. M., Liu, F., & Swan, S. H. (2008). Baby care products: possible sources of infant phthalate exposure. *Pediatrics, 121*(2), e260–e268.

270 Test Certificate R18832/2, August 2018. Consumer Lab Denmark. Provided by Naturesutten CEO Anne-Dorthe Schroeder, May 15, 2019.

271 Victora, C. G., Behague, D. P., Barros, F. C., Olinto, M. T. A., & Weiderpass, E. (1997). Pacifier use and short breastfeeding duration: cause, consequence, or coincidence? *Pediatrics, 99*(3), 445–453.

Howard, C. R., Howard, F. M., Lanphear, B., deBlieck, E. A., Eberly, S., & Lawrence, R. A. (1999). The effects of early pacifier use on breastfeeding duration. *Pediatrics, 103*(3), E33.

Howard, C. R., Howard, F. M., Lanphear, B., Eberly, S., deBlieck, E. A., Oakes, D., & Lawrence, R. A. (2003). Randomized clinical trial of pacifier use and bottle-feeding or cupfeeding and their effect on breastfeeding. *Pediatrics-English Edition, 111*(3), 511–518.

272 Alm, B., Wennergren, G., Möllborg, P., & Lagercrantz, H. (2016). Breastfeeding and dummy use have a protective effect on sudden infant death syndrome. *Acta Paediatrica, 105*(1), 31–38.

Schubiger, G., Schwarz, U., Tönz, O., & Neonatal Study Group. (1997). UNICEF/WHO baby-friendly hospital initiative: does the use of bottles and pacifiers in the neonatal nursery prevent successful breastfeeding? *European Journal of Pediatrics, 156*(11), 874–877.

Kramer, M. S., Barr, R. G., Dagenais, S., Yang, H., Jones, P., Ciofani, L., & Jané, F. (2001). Pacifier use, early weaning, and cry/fuss behavior: a randomized controlled trial. *JAMA, 286*(3), 322–326.

Collins, C. T., Ryan, P., Crowther, C. A., McPhee, A. J., Paterson, S., & Hiller, J. E. (2004). Effect of bottles, cups, and dummies on breast feeding in preterm infants: a randomised controlled trial. *BMJ, 329*(7459), 193–198.

Jenik, A. G., Vain, N. E., Gorestein, A. N., Jacobi, N. E., & Pacifier and Breastfeeding Trial Group. (2009). Does the recommendation to use a pacifier influence the prevalence of breastfeeding?. *The Journal of Pediatrics, 155*(3), 350–354.

273 Kair, L. R., Kenron, D., Etheredge, K., Jaffe, A. C., & Phillipi, C. A. (2013). Pacifier restriction and exclusive breastfeeding. *Pediatrics, 131*(4), e1101–e1107.

274 Sipsma, H. L., Kornfeind, K., & Kair, L. R. (2017). Pacifiers and Exclusive Breastfeeding: Does Risk for Postpartum Depression Modify the Association?. *Journal of Human Lactation, 33*(4), 692–700.

275 Bass, J. L., Gartley, T., & Kleinman, R. (2016). Unintended consequences of current breastfeeding initiatives. *JAMA Pediatrics, 170*(10), 923-924.

276 Hauck, F. R., Omojokun, O. O., & Siadaty, M. S. (2005). Do pacifiers reduce the risk of sudden infant death syndrome? A meta-analysis. *Pediatrics, 116*(5), 1211.

Mitchell, E. A., Blair, P. S., & L'Hoir, M. P. (2006). Should pacifiers be recommended to prevent sudden infant death syndrome? *Pediatrics, 117*(5), 1755–1758.

Moon, R. Y., Tanabe, K. O., Yang, D. C., Young, H. A., & Hauck, F. R. (2012). Pacifier use and SIDS: evidence for a consistently reduced risk. *Maternal and Child Health Journal, 16*(3), 609–614.

Alm, B., Wennergren, G., Möllborg, P., & Lagercrantz, H. (2016). Breastfeeding and dummy use have a protective effect on sudden infant death syndrome. *Acta Paediatrica, 105*(1), 31–38

277 Task Force on Sudden Infant Death Syndrome. (2016). SIDS and other sleep-related infant deaths: Updated 2016 recommendations

for a safe infant sleeping environment. *Pediatrics, 138*(5), e20162938.

278 Bass, J. L., Gartley, T., & Kleinman, R. (2016). Unintended consequences of current breastfeeding initiatives. *JAMA Pediatrics, 170*(10), 923–924

279 Spiesel, S (2006). Your Health This Month. *Slate*. January 2, 2006.

280 Mertens, B., Van Hoeck, E., Blaude, M. N., Simon, C., Onghena, M., Vandermarken, T., ... & Scippo, M. L. (2016). Evaluation of the potential health risks of substances migrating from polycarbonate replacement baby bottles. *Food and Chemical Toxicology, 97*, 108–119.
Yang, C. Z., Yaniger, S. I., Jordan, V. C., Klein, D. J., & Bittner, G. D. (2011). Most plastic products release estrogenic chemicals: a potential health problem that can be solved. *Environmental Health Perspectives, 119*(7), 989–996.

Chapter 13: Breastfeeding and the Formula Wars

281 Jung, C. (2015). Overselling Breast-Feeding. *The New York Times*.
282 Kramer, M. S., Chalmers, B., Hodnett, E. D., Sevkovskaya, Z., Dzikovich, I., Shapiro, S., ... & Shishko, G. (2001). Promotion of Breastfeeding Intervention Trial (PROBIT): a randomized trial in the Republic of Belarus. *JAMA, 285*(4), 413–420.
Kramer, M. S., Aboud, F., Mironova, E., Vanilovich, I., Platt, R. W., Matush, L., ... & Collet, J. P. (2008). Breastfeeding and child cognitive development: new evidence from a large randomized trial. *Archives of General Psychiatry, 65*(5), 578–584.

283 Evenhouse, E., & Reilly, S. (2005). Improved estimates of the benefits of breastfeeding using sibling comparisons to reduce selection bias. *Health Services Research, 40*(6p1), 1781–1802.

284 Anderson, J. W., Johnstone, B. M., & Remley, D. T. (1999). Breast-feeding and cognitive development: a meta-analysis. *The American Journal of Clinical Nutrition, 70*(4), 525–535.

285 Duijts, L., Jaddoe, V. W., Hofman, A., & Moll, H. A. (2010). Prolonged and exclusive breastfeeding reduces the risk of infectious diseases in infancy. *Pediatrics, peds-2008*.
Kramer, M. S., Chalmers, B., Hodnett, E. D., Sevkovskaya, Z., Dzikovich, I., Shapiro, S., ... & Shishko, G. (2001). Promotion of

Breastfeeding Intervention Trial (PROBIT): a randomized trial in the Republic of Belarus. *JAMA, 285*(4), 413–420.

Wilson, J. L., & Wilson, B. H. (2018). Is the" breast is best" mantra an oversimplification?. *The Journal of Family Practice, 67*(6), E1–E9.

286   Spiesel, S. Z. (2006). Tales From the Nursery:The health benefits of breast-feeding may not be what you think. *Slate*, March 27, 2006.

287   Van de Perre, P. (2003). Transfer of antibody via mother's milk. *Vaccine, 21*(24), 3374–3376.

288   Simister, N. E. (2003). Placental transport of immunoglobulin G. *Vaccine, 21*(24), 3365–3369.

289   Spiesel, S. Z. (2006). Tales From the Nursery:The health benefits of breast-feeding may not be what you think. *Slate*, March 27, 2006

290   Raissian, K. M., & Su, J. H. (2018). The best of intentions: Prenatal breastfeeding intentions and infant health. *SSM-Population Health, 5*, 86–100.

291   Tuteur, A. (2018). *Mothers who intended to breastfeed had infants with better health outcomes even if they DIDN'T breastfeed!* http://www.skepticalob.com/2018/09/mothers-who-intended-to-breastfeed-had-infants-with-better-health-outcomes-even-if-they-didnt-breastfeed.html

292   Van Odijk, J., Kull, I., Borres, M. P., Brandtzaeg, P., Edberg, U., Hanson, L. Å., ... & Sundell, J. (2003). Breastfeeding and allergic disease: a multidisciplinary review of the literature (1966–2001) on the mode of early feeding in infancy and its impact on later atopic manifestations. *Allergy, 58*(9), 833–843.

293   Lodge, C. J., Tan, D. J., Lau, M. X. Z., Dai, X., Tham, R., Lowe, A. J., ... & Dharmage, S. C. (2015). Breastfeeding and asthma and allergies: a systematic review and meta-analysis. *Acta Paediatrica, 104*, 38–53.

Van Odijk, J., Kull, I., Borres, M. P., Brandtzaeg, P., Edberg, U., Hanson, L. Å., ... & Sundell, J. (2003). Breastfeeding and allergic disease: a multidisciplinary review of the literature (1966–2001) on the mode of early feeding in infancy and its impact on later atopic manifestations. *Allergy, 58*(9), 833–843.

294   Bezirtzoglou, E., Tsiotsias, A., & Welling, G. W. (2011). Microbiota profile in feces of breast-and formula-fed newborns

by using fluorescence in situ hybridization (FISH). *Anaerobe, 17*(6), 478–482.

Mackie, R. I., Sghir, A., & Gaskins, H. R. (1999). Developmental microbial ecology of the neonatal gastrointestinal tract. *The American Journal of Clinical Nutrition, 69*(5), 1035s–1045s.

295 Lodge, C. J., Tan, D. J., Lau, M. X. Z., Dai, X., Tham, R., Lowe, A. J., ... & Dharmage, S. C. (2015). Breastfeeding and asthma and allergies: a systematic review and meta-analysis. *Acta Paediatrica, 104*, 38–53.

296 Arslanoglu, S., Moro, G. E., Schmitt, J., Tandoi, L., Rizzardi, S., & Boehm, G. (2008). Early dietary intervention with a mixture of prebiotic oligosaccharides reduces the incidence of allergic manifestations and infections during the first two years of life. *The Journal of Nutrition, 138*(6), 1091–1095.

Osborn, D. A., & Sinn, J. K. (2013). Prebiotics in infants for prevention of allergy. *Cochrane Database of Systematic Reviews*, (3).

Moro, G., Arslanoglu, S., Stahl, B., Jelinek, J., Wahn, U., & Boehm, G. (2006). A mixture of prebiotic oligosaccharides reduces the incidence of atopic dermatitis during the first six months of age. *Archives of Disease in Childhood, 91*(10), 814–819.

Bruzzese, E., Volpicelli, M., Squeglia, V., Bruzzese, D., Salvini, F., Bisceglia, M., ... & Guarino, A. (2009). A formula containing galacto-and fructo-oligosaccharides prevents intestinal and extra-intestinal infections: an observational study. *Clinical Nutrition, 28*(2), 156–161.

297 Jensen, C. L., Voigt, R. G., Prager, T. C., Zou, Y. L., Fraley, J. K., Rozelle, J. C., ... & Heird, W. C. (2005). Effects of maternal docosahexaenoic acid intake on visual function and neurodevelopment in breastfed term infants. *The American Journal of Clinical Nutrition, 82*(1), 125–132.

Cunnane, S. C., Francescutti, V., Brenna, J. T., & Crawford, M. A. (2000). Breast-fed infants achieve a higher rate of brain and whole body docosahexaenoate accumulation than formula-fed infants not consuming dietary docosahexaenoate. *Lipids, 35*(1), 105–111.

298 Birch, E. E., Garfield, S., Castañeda, Y., Hughbanks-Wheaton, D., Uauy, R., & Hoffman, D. (2007). Visual acuity and cognitive outcomes at 4 years of age in a double-blind, randomized trial of long-chain polyunsaturated fatty acid-supplemented infant formula. *Early Human Development, 83*(5), 279–284.

Qawasmi, A., Landeros-Weisenberger, A., Leckman, J. F., & Bloch, M. H. (2012). Meta-analysis of long-chain polyunsaturated fatty acid supplementation of formula and infant cognition. *Pediatrics, 129*(6), 1141–1149.

299   Timby, N., Domellöf, E., Hernell, O., Lönnerdal, B., & Domellöf, M. (2014). Neurodevelopment, nutrition, and growth until 12 mo of age in infants fed a low-energy, low-protein formula supplemented with bovine milk fat globule membranes: a randomized controlled trial. *The American Journal of Clinical Nutrition, 99*(4), 860–868.

300   Hernell, O., Domellöf, M., Grip, T., Lönnerdal, B., & Timby, N. (2019). Physiological Effects of Feeding Infants and Young Children Formula Supplemented with Milk Fat Globule Membranes. *In Human Milk: Composition, Clinical Benefits and Future Opportunities* (Vol. 90, pp. 35–42). Karger Publishers.

301   Centers for Disease Control. (2019) *Nationwide Breastfeeding Data & Statistics.* https://www.cdc.gov/breastfeeding/data/facts.html

302   Jung, C. (2015). Overselling Breast-Feeding. *The New York Times.*

303   Bass, J. L., Gartley, T., & Kleinman, R. (2016). Unintended consequences of current breastfeeding initiatives. *JAMA pediatrics, 170*(10), 923–924.

304   Tuteur, A. (2019). *(Nearly) everything wrong with the Baby Friendly Hospital Initative explained in one paper.* https://www.skepticalob.com/2019/03/nearly-everything-wrong-with-the-baby-friendly-hospital-initative-explained-in-one-paper.html

305   Ebinger, J., Castleberry, L., & Cai, B. (2017). Is' Baby-Friendly'Actually'Mommy-Friendly?'The Baby-Friendly Initiative and Effect on Patient Satisfaction. *Obstetrics & Gynecology, 129*(5), S156.
      Preston-Roedder, E., Fagen, H., Martucci, J., & Barnhill, A. (2019) Understanding the Baby-Friendly Hospital Initiative: A Multi-Disciplinary Analysis. *International Journal of Feminist Approaches to Bioethics.*

306   Neifert, M. R. (2001). Prevention of breastfeeding tragedies. *Pediatric Clinics, 48*(2), 273–297.

307   Johns Hopkins Medicine. Breastfeeding and Delayed Milk Production. https://www.hopkinsmedicine.org/health/conditions-and-diseases/breastfeeding-and-delayed-milk-production.

308 *Shared with permission.* del Castillo-Hegyi (2015). https://
fedisbest.org/2015/04/letter-to-doctors-and-parents-about-the-
dangers-of-insufficient-exclusive-breastfeeding/

309 Seske, L. M., Merhar, S. L., & Haberman, B. E. (2015). Late-
onset hypoglycemia in term newborns with poor breastfeeding.
Hospital Pediatrics, 5(9), 501–504.

310 Flaherman, V. J., Aby, J., Burgos, A. E., Lee, K. A., Cabana, M.
D., & Newman, T. B. (2013). Effect of early limited formula on
duration and exclusivity of breastfeeding in at-risk infants: an
RCT. *Pediatrics, peds-2012.*

311 Flaherman, V. J., Cabana, M. D., McCulloch, C. E., & Paul, I. M.
Effect of Early Limited Formula on Breastfeeding Duration in the
First Year of Life. *JAMA Pediatrics,* 2019.
Flaherman, V. J., Narayan, N. R., Hartigan-O'Connor, D.,
Cabana, M. D., McCulloch, C. E., & Paul, I. M. (2018). The effect
of early limited formula on breastfeeding, readmission, and
intestinal microbiota: a randomized clinical trial. *The Journal of
Pediatrics, 196,* 84–90.

312 Flaherman, V. J., Narayan, N. R., Hartigan-O'Connor, D.,
Cabana, M. D., McCulloch, C. E., & Paul, I. M. (2018). The effect
of early limited formula on breastfeeding, readmission, and
intestinal microbiota: a randomized clinical trial. *The Journal of
Pediatrics, 196,* 84–90.

313 Tam, E. W., Haeusslein, L. A., Bonifacio, S. L., Glass, H.
C., Rogers, E. E., Jeremy, R. J., ... & Ferriero, D. M. (2012).
Hypoglycemia is associated with increased risk for brain injury
and adverse neurodevelopmental outcome in neonates at risk for
encephalopathy. *The Journal of Pediatrics, 161*(1), 88–93.

314 Tam, E. W., Haeusslein, L. A., Bonifacio, S. L., Glass, H.
C., Rogers, E. E., Jeremy, R. J., ... & Ferriero, D. M. (2012).
Hypoglycemia is associated with increased risk for brain injury
and adverse neurodevelopmental outcome in neonates at risk for
encephalopathy. *The Journal of Pediatrics, 161*(1), 88–93.

315 McKinlay, C. J., Alsweiler, J. M., Anstice, N. S., Burakevych, N.,
Chakraborty, A., Chase, J. G., ... & Paudel, N. (2017). Association
of neonatal glycemia with neurodevelopmental outcomes at 4.5
years. *JAMA Pediatrics, 171*(10), 972–983.

316 Fed is Best Foundation (2018) https://fedisbest.org/wp-content/
uploads/2018/09/2018-Edition-Feeding-Plan-for-Baby-2.pdf

317 Flaherman, V. J., Cabana, M. D., McCulloch, C. E., & Paul, I. M. Effect of Early Limited Formula on Breastfeeding Duration in the First Year of Life. *JAMA Pediatrics*, 2019; Flaherman, V. J., Narayan, N. R., Hartigan-O'Connor, D., Cabana, M. D., McCulloch, C. E., & Paul, I. M. (2018). The effect of early limited formula on breastfeeding, readmission, and intestinal microbiota: a randomized clinical trial. *The Journal of Pediatrics, 196*, 84–90.

Chapter 14. Choosing a Formula

318 Tolia, V., Lin, C. H., & Kuhns, L. R. (1992). Gastric emptying using three different formulas in infants with gastroesophageal reflux. *Journal of Pediatric Gastroenterology and Nutrition, 15*(3), 297–301.

319 Petschow, B. W., & Talbott, R. D. (1990). Growth promotion of Bifidobacterium species by whey and casein fractions from human and bovine milk. *Journal of Clinical Microbiology, 28*(2), 287–292.

320 Alexander, D. D., & Cabana, M. D. (2010). Partially hydrolyzed 100% whey protein infant formula and reduced risk of atopic dermatitis: a meta-analysis. *Journal of Pediatric Gastroenterology and Nutrition, 50*(4), 422–430.
von Berg, A., Filipiak-Pittroff, B., Krämer, U., Hoffmann, B., Link, E., Beckmann, C., ... & Wichmann, H. E. (2013). Allergies in high-risk schoolchildren after early intervention with cow's milk protein hydrolysates: 10-year results from the German Infant Nutritional Intervention (GINI) study. *Journal of Allergy and Clinical Immunology, 131*(6), 1565–1573.
Von Berg, A., Filipiak-Pittroff, B., Schulz, H., Hoffmann, U., Link, E., Sußmann, M., ... & Hoffmann, B. (2016). Allergic manifestation 15 years after early intervention with hydrolyzed formulas–the GINI Study. *Allergy, 71*(2), 210–219.
Jin, Y. Y., Cao, R. M., Chen, J., Kaku, Y., Wu, J., Cheng, Y., Shimizu, T., Takase, M., Wu, S. M., and Chen, T. X. (2011) Partially hydrolyzed cow's milk formula has a therapeutic effect on the infants with mild to moderate atopic dermatitis: a randomized, double-blind study. *Pediatr. Allergy Immunol. 22*, 688–694

Greer, F. R., Sicherer, S. H., Burks, A. W., American Academy of Pediatrics Committee on, N., American Academy of Pediatrics Section on, A., and Immunology. (2008) Effects of early nutritional interventions on the development of atopic disease in infants and children: the role of maternal dietary restriction, breastfeeding, timing of introduction of complementary foods, and hydrolyzed formulas. *Pediatrics 121*, 183–191

321 Maclean Jr, W. C., Fink, B. B., Schoeller, D. A., Wong, W., & Klein, P. D. (1983). Lactose assimilation by full-term infants: relation of [13 C] and H 2 breath tests with fecal [13 C] excretion. *Pediatric Research, 17*(8), 629.

322 Kanabar, D., Randhawa, M., & Clayton, P. (2001). Improvement of symptoms in infant colic following reduction of lactose load with lactase. *Journal of Human Nutrition and Dietetics, 14*(5), 359–363.
Ståhlberg, M. R., & Savilahti, E. (1986). Infantile colic and feeding. *Archives of Disease in Childhood, 61*(12), 1232–1233.
Miller JJ, McVeagh P, Fleet GH, et al. Effect of yeast lactase enzyme on "colic" in infants fed human milk. *J Pediatr 1990; 117* (2 Pt 1), 261–263

323 Francavilla, R., Calasso, M., Calace, L., Siragusa, S., Ndagijimana, M., Vernocchi, P., ... & Indrio, F. (2012). Effect of lactose on gut microbiota and metabolome of infants with cow's milk allergy. *Pediatric Allergy and Immunology, 23*(5), 420–427.

324 Ben, X. M., Li, J., Feng, Z. T., Shi, S. Y., Lu, Y. D., Chen, R., & Zhou, X. Y. (2008). Low level of galacto-oligosaccharide in infant formula stimulates growth of intestinal Bifidobacteria and Lactobacilli. *World Journal of Gastroenterology: WJG, 14*(42), 6564.
Matsuki, T., Tajima, S., Hara, T., Yahagi, K., Ogawa, E., & Kodama, H. (2016). Infant formula with galacto-oligosaccharides (OM55N) stimulates the growth of indigenous bifidobacteria in healthy term infants. *Beneficial Microbes, 7*(4), 453–461.
Cai, J. W., Lu, Y. D., & Ben, X. M. (2008). Effects of infant formula containing galacto-oligosaccharides on the intestinal microflora in infants. *Zhongguo dang dai er ke za zhi= Chinese Journal of Contemporary Pediatrics, 10*(5), 629–632.
Rinne, M. M., Gueimonde, M., Kalliomäki, M., Hoppu, U., Salminen, S. J., & Isolauri, E. (2005). Similar bifidogenic effects of prebiotic-supplemented partially hydrolyzed infant formula and

breastfeeding on infant gut microbiota. *FEMS Immunology & Medical Microbiology, 43*(1), 59–65.

325 Arslanoglu, S., Moro, G. E., Schmitt, J., Tandoi, L., Rizzardi, S., & Boehm, G. (2008). Early dietary intervention with a mixture of prebiotic oligosaccharides reduces the incidence of allergic manifestations and infections during the first two years of life. *The Journal of Nutrition, 138*(6), 1091–1095.
Osborn, D. A., & Sinn, J. K. (2013). Prebiotics in infants for prevention of allergy. *Cochrane Database of Systematic Reviews*, (3).
Moro, G., Arslanoglu, S., Stahl, B., Jelinek, J., Wahn, U., & Boehm, G. (2006). A mixture of prebiotic oligosaccharides reduces the incidence of atopic dermatitis during the first six months of age. *Archives of Disease in Childhood, 91*(10), 814–819.
Bruzzese, E., Volpicelli, M., Squeglia, V., Bruzzese, D., Salvini, F., Bisceglia, M., ... & Guarino, A. (2009). A formula containing galacto-and fructo-oligosaccharides prevents intestinal and extra-intestinal infections: an observational study. *Clinical Nutrition, 28*(2), 156–161.

326 Ivakhnenko, O. S., & Nyankovskyy, S. L. (2013). Effect of the specific infant formula mixture of oligosaccharides on local immunity and development of allergic and infectious disease in young children: randomized study. *Pediatria Polska, 88*(5), 398–404.

327 Cuello-Garcia, C. A., Fiocchi, A., Pawankar, R., Yepes-Nuñez, J. J., Morgano, G. P., Zhang, Y., ... & Beyer, K. (2016). World allergy organization-McMaster University guidelines for allergic disease prevention (GLAD-P): Prebiotics. *World Allergy Organization Journal, 9*(1), 10.

328 Scalabrin, D. M., Mitmesser, S. H., Welling, G. W., Harris, C. L., Marunycz, J. D., Walker, D. C., ... & Vanderhoof, J. A. (2012). New prebiotic blend of polydextrose and galacto-oligosaccharides has a bifidogenic effect in young infants. *Journal of Pediatric Gastroenterology and Nutrition, 54*(3), 343–352.

329 Timby, N., Domellöf, E., Hernell, O., Lönnerdal, B., & Domellöf, M. (2014). Neurodevelopment, nutrition, and growth until 12 mo of age in infants fed a low-energy, low-protein formula supplemented with bovine milk fat globule membranes: a randomized controlled trial. *The American Journal of Clinical Nutrition, 99*(4), 860–868.

330 Bhinder, G., Allaire, J. M., Garcia, C., Lau, J. T., Chan, J. M., Ryz, N. R., ... & Berkmann, J. C. (2017). Milk fat globule membrane supplementation in formula modulates the neonatal gut microbiome and normalizes intestinal development. *Scientific Reports, 7,* 45274

331 Ochoa, T. J., Chea-Woo, E., Baiocchi, N., Pecho, I., Campos, M., Prada, A., ... & Cleary, T. G. (2013). Randomized double-blind controlled trial of bovine lactoferrin for prevention of diarrhea in children. *The Journal of Pediatrics, 162*(2), 349–356.
Pammi, M., & Suresh, G. (2017). Enteral lactoferrin supplementation for prevention of sepsis and necrotizing enterocolitis in preterm infants. *Cochrane Database of Systematic Reviews,* (6).
Donovan, S. M. (2016). The role of lactoferrin in gastrointestinal and immune development and function: a preclinical perspective. *The Journal of Pediatrics, 173,* S16–S28.
Pammi, M., & Abrams, S. A. (2015). Oral lactoferrin for the prevention of sepsis and necrotizing enterocolitis in preterm infants. *Cochrane Database of Systematic Reviews,* (2).

332 *Docosahexaenoic Acid (DHA) Algal Oil Technical Evaluation Report (2011).* Compiled by ICF International for the USDA National Organic Program.

333 Melgar, M. J., Santaeufemia, M., & García, M. A. (2010). Organophosphorus pesticide residues in raw milk and infant formulas from Spanish northwest. *Journal of Environmental Science and Health Part B, 45*(7), 595–600.

334 Cressey, P. J., & Vannoort, R. W. (2003). Pesticide content of infant formulae and weaning foods available in New Zealand. *Food Additives & Contaminants, 20*(1), 57–64.
Gelardi, R. C., & Mountford, M. K. (1993). Infant formulas: evidence of the absence of pesticide residues. *Regulatory Toxicology and Pharmacology, 17*(2), 181–192.
Chen, X., Panuwet, P., Hunter, R. E., Riederer, A. M., Bernoudy, G. C., Barr, D. B., & Ryan, P. B. (2014). Method for the quantification of current use and persistent pesticides in cow milk, human milk and baby formula using gas chromatography tandem mass spectrometry. *Journal of Chromatography B, 970,* 121–130.

335 Pico, Y., Viana, E., Font, G., & Manes, J. (1995). Determination of organochlorine pesticide content in human milk and

infant formulas using solid phase extraction and capillary gas chromatography. *Journal of Agricultural and Food Chemistry, 43*(6), 1610–1615.

336   Chesney, R. W., Helms, R. A., Christensen, M., Budreau, A. M., Han, X., & Sturman, J. A. (1998). The role of taurine in infant nutrition. In *Taurine 3* (pp. 463–476). Springer, Boston, MA. Chapman, G. E., & Greenwood, C. E. (1988). Taurine in nutrition and brain development. *Nutrition Research, 8*(8), 955–968.

337   Rigo, J., & Senterre, J. (1977). Is taurine essential for the neonates?. *Neonatology, 32*(1-2), 73–76.

Chapter 15. Pain & Fever Relief for Babies

338   Orlowski, J. P., Hanhan, U. A., & Fiallos, M. R. (2002). Is Aspirin a Cause of Reye's Syndrome? *Drug Safety, 25*(4), 225-231. Schrör, K. (2007). Aspirin and Reye Syndrome. *Pediatric Drugs, 9*(3), 195–204.

339   Shapiro, E. (1999). Circumcision policy statement. American Academy of Pediatrics. Task Force on Circumcision. *Pediatrics, 103*(3), 686–693.

340   Schultz, S. T., Klonoff-Cohen, H. S., Wingard, D. L., Akshoomoff, N. A., Macera, C. A., & Ji, M. (2008). Acetaminophen (paracetamol) use, measles-mumps-rubella vaccination, and autistic disorder: the results of a parent survey. *Autism, 12*(3), 293–307. Schultz, S. T., & Gould, G. G. (2016). Acetaminophen use for fever in children associated with autism spectrum disorder. *Autism-Open Access, 6*(2).

341   Posadas, I., Santos, P., Blanco, A., Muñoz-Fernández, M., & Ceña, V. (2010). Acetaminophen induces apoptosis in rat cortical neurons. *PloS One, 5*(12), e15360. Ghanem, C. I., Pérez, M. J., Manautou, J. E., & Mottino, A. D. (2016). Acetaminophen from liver to brain: new insights into drug pharmacological action and toxicity. *Pharmacological Research, 109*, 119–131.

342   Viberg, H., Eriksson, P., Gordh, T., & Fredriksson, A. (2013). Paracetamol (acetaminophen) administration during neonatal brain development affects cognitive function and alters its analgesic and anxiolytic response in adult male mice. *Toxicological Sciences, 138*(1), 139–147.

343 Interview with W. Parker. 6/10/2019.
344 Bittker, S. S., & Bell, K. R. (2018). acetaminophen, antibiotics, ear infection, breastfeeding, vitamin D drops, and autism: an epidemiological study. *Neuropsychiatric Disease and Treatment, 14*, 1399.
345 Frisch, M., & Simonsen, J. (2015). Ritual circumcision and risk of autism spectrum disorder in 0-to 9-year-old boys: national cohort study in Denmark. *Journal of the Royal Society of Medicine, 108*(7), 266–279.
346 Morris, B. J., & Wiswell, T. E. (2015). 'Circumcision pain'unlikely to cause autism. *Journal of the Royal Society of Medicine; 2015, 108*(8) 297–298
347 Bauer, A. Z., & Kriebel, D. (2013). Prenatal and perinatal analgesic exposure and autism: an ecological link. *Environmental Health, 12*(1), 41.
348 Becker, K. G., & Schultz, S. T. (2010). Similarities in features of autism and asthma and a possible link to acetaminophen use. *Medical Hypotheses, 74*(1), 7–11.
Bauer, A. Z., & Kriebel, D. (2013). Prenatal and perinatal analgesic exposure and autism: an ecological link. *Environmental Health, 12*(1), 41.
349 Interview with W. Parker. 6/10/2019.
350 Parker, W., Hornik, C. D., Bilbo, S., Holzknecht, Z. E., Gentry, L., Rao, R., ... & Nevison, C. D. (2017). The role of oxidative stress, inflammation and acetaminophen exposure from birth to early childhood in the induction of autism. *Journal of International Medical Research, 45*(2), 407–438.
351 Parker, W., Hornik, C. D., Bilbo, S., Holzknecht, Z. E., Gentry, L., Rao, R., ... & Nevison, C. D. (2017). The role of oxidative stress, inflammation and acetaminophen exposure from birth to early childhood in the induction of autism. *Journal of International Medical Research, 45*(2), 407–438.
352 Dang, D., Wang, D., Zhang, C., Zhou, W., Zhou, Q., & Wu, H. (2013). Comparison of oral paracetamol versus ibuprofen in premature infants with patent ductus arteriosus: a randomized controlled trial. *PloS One, 8*(11), e77888.
Mulberg, A. E., Linz, C., Bern, E., Tucker, L., Verhave, M., & Grand, R. J. (1993). Identification of nonsteroidal antiinflammatory drug-induced gastroduodenal injury in

children with juvenile rheumatoid arthritis. *The Journal of Pediatrics, 122*(4), 647–649.

Lesko, S. M., & Mitchell, A. A. (1995). An assessment of the safety of pediatric ibuprofen: a practitioner-based randomized clinical trial. *JAMA, 273*(12), 929–933.

353 Ohlsson, A., & Shah, P. S. (2015). Paracetamol (acetaminophen) for patent ductus arteriosus in preterm or low-birth-weight infants. *Cochrane Database of Systematic Reviews*, (3).

354 McCullough, H. N. (1998). Acetaminophen and ibuprofen in the management of fever and mild to moderate pain in children. *Paediatrics & Child Health, 3*(4), 246–250.

355 Howard, C. R., Weitzman, M. L., & Howard, F. M. (1994). Acetaminophen analgesia in neonatal circumcision: the effect on pain. *Pediatrics, 93*(4), 641–646.

356 Brady-Fryer, B., Wiebe, N., & Lander, J. A. (2004). Pain relief for neonatal circumcision. *Cochrane Database of Systematic Reviews*, (3).

357 Sullivan, J. E., & Farrar, H. C. (2011). Fever and antipyretic use in children. *Pediatrics, 127*(3), 580–587.

358 Sullivan, J. E., & Farrar, H. C. (2011). Fever and antipyretic use in children. *Pediatrics, 127*(3), 580–587.

359 Smith, J. (2014). *My Child Has a Fever. Should We Go to the ER? Cook Children's Checkup Newsroom*. https://www.checkupnewsroom.com/my-child-has-a-fever/

360 Cannell, F. J. J. (2014). Letter to the Editor Paracetamol, oxidative stress, vitamin D and autism spectrum disorders. *International Journal of Epidemiology, 1*, 2.

W. Parker. Interview 6/10/2019. Acetaminophen more likely to contribute to autism when given to children who are already experiencing oxidative stress.

Chapter 16. Infant Vaccines

361 HogenEsch, H. (2013). Mechanism of immunopotentiation and safety of aluminum adjuvants. *Frontiers in Immunology, 3*, 406.

362 Tomljenovic, L., & Shaw, C. A. (2011). Do aluminum vaccine adjuvants contribute to the rising prevalence of autism? *Journal of Inorganic Biochemistry, 105*(11), 1489–1499.

363 Nevison, C. D. (2014). A comparison of temporal trends in United States autism prevalence to trends in suspected environmental factors. *Environmental Health, 13*(1), 73. Tomljenovic, L., & Shaw, C. A. (2011). Do aluminum vaccine adjuvants contribute to the rising prevalence of autism? *Journal of Inorganic Biochemistry, 105*(11), 1489–1499.

364 https://www.who.int/vaccine_safety/committee/topics/adjuvants/Jun_2012/en/

365 Bishop, N. J., Morley, R., Day, J. P., & Lucas, A. (1997). Aluminum neurotoxicity in preterm infants receiving intravenous-feeding solutions. *New England Journal of Medicine, 336*(22), 1557–1562. Erasmus, R. T., Kusnir, J., Stevenson, W. C., Lobo, P., Herman, M. M., Wills, M. R., & Savory, J. (1995). Hyperaluminemia associated with liver transplantation and acute renal failure. *Clinical Transplantation, 9*(4), 307–311. Bondy, S. C. (2010). The neurotoxicity of environmental aluminum is still an issue. *Neurotoxicology, 31*(5), 575–581. Erasmus, R. T., Savory, J., Wills, M. R., & Herman, M. M. (1993). Aluminum neurotoxicity in experimental animals. *Therapeutic Drug Monitoring, 15*(6), 588–592. Marquis, J. K. (1982). Aluminum neurotoxicity: an experimental perspective. *Bulletin of Environmental Contamination and Toxicology, 29*(1), 43–49. Hänninen, H., Matikainen, E., Kovala, T., Valkonen, S., & Riihimäki, V. (1994). Internal load of aluminum and the central nervous system function of aluminum welders. *Scandinavian Journal of Work, Environment & Health*, 279–285. Arieff, A. I. (1985). Aluminum and the pathogenesis of dialysis encephalopathy. *American Journal of Kidney Diseases, 6*(5), 317–321

366 Arieff, A. I. (1985). Aluminum and the pathogenesis of dialysis encephalopathy. *American Journal of Kidney Diseases, 6*(5), 317–321.

367 Quinby, W. (2018), *Aluminum toxicity in chronic kidney disease, UpToDate.* https://www.uptodate.com/contents/aluminum-toxicity-in-chronic-kidney-disease

368 Inbar, R., Weiss, R., Tomljenovic, L., Arango, M. T., Deri, Y., Shaw, C. A., … & Shoenfeld, Y. (2016). WITHDRAWN: Behavioral abnormalities in young female mice following

administration of aluminum adjuvants and the human papillomavirus (HPV) vaccine Gardasil. *Vaccine.*

369   Hawkes, D., Benhamu, J., Sidwell, T., Miles, R., & Dunlop, R. A. (2015). Revisiting adverse reactions to vaccines: A critical appraisal of Autoimmune Syndrome Induced by Adjuvants (ASIA). *Journal of Autoimmunity, 59*, 77–84.

370   Lu, F., & HogenEsch, H. (2013). Kinetics of the inflammatory response following intramuscular injection of aluminum adjuvant. *Vaccine, 31*(37), 3979–3986.
      Li, H., Willingham, S. B., Ting, J. P. Y., & Re, F. (2008). Cutting edge: inflammasome activation by alum and alum's adjuvant effect are mediated by NLRP3. *The Journal of Immunology, 181*(1), 17–21.
      Harris, J., Sharp, F. A., & Lavelle, E. C. (2010). The role of inflammasomes in the immunostimulatory effects of particulate vaccine adjuvants. *European Journal of Immunology, 40*(3), 634–638.
      Oleszycka, E., Moran, H. B., Tynan, G. A., Hearnden, C. H., Coutts, G., Campbell, M., … & Lavelle, E. C. (2016). IL-1α and inflammasome-independent IL-1β promote neutrophil infiltration following alum vaccination. *The FEBS Journal, 283*(1), 9–24.
      HogenEsch, H. (2013). Mechanism of immunopotentiation and safety of aluminum adjuvants. *Frontiers in Immunology, 3*, 406.

371   Meltzer, A., & Van de Water, J. (2017). The role of the immune system in autism spectrum disorder. *Neuropsychopharmacology, 42*(1), 284.
      van der Burg, J. W., Sen, S., Chomitz, V. R., Seidell, J. C., Leviton, A., & Dammann, O. (2015). The role of systemic inflammation linking maternal BMI to neurodevelopment in children. *Pediatric research, 79*(1-1), 3.
      Spencer, S. J., & Meyer, U. (2017). Perinatal programming by inflammation. *Brain, Behavior, and Immunity, 63*, 1–7.
      Matelski, L., & Van de Water, J. (2016). Risk factors in autism: Thinking outside the brain. *Journal of Autoimmunity, 67*, 1–7.
      Edmiston, E., Ashwood, P., & Van de Water, J. (2017). Autoimmunity, autoantibodies, and autism spectrum disorder. *Biological Psychiatry, 81*(5), 383–390.

372   https://www.chop.edu/centers-programs/vaccine-education-center/vaccine-ingredients/aluminum

373 Flarend, R. E., Hem, S. L., White, J. L., Elmore, D., Suckow, M. A., Rudy, A. C., & Dandashli, E. A. (1997). In vivo absorption of aluminium-containing vaccine adjuvants using 26Al. *Vaccine, 15*(12-13), 1314–1318.
Gherardi, R. K., Eidi, H., Crépeaux, G., Authier, F. J., & Cadusseau, J. (2015). Biopersistence and brain translocation of aluminum adjuvants of vaccines. *Frontiers in Neurology, 6*, 4.
Rigolet, M., Aouizerate, J., Couette, M., Ragunathan-Thangarajah, N., Aoun-Sebaiti, M., Gherardi, R. K., ... & Authier, F. J. (2014). Clinical features in patients with long-lasting macrophagic myofasciitis. *Frontiers in Neurology, 5*, 230.
374 Code of Federal Regulations Title 21, Volume 4. Sec. 201.323 *Aluminum in large and small volume parenterals used in total parenteral nutrition.* Revised as of April 1, 2018. https://www.accessdata.fda.gov/scripts/cdrh/cfdocs/cfcfr/CFRSearch.cfm?fr=201.323
375 Bishop, N. J., Morley, R., Day, J. P., & Lucas, A. (1997). Aluminum neurotoxicity in preterm infants receiving intravenous-feeding solutions. *New England Journal of Medicine, 336*(22), 1557–1562.
376 Poole, R., Pieroni, K., Gaskari, S., Dixon, T., & Kerner, J. (2012). Aluminum exposure in neonatal patients using the least contaminated parenteral nutrition solution products. *Nutrients, 4*(11), 1566–1574.
377 Karwowski, M. P., Stamoulis, C., Wenren, L. M., Faboyede, G. M., Quinn, N., Gura, K. M., ... & Woolf, A. D. (2018). Blood and hair aluminum levels, vaccine history, and early infant development: A cross-sectional study. Academic pediatrics, 18(2), 161-165.
Lyons-Weiler, J., & Ricketson, R. (2018). Reconsideration of the immunotherapeutic pediatric safe dose levels of aluminum. *Journal of Trace Elements in Medicine and Biology, 48*, 67–73.
Mitkus, R. J., King, D. B., Hess, M. A., Forshee, R. A., & Walderhaug, M. O. (2011). Updated aluminum pharmacokinetics following infant exposures through diet and vaccination. *Vaccine, 29*(51), 9538–9543.
Hoyt, A. E., Schuyler, A. J., Heymann, P. W., Platts-Mills, T. A., & Commins, S. P. (2016). Alum-Containing Vaccines Increase Total and Food Allergen-Specific IgE, and Cow's Milk Oral Desensitization Increases Bosd4 IgG4 While Peanut Avoidance Increases Arah2 IgE: The Complexity of Today's Child with Food

Allergy. *Journal of Allergy and Clinical Immunology, 137*(2), AB151.

378   Hviid, A., Hansen, J. V., Frisch, M., & Melbye, M. (2019). Measles, Mumps, Rubella Vaccination and Autism: A Nationwide Cohort Study. *Annals of Internal Medicine.*
Jain, A., Marshall, J., Buikema, A., Bancroft, T., Kelly, J. P., & Newschaffer, C. J. (2015). Autism occurrence by MMR vaccine status among US children with older siblings with and without autism. *JAMA, 313*(15), 1534–1540.
Taylor, L. E., Swerdfeger, A. L., & Eslick, G. D. (2014). Vaccines are not associated with autism: an evidence-based meta-analysis of case-control and cohort studies. *Vaccine, 32*(29), 3623–3629.
Madsen, K. M., Hviid, A., Vestergaard, M., Schendel, D., Wohlfahrt, J., Thorsen, P., … & Melbye, M. (2002). A population-based study of measles, mumps, and rubella vaccination and autism. *New England Journal of Medicine, 347*(19), 1477–1482.

379   Hviid, A., Hansen, J. V., Frisch, M., & Melbye, M. (2019). Measles, Mumps, Rubella Vaccination and Autism: A Nationwide Cohort Study. *Annals of Internal Medicine.*

380   Jain, A., Marshall, J., Buikema, A., Bancroft, T., Kelly, J. P., & Newschaffer, C. J. (2015). Autism occurrence by MMR vaccine status among US children with older siblings with and without autism. *JAMA, 313*(15), 1534–1540.

381   Bazzano, A., Zeldin, A., Schuster, E., Barrett, C., & Lehrer, D. (2012). Vaccine-related beliefs and practices of parents of children with autism spectrum disorders. *American Journal on Intellectual and Developmental Disabilities, 117*(3), 233–242.

382   Hooker, B. S. (2014). Measles-mumps-rubella vaccination timing and autism among young african american boys: a reanalysis of CDC data. *Translational Neurodegeneration, 3*(1), 16.

383   Madsen, K. M., Hviid, A., Vestergaard, M., Schendel, D., Wohlfahrt, J., Thorsen, P., … & Melbye, M. (2002). A population-based study of measles, mumps, and rubella vaccination and autism. *New England Journal of Medicine, 347*(19), 1477–1482.

384   U.S. Health Resources and Services Administration (2019). *Vaccine Injury Compensation Program Data and Statistics, June 2019.* https://www.hrsa.gov/sites/default/files/hrsa/vaccine-compensation/data/monthly-stats-june-2019.pdf

385   U.S. Health Resources and Services Administration (2019). *Vaccine Injury Compensation Program Data and Statistics,*

June 2019. https://www.hrsa.gov/sites/default/files/hrsa/vaccine-compensation/data/monthly-stats-june-2019.pdf

386 Child vs. Secretary of Health and Human Services, United States Court of Federal Claims. November 9, 2007

Chapter 17. Safeguarding the Microbiome

387 Kang, D. W., Adams, J. B., Gregory, A. C., Borody, T., Chittick, L., Fasano, A., ... & Pollard, E. L. (2017). Microbiota Transfer Therapy alters gut ecosystem and improves gastrointestinal and autism symptoms: an open-label study. *Microbiome, 5*(1), 10.

388 Kang, D. W., Adams, J. B., Coleman, D. M., Pollard, E. L., Maldonado, J., McDonough-Means, S., ... & Krajmalnik-Brown, R. (2019). Long-term benefit of Microbiota Transfer Therapy on autism symptoms and gut microbiota. *Scientific Reports, 9*(1), 5821.

389 *Press Release by Arizona State University (2019).* https://biodesign.asu.edu/news/autism-symptoms-reduced-nearly-50-two-years-after-fecal-transplant

390 Yano, J. M., Yu, K., Donaldson, G. P., Shastri, G. G., Ann, P., Ma, L., ... & Hsiao, E. Y. (2015). Indigenous bacteria from the gut microbiota regulate host serotonin biosynthesis. *Cell, 161*(2), 264–276.

391 Carabotti, M., Scirocco, A., Maselli, M. A., & Severi, C. (2015). The gut-brain axis: interactions between enteric microbiota, central and enteric nervous systems. Annals of gastroenterology: quarterly publication of the *Hellenic Society of Gastroenterology, 28*(2), 203.

392 The Nemechek Protocol for Autism and Developmental Disorders: A How-To Guide For Restoring Neurological Function (2017).

393 Atarashi, K., Tanoue, T., Oshima, K., Suda, W., Nagano, Y., Nishikawa, H., ... & Kim, S. (2013). T reg induction by a rationally selected mixture of Clostridia strains from the human microbiota. *Nature, 500*(7461), 232.
Furusawa, Y., Obata, Y., Fukuda, S., Endo, T. A., Nakato, G., Takahashi, D., ... & Takahashi, M. (2013). Commensal microbe-derived butyrate induces the differentiation of colonic regulatory T cells. *Nature, 504*(7480), 446.

394 van den Munckhof, I. C. L., Kurilshikov, A., Ter Horst, R.,
Riksen, N. P., Joosten, L. A. B., Zhernakova, A., ... & Rutten,
J. H. W. (2018). Role of gut microbiota in chronic low-
grade inflammation as potential driver for atherosclerotic
cardiovascular disease: a systematic review of human studies.
Obesity Reviews, 19(12), 1719–1734.

Zacarías, M. F., Collado, M. C., Gómez-Gallego, C., Flinck, H.,
Aittoniemi, J., Isolauri, E., & Salminen, S. (2018). Pregestational
overweight and obesity are associated with differences in gut
microbiota composition and systemic inflammation in the third
trimester. *PloS One, 13*(7), e0200305.

Van Den Elsen, L. W., Poyntz, H. C., Weyrich, L. S., Young, W.,
& Forbes-Blom, E. E. (2017). Embracing the gut microbiota: the
new frontier for inflammatory and infectious diseases. *Clinical &
Translational Immunology, 6*(1), e125.

395 Romero, R., Espinoza, J., Gonçalves, L. F., Kusanovic, J. P., Friel,
L. A., & Nien, J. K. (2006, October). Inflammation in preterm
and term labour and delivery. *In Seminars in Fetal and Neonatal
Medicine, 11*(5), 317–326. WB Saunders.

Scholl, T. O., Chen, X., Goldberg, G. S., Khusial, P. R., & Stein, T.
P. (2011). Maternal diet, C-reactive protein, and the outcome of
pregnancy. *Journal of the American College of Nutrition, 30*(4),
233–240.

Nordqvist, M., Jacobsson, B., Brantsæter, A. L., Myhre, R.,
Nilsson, S., & Sengpiel, V. (2018). Timing of probiotic milk
consumption during pregnancy and effects on the incidence of
preeclampsia and preterm delivery: a prospective observational
cohort study in Norway. *BMJ Open, 8*(1), e018021.

396 Harmon, A. C., Cornelius, D. C., Amaral, L. M., Faulkner, J. L.,
Cunningham, M. W., Wallace, K., & LaMarca, B. (2016). The
role of inflammation in the pathology of preeclampsia. *Clinical
Science, 130*(6), 409–419.

Redman CWH, Sacks GP, Sargent IL. Preeclampsia: an excessive
maternal inflammatory response to pregnancy. *Am J Obstet
Gynecol 1999; 180*(2): 499–506.

Nordqvist, M., Jacobsson, B., Brantsæter, A. L., Myhre, R.,
Nilsson, S., & Sengpiel, V. (2018). Timing of probiotic milk
consumption during pregnancy and effects on the incidence of
preeclampsia and preterm delivery: a prospective observational
cohort study in Norway. *BMJ Open, 8*(1), e018021.

397 Instanes, J. T., Halmøy, A., Engeland, A., Haavik, J., Furu, K., & Klungsøyr, K. (2017). Attention-deficit/hyperactivity disorder in offspring of mothers with inflammatory and immune system diseases. *Biological Psychiatry, 81*(5), 452–459.

398 Lammert, C. R., Frost, E. L., Bolte, A. C., Paysour, M. J., Shaw, M. E., Bellinger, C. E., … & Lukens, J. R. (2018). Cutting edge: critical roles for microbiota-mediated regulation of the immune system in a prenatal immune activation model of autism. *The Journal of Immunology, 201*(3), 845–850.

Lukens, J. R., Lammert, C. R., Frost, E. L., & Bellinger, C. E. (2018). Critical roles for microbiota-mediated regulation of Th17 responses in a maternal immune activation model of autism. *Journal of Immunology, 200* (supp), 166–36.

Vuong, H. E., & Hsiao, E. Y. (2017). Emerging roles for the gut microbiome in autism spectrum disorder. *Biological Psychiatry, 81*(5), 411–423.

Doenyas, C. (2018). Gut microbiota, inflammation, and probiotics on neural development in autism spectrum disorder. *Neuroscience, 374*, 271–286.

399 Graciarena, M., Depino, A. M., & Pitossi, F. J. (2010). Prenatal inflammation impairs adult neurogenesis and memory related behavior through persistent hippocampal TGFβ1 downregulation. *Brain, Behavior, and Immunity, 24*(8), 1301–1309.

Hao, L. Y., Hao, X. Q., Li, S. H., & Li, X. H. (2010). Prenatal exposure to lipopolysaccharide results in cognitive deficits in age-increasing offspring rats. *Neuroscience, 166*(3), 763–770.

Richetto, J., & Riva, M. A. (2014). Prenatal maternal factors in the development of cognitive impairments in the offspring. *Journal of Reproductive Immunology, 104*, 20–25.

400 King, D. E., Egan, B. M., Woolson, R. F., Mainous, A. G., Al-Solaiman, Y., & Jesri, A. (2007). Effect of a high-fiber diet vs a fiber-supplemented diet on C-reactive protein level. *Archives of Internal Medicine, 167*(5), 502–506.

Ma, Y., Hébert, J. R., Li, W., Bertone-Johnson, E. R., Olendzki, B., Pagoto, S. L., … & Griffith, J. A. (2008). Association between dietary fiber and markers of systemic inflammation in the Women's Health Initiative Observational Study. *Nutrition, 24*(10), 941–949.

Vitaglione, P., Mennella, I., Ferracane, R., Rivellese, A. A., Giacco, R., Ercolini, D., … & Thielecke, F. (2014). Whole-grain wheat consumption reduces inflammation in a randomized controlled trial on overweight and obese subjects with unhealthy dietary and lifestyle behaviors: role of polyphenols bound to cereal dietary fiber. *The American Journal of Clinical Nutrition, 101*(2), 251–261.

401 Qiu, C., Coughlin, K. B., Frederick, I. O., Sorensen, T. K., & Williams, M. A. (2008). Dietary fiber intake in early pregnancy and risk of subsequent preeclampsia. *American Journal of Hypertension, 21*(8), 903–909.

Frederick, I. O., Williams, M. A., Dashow, E., Kestin, M., Zhang, C., & Leisenring, W. M. (2005). Dietary fiber, potassium, magnesium and calcium in relation to the risk of preeclampsia. *The Journal of Reproductive Medicine, 50*(5), 332-344.

Zhang, C., Liu, S., Solomon, C. G., & Hu, F. B. (2006). Dietary fiber intake, dietary glycemic load, and the risk for gestational diabetes mellitus. *Diabetes Care, 29*(10), 2223–2230.

Gabbe, S. G., Cohen, A. W., Herman, G. O., & Schwartz, S. (1982). Effect of dietary fiber on the oral glucose tolerance test in pregnancy. *American Journal of Obstetrics and Gynecology, 143*(5), 514–517.

402 Maia, L. P., Levi, Y. L. D. A. S., do Prado, R. L., dos Santos Santinoni, C., & Marsicano, J. A. (2019). Effects of probiotic therapy on serum inflammatory markers: A systematic review and meta-analysis. *Journal of Functional Foods, 54*, 466–478.

Badehnoosh, B., Karamali, M., Zarrati, M., Jamilian, M., Bahmani, F., Tajabadi-Ebrahimi, M., ... & Asemi, Z. (2018). The effects of probiotic supplementation on biomarkers of inflammation, oxidative stress and pregnancy outcomes in gestational diabetes. *The Journal of Maternal-Fetal & Neonatal Medicine, 31*(9), 1128–1136.

Karamali, M., Nasiri, N., Shavazi, N. T., Jamilian, M., Bahmani, F., Tajabadi-Ebrahimi, M., & Asemi, Z. (2018). The effects of synbiotic supplementation on pregnancy outcomes in gestational diabetes. *Probiotics and Antimicrobial Proteins, 10*(3), 496–503.

Asemi, Z., Jazayeri, S., Najafi, M., Samimi, M., Mofid, V., Shidfar, F., ... & Shahaboddin, M. E. (2011). Effects of daily consumption of probiotic yoghurt on inflammatory factors in pregnant women: a randomized controlled trial. *Pakistan Journal of Biological Sciences, 14*(8), 476.

403 Azad, M. B., Konya, T., Persaud, R. R., Guttman, D. S., Chari, R. S., Field, C. J., ... & Becker, A. B. (2016). Impact of maternal intrapartum antibiotics, method of birth and breastfeeding on gut microbiota during the first year of life: a prospective cohort study. *BJOG: An International Journal of Obstetrics & Gynaecology, 123*(6), 983–993.

404 Thomas, P., & Margulis, J. (2016). *The Vaccine-friendly Plan: Dr. Paul's Safe and Effective Approach to Immunity and Health- from Pregnancy Through Your Child's Teen Years.* Ballantine Books.

405 Ho, M., Chang, Y. Y., Chang, W. C., Lin, H. C., Wang, M. H., Lin, W. C., & Chiu, T. H. (2016). Oral Lactobacillus rhamnosus GR-1 and Lactobacillus reuteri RC-14 to reduce group B Streptococcus colonization in pregnant women: a randomized controlled trial. *Taiwanese Journal of Obstetrics and Gynecology, 55*(4), 515–518.

406 Petricevic, L., Unger, F. M., Viernstein, H., & Kiss, H. (2008). Randomized, double-blind, placebo-controlled study of oral lactobacilli to improve the vaginal flora of postmenopausal women. *European Journal of Obstetrics & Gynecology and Reproductive Biology, 141*(1), 54–57.
Anukam, K. C., Osazuwa, E., Osemene, G. I., Ehigiagbe, F., Bruce, A. W., & Reid, G. (2006). Clinical study comparing probiotic Lactobacillus GR-1 and RC-14 with metronidazole vaginal gel to treat symptomatic bacterial vaginosis. *Microbes and Infection, 8*(12-13), 2772–2776.
Martinez, R. C. R., Franceschini, S. A., Patta, M. C., Quintana, S. M., Candido, R. C., Ferreira, J. C., ... & Reid, G. (2009). Improved treatment of vulvovaginal candidiasis with fluconazole plus probiotic Lactobacillus rhamnosus GR-1 and Lactobacillus reuteri RC-14. *Letters in Applied Microbiology, 48*(3), 269–274.

407 Bager, P., Wohlfahrt, J., & Westergaard, T. (2008). Caesarean delivery and risk of atopy and allergic disesase: meta-analyses. *Clinical & Experimental Allergy, 38*(4), 634-642.
Azad, M. B., Konya, T., Guttman, D. S., Field, C. J., Sears, M. R., HayGlass, K. T., ... & Scott, J. A. (2015). Infant gut microbiota and food sensitization: associations in the first year of life. *Clinical & Experimental Allergy, 45*(3), 632–643.

Metsälä, J., Lundqvist, A., Virta, L. J., Kaila, M., Gissler, M., & Virtanen, S. M. (2013). Mother's and offspring's use of antibiotics and infant allergy to cow's milk. *Epidemiology*, 303–309.

Sjögren, Y. M., Jenmalm, M. C., Böttcher, M. F., Björkstén, B., & Sverremark⊠Ekström, E. (2009). Altered early infant gut microbiota in children developing allergy up to 5 years of age. *Clinical & Experimental Allergy, 39*(4), 518–526.

Abrahamsson, T. R., Jakobsson, H. E., Andersson, A. F., Björkstén, B., Engstrand, L., & Jenmalm, M. C. (2012). Low diversity of the gut microbiota in infants with atopic eczema. *Journal of Allergy and Clinical Immunology, 129*(2), 434–440.

Penders, J., Gerhold, K., Stobberingh, E. E., Thijs, C., Zimmermann, K., Lau, S., & Hamelmann, E. (2013). Establishment of the intestinal microbiota and its role for atopic dermatitis in early childhood. *Journal of Allergy and Clinical Immunology, 132*(3), 601–607.

Guaraldi, F., & Salvatori, G. (2012). Effect of breast and formula feeding on gut microbiota shaping in newborns. *Frontiers in Cellular and Infection Microbiology, 2*, 94.

408   Adams, J. B., Johansen, L. J., Powell, L. D., Quig, D., & Rubin, R. A. (2011). Gastrointestinal flora and gastrointestinal status in children with autism–comparisons to typical children and correlation with autism severity. *BMC Gastroenterology, 11*(1), 22.

Wang, L., Christophersen, C. T., Sorich, M. J., Gerber, J. P., Angley, M. T., & Conlon, M. A. (2011). Low relative abundances of the mucolytic bacterium Akkermansia muciniphila and Bifidobacterium spp. in feces of children with autism. Appl. Environ. *Microbiol., 77*(18), 6718–6721.

409   Finegold SM, et al. Pyrosequencing study of fecal microflora of autistic and control children. *Anaerobe. 2011;16*:444–453.

Parracho HM, Bingham MO, Gibson GR, McCartney AL. Differences between the gut microflora of children with autistic spectrum disorders and that of healthy children. *J Med Microbiol. 2005; 54*:987–991.

34. Song Y, Liu C, Finegold SM. Real-time PCR quantitation of clostridia in feces of autistic children. *Appl Environ Microbiol. 2004; 70*:6459–6465

410   Chaidez, V., Hansen, R. L., & Hertz-Picciotto, I. (2014). Gastrointestinal problems in children with autism, developmental

delays or typical development. *Journal of Autism and Developmental Disorders, 44*(5), 1117–1127.

Adams, J. B., Johansen, L. J., Powell, L. D., Quig, D., & Rubin, R. A. (2011). Gastrointestinal flora and gastrointestinal status in children with autism–comparisons to typical children and correlation with autism severity. *BMC Gastroenterology, 11*(1), 22.

Kang, D. W., Adams, J. B., Gregory, A. C., Borody, T., Chittick, L., Fasano, A., … & Pollard, E. L. (2017). Microbiota Transfer Therapy alters gut ecosystem and improves gastrointestinal and autism symptoms: an open-label study. *Microbiome, 5*(1), 10.

411 Sandler, R. H., Finegold, S. M., Bolte, E. R., Buchanan, C. P., Maxwell, A. P., Väisänen, M. L., … & Wexler, H. M. (2000). Short-term benefit from oral vancomycin treatment of regressive-onset autism. *Journal of Child Neurology, 15*(7), 429–435.

412 Kang, D. W., Adams, J. B., Coleman, D. M., Pollard, E. L., Maldonado, J., McDonough-Means, S., … & Krajmalnik-Brown, R. (2019). Long-term benefit of Microbiota Transfer Therapy on autism symptoms and gut microbiota. *Scientific Reports, 9*(1), 5821.

413 Azad, M. B., Konya, T., Maughan, H., Guttman, D. S., Field, C. J., Sears, M. R., … & Kozyrskyj, A. L. (2013). Infant gut microbiota and the hygiene hypothesis of allergic disease: impact of household pets and siblings on microbiota composition and diversity. *Allergy, Asthma & Clinical Immunology, 9*(1), 15.

414 Ben, X. M., Li, J., Feng, Z. T., Shi, S. Y., Lu, Y. D., Chen, R., & Zhou, X. Y. (2008). Low level of galacto-oligosaccharide in infant formula stimulates growth of intestinal Bifidobacteria and Lactobacilli. *World Journal of Gastroenterology: WJG, 14*(42), 6564.

Matsuki, T., Tajima, S., Hara, T., Yahagi, K., Ogawa, E., & Kodama, H. (2016). Infant formula with galacto-oligosaccharides (OM55N) stimulates the growth of indigenous bifidobacteria in healthy term infants. *Beneficial Microbes, 7*(4), 453–461.

Cai, J. W., Lu, Y. D., & Ben, X. M. (2008). Effects of infant formula containing galacto-oligosaccharides on the intestinal microflora in infants. *Zhongguo dang dai er ke za zhi= Chinese Journal of Contemporary Pediatrics, 10*(5), 629–632.

Rinne, M. M., Gueimonde, M., Kalliomäki, M., Hoppu, U., Salminen, S. J., & Isolauri, E. (2005). Similar bifidogenic effects of prebiotic-supplemented partially hydrolyzed infant formula and breastfeeding on infant gut microbiota. *FEMS Immunology & Medical Microbiology, 43*(1), 59–65.

Arslanoglu, S., Moro, G. E., Schmitt, J., Tandoi, L., Rizzardi, S., & Boehm, G. (2008). Early dietary intervention with a mixture of prebiotic oligosaccharides reduces the incidence of allergic manifestations and infections during the first two years of life. *The Journal of Nutrition, 138*(6), 1091–1095.

Osborn, D. A., & Sinn, J. K. (2013). Prebiotics in infants for prevention of allergy. *Cochrane Database of Systematic Reviews*, (3).

Moro, G., Arslanoglu, S., Stahl, B., Jelinek, J., Wahn, U., & Boehm, G. (2006). A mixture of prebiotic oligosaccharides reduces the incidence of atopic dermatitis during the first six months of age. *Archives of Disease in Childhood, 91*(10), 814–819.

Bruzzese, E., Volpicelli, M., Squeglia, V., Bruzzese, D., Salvini, F., Bisceglia, M., ... & Guarino, A. (2009). A formula containing galacto-and fructo-oligosaccharides prevents intestinal and extra-intestinal infections: an observational study. *Clinical Nutrition, 28*(2), 156–161.

Ivakhnenko, O. S., & Nyankovskyy, S. L. (2013). Effect of the specific infant formula mixture of oligosaccharides on local immunity and development of allergic and infectious disease in young children: randomized study. *Pediatria Polska, 88*(5), 398–404.

Scalabrin, D. M., Mitmesser, S. H., Welling, G. W., Harris, C. L., Marunycz, J. D., Walker, D. C., ... & Vanderhoof, J. A. (2012). New prebiotic blend of polydextrose and galacto-oligosaccharides has a bifidogenic effect in young infants. *Journal of Pediatric Gastroenterology and Nutrition, 54*(3), 343–352

415 Arslanoglu, S., Moro, G. E., Schmitt, J., Tandoi, L., Rizzardi, S., & Boehm, G. (2008). Early dietary intervention with a mixture of prebiotic oligosaccharides reduces the incidence of allergic manifestations and infections during the first two years of life. *The Journal of Nutrition, 138*(6), 1091–1095.

Osborn, D. A., & Sinn, J. K. (2013). Prebiotics in infants for prevention of allergy. *Cochrane Database of Systematic Reviews*, (3).

Moro, G., Arslanoglu, S., Stahl, B., Jelinek, J., Wahn, U., & Boehm, G. (2006). A mixture of prebiotic oligosaccharides reduces the incidence of atopic dermatitis during the first six months of age. *Archives of Disease in Childhood, 91*(10), 814–819.

Bruzzese, E., Volpicelli, M., Squeglia, V., Bruzzese, D., Salvini, F., Bisceglia, M., ... & Guarino, A. (2009). A formula containing galacto-and fructo-oligosaccharides prevents intestinal and extra-intestinal infections: an observational study. *Clinical Nutrition, 28*(2), 156–161.

416 Castanys-Muñoz, E., Martin, M. J., & Prieto, P. A. (2013). 2'-Fucosyllactose: an abundant, genetically determined soluble glycan present in human milk. *Nutrition Reviews, 71*(12), 773–789.

417 Yu, Z. T., Chen, C., Kling, D. E., Liu, B., McCoy, J. M., Merighi, M., ... & Newburg, D. S. (2012). The principal fucosylated oligosaccharides of human milk exhibit prebiotic properties on cultured infant microbiota. *Glycobiology, 23*(2), 169–177.
Wang, M., Li, M., Wu, S., Lebrilla, C. B., Chapkin, R. S., Ivanov, I., & Donovan, S. M. (2015). Fecal microbiota composition of breast-fed infants is correlated with human milk oligosaccharides consumed. *Journal of Pediatric Gastroenterology and Nutrition, 60*(6), 825.

418 Dermyshi, E., Wang, Y., Yan, C., Hong, W., Qiu, G., Gong, X., & Zhang, T. (2017). The "golden age" of probiotics: a systematic review and meta-analysis of randomized and observational studies in preterm infants. *Neonatology, 112*(1), 9–23.

419 Underwood, M. A. (2019). Arguments for routine administration of probiotics for NEC prevention. *Current Opinion in Pediatrics, 31*(2), 188–194.

420 Neu, J. (2018) Necrotizing enterocolitis. *Semin Fetal Neonatal Med 23*, 369 pii: S1744-165X(18)30105-7.
Strunk, T., Inder, T., Wang, X., Burgner, D., Mallard, C., and Levy, O. (2014) Infection-induced inflammation and cerebral injury in preterm infants. *Lancet Infect Dis 14*: 751–762.
Athalye-Jape, G., & Patole, S. (2019). Probiotics for preterm infants–time to end all controversies. *Microbial Biotechnology, 12*(2), 249–253.

421 Manzoni, P., Mostert, M., Leonessa, M. L., Priolo, C., Farina, D., Monetti, C., ... & Gomirato, G. (2006). Oral supplementation with Lactobacillus casei subspecies rhamnosus prevents enteric colonization by Candida species in preterm neonates: a randomized study. *Clinical Infectious Diseases, 42*(12), 1735–1742.

422 Underwood, M. A., German, J. B., Lebrilla, C. B., & Mills, D. A. (2015). Bifidobacterium longum subspecies infantis: champion colonizer of the infant gut. *Pediatric Research, 77*(1–2), 229.

Bin-Nun, A., Bromiker, R., Wilschanski, M., Kaplan, M., Rudensky, B., Caplan, M., & Hammerman, C. (2005). Oral probiotics prevent necrotizing enterocolitis in very low birth weight neonates. *The Journal of Pediatrics, 147*(2), 192–196.

Lin, H. C., Su, B. H., Chen, A. C., Lin, T. W., Tsai, C. H., Yeh, T. F., & Oh, W. (2005). Oral probiotics reduce the incidence and severity of necrotizing enterocolitis in very low birth weight infants. *Pediatrics, 115*(1), 1–4.

Kanic, Z., Turk, D. M., Burja, S., Kanic, V., & Dinevski, D. (2015). Influence of a combination of probiotics on bacterial infections in very low birthweight newborns. *Wiener Klinische Wochenschrift, 127*(5), 210–215.

Dermyshi, E., Wang, Y., Yan, C., Hong, W., Qiu, G., Gong, X., & Zhang, T. (2017). The "golden age" of probiotics: a systematic review and meta-analysis of randomized and observational studies in preterm infants. *Neonatology, 112*(1), 9–23.

423 Underwood, M. A., German, J. B., Lebrilla, C. B., & Mills, D. A. (2015). Bifidobacterium longum subspecies infantis: champion colonizer of the infant gut. *Pediatric Research, 77*(1-2), 229.

Ganguli, K., Collado, M. C., Rautava, J., Lu, L., Satokari, R., von Ossowski, I., ... & Salminen, S. (2015). Lactobacillus rhamnosus GG and its SpaC pilus adhesin modulate inflammatory responsiveness and TLR-related gene expression in the fetal human gut. *Pediatric Research, 77*(4), 528.

Capurso, L. (2019). Thirty Years of Lactobacillus rhamnosus GG: A Review. *Journal of Clinical Gastroenterology, 53*, S1–S41.

De Andrés, J., Manzano, S., García, C., Rodríguez, J. M., Espinosa-Martos, I., & Jiménez, E. (2018). Modulatory effect of three probiotic strains on infants' gut microbial composition and immunological parameters on a placebo-controlled, double-blind, randomised study. *Beneficial Microbes, 9*(4), 573–584.

424 Underwood, M. A., German, J. B., Lebrilla, C. B., & Mills, D. A. (2015). Bifidobacterium longum subspecies infantis: champion colonizer of the infant gut. *Pediatric Research, 77*(1–2), 229.

425 Henrick, B. M., Hutton, A. A., Palumbo, M. C., Casaburi, G., Mitchell, R. D., Underwood, M. A., ... & Frese, S. A. (2018). Elevated fecal pH indicates a profound change in the breastfed infant gut microbiome due to reduction of Bifidobacterium over the past century. *mSphere, 3*(2), e00041–18.

426 Henrick, B. M., Hutton, A. A., Palumbo, M. C., Casaburi, G., Mitchell, R. D., Underwood, M. A., ... & Frese, S. A. (2018). Elevated fecal pH indicates a profound change in the breastfed infant gut microbiome due to reduction of Bifidobacterium over the past century. *mSphere, 3*(2), e00041-18.

427 Frese, S. A., Hutton, A. A., Contreras, L. N., Shaw, C. A., Palumbo, M. C., Casaburi, G., ... & Freeman, S. L. (2017). Persistence of Supplemented Bifidobacterium longum subsp. infantis EVC001 in Breastfed Infants. *mSphere, 2*(6), e00501-17. Casaburi, G., & Frese, S. A. (2018). Colonization of breastfed infants by Bifidobacterium longum subsp. infantis EVC001 reduces virulence gene abundance. *Human Microbiome Journal, 9*, 7-10. Karav, S., Casaburi, G., & Frese, S. A. (2018). Reduced colonic mucin degradation in breastfed infants colonized by Bifidobacterium longum subsp. infantis EVC001. *FEBS Open Bio, 8*(10), 1649-1657. Pärtty, A., Kalliomäki, M., Wacklin, P., Salminen, S., & Isolauri, E. (2015). A possible link between early probiotic intervention and the risk of neuropsychiatric disorders later in childhood: a randomized trial. *Pediatric Research, 77*(6), 823

428 Korpela, K., Salonen, A., Vepsäläinen, O., Suomalainen, M., Kolmeder, C., Varjosalo, M., ... & de Vos, W. M. (2018). Probiotic supplementation restores normal microbiota composition and function in antibiotic-treated and in caesarean-born infants. *Microbiome, 6*(1), 182.

429 Rhoads, J. M., Collins, J., Fatheree, N. Y., Hashmi, S. S., Taylor, C. M., Luo, M., ... & Liu, Y. (2018). Infant colic represents gut inflammation and dysbiosis. *The Journal of Pediatrics, 203*, 55–61.

430 Rhoads, J. M. (2018). Probiotic Lactobacillus reuteri effective in treating infantile colic and is associated with inflammatory marker reduction. *The Journal of Pediatrics, 196*, 324–327.

431 Savino, F., Garro, M., Montanari, P., Galliano, I., & Bergallo, M. (2018). Crying time and RORγ/FOXP3 expression in Lactobacillus reuteri DSM17938-treated infants with colic: a randomized trial. *The Journal of Pediatrics, 192*, 171–177.

432 Pärtty, A., Kalliomäki, M., Endo, A., Salminen, S., & Isolauri, E. (2012). Compositional development of Bifidobacterium and Lactobacillus microbiota is linked with crying and fussing in early infancy. *PloS One, 7*(3), e32495.

433 Evivo Purchaser's Surve, 3/21/18-9/19/18; n=469.

434 Mitre, E., Susi, A., Kropp, L. E., Schwartz, D. J., Gorman, G. H., & Nylund, C. M. (2018). Association between use of acid-suppressive medications and antibiotics during infancy and allergic diseases in early childhood. *JAMA Pediatrics, 172*(6), e180315–e180315.

435 Weizman, Z. V. I., Alkrinawi, S., Goldfarb, D. A. N., & Bitran, C. (1993). Efficacy of herbal tea preparation in infantile colic. *The Journal of Pediatrics, 122*(4), 650–652.

436 Mitre, E., Susi, A., Kropp, L. E., Schwartz, D. J., Gorman, G. H., & Nylund, C. M. (2018). Association between use of acid-suppressive medications and antibiotics during infancy and allergic diseases in early childhood. *JAMA Pediatrics, 172*(6), e180315–e180315.

Droste, J. H. J., Wieringa, M. H., Weyler, J. J., Nelen, V. J., Vermeire, P. A., & Van Bever, H. P. (2000). Does the use of antibiotics in early childhood increase the risk of asthma and allergic disease?. Clinical & Experimental Allergy, 30(11), 1548–1553.

Kozyrskyj, A. L., Ernst, P., & Becker, A. B. (2007). Increased risk of childhood asthma from antibiotic use in early life. *Chest, 131*(6), 1753–1759.

Kronman, M. P., Zaoutis, T. E., Haynes, K., Feng, R., & Coffin, S. E. (2012). Antibiotic exposure and IBD development among children: a population-based cohort study. *Pediatrics, 130*(4), e794.

437 Lieberthal, A. S., Carroll, A. E., Chonmaitree, T., Ganiats, T. G., Hoberman, A., Jackson, M. A., ... & Schwartz, R. H. (2013). The diagnosis and management of acute otitis media. *Pediatrics, 131*(3), e964–e999.

438 Engelbrektson, A., Korzenik, J. R., Pittler, A., Sanders, M. E., Klaenhammer, T. R., Leyer, G., & Kitts, C. L. (2009). Probiotics to minimize the disruption of faecal microbiota in healthy subjects undergoing antibiotic therapy. *Journal of Medical Microbiology, 58*(5), 663–670.

439 Cremonini, F., Di Caro, S., Nista, E. C., Bartolozzi, F., Capelli, G. Gasbarrini, G., & Gasbarrini, A.(2002). Meta-analysis: the effect of probiotic administration on antibiotic-associated diarrhoea. *Alimentary Pharmacology & Therapeutics, 16*(8), 1461–1467.

Szajewska, H., Canani, R. B., Guarino, A., Hojsak, I., Indrio, F., Kolacek, S., ... & Weizman, Z. (2016). Probiotics for the prevention of antibiotic-associated diarrhea in children. *Journal of Pediatric Gastroenterology and Nutrition, 62*(3), 495–506.

440 Kabbani, T. A., Pallav, K., Dowd, S. E., Villafuerte-Galvez, J., Vanga, R. R., Castillo, N. E., ... & Kelly, C. P. (2017). Prospective randomized controlled study on the effects of Saccharomyces boulardii CNCM I-745 and amoxicillin-clavulanate or the combination on the gut microbiota of healthy volunteers. *Gut Microbes, 8*(1), 17–32.
Korpela, K., Salonen, A., Virta, L. J., Kumpu, M., Kekkonen, R. A., & De Vos, W. M. (2016). Lactobacillus rhamnosus GG intake modifies preschool children's intestinal microbiota, alleviates penicillin-associated changes, and reduces antibiotic use. *PloS One, 11*(4), e0154012.
Szajewska, H., & Kołodziej, M. (2015). Systematic review with meta-analysis: Lactobacillus rhamnosus GG in the prevention of antibiotic-associated diarrhoea in children and adults. *Alimentary Pharmacology & Therapeutics, 42*(10), 1149–1157.

441 Collignon, A., Sandre, C., & Barc, M. C. (2010). Saccharomyces boulardii modulates dendritic cell properties and intestinal microbiota disruption after antibiotic treatment. *Gastroentérologie Clinique et Biologique, 34*, S71–S78.
Bruzzese, E., Callegari, M. L., Raia, V., Viscovo, S., Scotto, R., Ferrari, S., ... & Guarino, A. (2014). Disrupted intestinal microbiota and intestinal inflammation in children with cystic fibrosis and its restoration with Lactobacillus GG: a randomised clinical trial. *PLoS One, 9*(2), e87796.

442 Demirel, G., Celik, I. H., Erdeve, O., Saygan, S., Dilmen, U., & Canpolat, F. E. (2013). Prophylactic Saccharomyces boulardii versus nystatin for the prevention of fungal colonization and invasive fungal infection in premature infants. *European Journal of Pediatrics, 172*(10), 1321–1326.
Demirel, G., Erdeve, O., Celik, I. H., & Dilmen, U. (2013). Saccharomyces boulardii for prevention of necrotizing enterocolitis in preterm infants: a randomized, controlled study. *Acta Paediatrica, 102*(12), e560–e565.
Xu, L., Wang, Y., Wang, Y., Fu, J., Sun, M., Mao, Z., & Vandenplas, Y. (2016). A double-blinded randomized trial on growth and feeding tolerance with Saccharomyces boulardii CNCM I-745 in formula-fed preterm infants. *Jornal de Pediatria (Versão em Português), 92*(3), 296–301.

443 Urashima, M., Segawa, T., Okazaki, M., Kurihara, M., Wada, Y., & Ida, H. (2010). Randomized trial of vitamin D supplementation

to prevent seasonal influenza A in schoolchildren. *The American journal of Clinical Nutrition, 91*(5), 1255–1260.

444 Zipitis, C. S., & Akobeng, A. K. (2008). Vitamin D supplementation in early childhood and risk of type 1 diabetes: a systematic review and meta-analysis. *Archives of Disease in Childhood, 93*(6), 512–517.

Schmidt, R. J., Hansen, R. L., Hartiala, J., Allayee, H., Sconberg, J. L., Schmidt, L. C., ... & Tassone, F. (2015). Selected vitamin D metabolic gene variants and risk for autism spectrum disorder in the CHARGE Study. *Early Human Development, 91*(8), 483–489.

Coşkun, S., Şimşek, Ş., Camkurt, M. A., Çim, A., & Çelik, S. B. (2016). Association of polymorphisms in the vitamin D receptor gene and serum 25-hydroxyvitamin D levels in children with autism spectrum disorder. *Gene, 588*(2), 109–114.

Cannell, J. J., & Grant, W. B. (2013). What is the role of vitamin D in autism?. *Dermato-Endocrinology, 5*(1), 199–204.

Kočovská, E., Andorsdóttir, G., Weihe, P., Halling, J., Fernell, E., Stóra, T., ... & Bourgeron, T. (2014). Vitamin D in the general population of young adults with autism in the Faroe Islands. *Journal of Autism and Developmental Disorders, 44*(12), 2996–3005.

Stubbs, G., Henley, K., & Green, J. (2016). Autism: will vitamin D supplementation during pregnancy and early childhood reduce the recurrence rate of autism in newborn siblings? *Medical Hypotheses, 88*, 74–78.

445 Gordon, C. M., Feldman, H. A., Sinclair, L., Williams, A. L., Kleinman, P. K., Perez-Rossello, J., & Cox, J. E. (2008). Prevalence of vitamin D deficiency among healthy infants and toddlers. *Archives of Pediatrics & Adolescent Medicine, 162*(6), 505-512.

446 Perrine, C. G., Sharma, A. J., Jefferds, M. E. D., Serdula, M. K., & Scanlon, K. S. (2010). Adherence to vitamin D recommendations among US infants. *Pediatrics, 125*(4), 627.

447 American Academy of Pediatrics. (2010). *Vitamin D Supplementation for Infants.* https://www.aap.org/en-us/about-the-aap/aap-press-room/pages/Vitamin-D-Supplementation-for-Infants.aspx

Printed in Great Britain
by Amazon

36355193R00192